ELIAS H. WIEBE ED. D.
PACIFIC COLLEGE
1717 S. CHESTNUT
FRESNO, CALIF, 93702

a question of competence

a question of competence

language, intelligence, and learning to read

justin fishbein
robert emans

SCIENCE RESEARCH ASSOCIATES, INC.
Chicago, Palo Alto
Toronto, Henley-on-Thames, Sydney
A Subsidiary of IBM

Library of Congress Catalog Card Number 72-76842

acknowledgments

Joseph Alsop: "A Condition of Enormous Improbability." Reprinted by permission of Joseph Alsop. Copyright ©1969 by Joseph Alsop. First appeared in THE NEW YORKER, March 8, 1969.

Moshe Anisfeld: "Language Skills in the Context of the Child's Cognitive Development," in *Project Literacy Reports* 2 (September 1964), Cornell University. Reprinted with the permission of the author.

E. James Archer: "The Psychological Nature of Concepts," in *Analyses of Concept Learning*, edited by Herbert J. Klausmeier and Chester W. Harris. ©1966 by Academic Press, Inc. Reprinted with the permission of the author and the publisher.

Ursula Bellugi: "Review of *Language in the Crib*," *Harvard Educational Review*, 34, Spring 1964, 332–334. Copyright ©1964 by President and Fellows of Harvard College. Reprinted with the permission of Ursula Bellugi and the *Harvard Educational Review*.

U. Bellugi-Klima: *The Acquisition of the System of Negation in Children's Speech*. Reprinted with the permission of the author.

D. E. Berlyne: *Structure and Direction in Thinking*. ©1965 by John Wiley & Sons, Inc. Reprinted with the permission of the publisher.

Thomas G. Bever and T. G. Bower: "How to Read without Listening," in *Project Literacy Reports* 6 (1966), Cornell University. Reprinted with the permission of the author.

Roger Brown and Ursula Bellugi: "Three Processes in the Child's Acquisition of Syntax," *Harvard Educational Review*, 34, Spring 1964, 133–151. Copyright ©1964 by President and Fellows of Harvard College. Reprinted with the permission of Roger Brown, Ursula Bellugi, and the *Harvard Educational Review*.

Jerome S. Bruner: *Toward a Theory of Instruction*. Reprinted with the permission of The Belknap Press of Harvard University Press.

John B. Carroll: *Language and Thought*. ©1964 by Prentice-Hall, Inc. Reprinted with the permission of the publisher.

John B. Carroll: "Words, Meanings and Concepts," *Harvard Educational Review*, 34, Spring 1964, 178–202. Copyright ©1964 by President and Fellows of Harvard College. Reprinted with the permission of John B. Carroll and the *Harvard Educational Review*.

Courtney B. Cazden: "Suggestions from Studies of Early Language Ac-

Arthur I. Gates: "What We Should Be Doing Soon," in the *Invitational Addresses*, 1965, International Reading Association. ©1965 by the International Reading Association. Reprinted with permission of Arthur I. Gates and the International Reading Association.

Jean Berko Gleason: "Language Development in Early Childhood," in *Oral Language and Reading*, edited by James Walden. Copyright ©1969 by the National Council of Teachers of English. Reprinted by permission of the publisher and Jean Berko Gleason.

Jean Berko Gleason in *Proceedings of International Conference on Oral Education of the Deaf*. Copyright ©1967. Reprinted by permission of the Alexander Graham Bell Association for the Deaf, Washington, D.C.

Kenneth S. Goodman: "Analysis of Oral Reading Miscues: Applied Psycholinguistics," in the *Reading Research Quarterly*, Fall 1969. ©1969 by the International Reading Association. Reprinted with permission of Kenneth S. Goodman and the International Reading Association.

Kellogg W. Hunt: *Grammatical Structures Written at Three Grade Levels*, Research Report 3. Copyright ©1965 by the National Council of Teachers of English. Reprinted by permission of the publisher and Kellogg W. Hunt.

Sumner Ives: "Syntax and Meaning," in *Recent Developments in Reading*. ©1965 by The University of Chicago. Reprinted with the permission of the author and The University of Chicago Press.

James J. Jenkins: "Meaningfulness and Concepts; Concepts and Meaningfulness," in *Analyses of Concept Learning*, edited by Herbert J. Klausmeier and Chester W. Harris. ©1966 by Academic Press, Inc. Reprinted with the permission of the author and the publisher.

Jerome Kagan: "A Developmental Approach to Conceptual Growth," in *Analyses of Concept Learning*, edited by Herbert J. Klausmeier and Chester W. Harris. ©1966 by Academic Press, Inc. Reprinted with the permission of the author and the publisher.

Jerrold J. Katz and Jerry A. Fodor: "The Structure of a Semantic Theory," in *Language* 39 (April–June 1963). Reprinted with the permission of the Linguistic Society of America.

Eric H. Lenneberg: *Biological Foundations of Language*. ©1967 by John Wiley & Sons, Inc. Reprinted with the permission of the publisher and Eric H. Lenneberg.

Eric H. Lenneberg: "The Capacity for Language Acquisition," an extended version of his article in S. Diamond (ed.): *Culture in History*, New York: Columbia University Press, 1960, pp. 869–93, appearing in Fodor and Katz: *The Structure of Language: Readings in the Philosophy of Language*, New York: Prentice-Hall, 1964. Reprinted by permission of the Columbia University Press and Prentice-Hall, Inc.

Walter D. Loban: *The Language of Elementary School Children*, Research Report 1. Copyright ©1963 by the National Council of Teachers of

table of contents

foreword

If we agree that the ability to read plays a major role in the learner's quest for self-actualization, it is abundantly clear that the child's first teacher in formal reading instruction must know about a child's mind and his language. For this is what the child brings to the classroom.

Because the different approaches to reading instruction work, and because children become capable of reading new material, an explanation in terms of the nature of the learner, not the method or the material, must be looked for.

Justin Fishbein and Robert Emans, in *A Question of Competence*, have asked that teachers contemplate these important questions: What must a child know if he is to read? What is the nature of the knower that permits him to read with understanding? What is his competence?

In order to enlighten teachers, the authors competently explore developmental psychology, psycholinguistics, and concept-attainment research, offering hypotheses to explain why various methods and materials will or will not work in terms of the *child's* competence.

This book does not offer the *what* or the *how* of reading materials and approaches. It does, however, present the *why* of materials and approaches, which, in my opinion, is the most fundamental and significant issue in self-actualization through reading.

This is an honest and an able work, one which bespeaks accountability to the child as learner, to the parents, to the teacher and the teaching profession, and to society itself.

Lester L. Van Gilder

Marquette University
Milwaukee, Wisconsin

introduction

This book focuses on one question: what does a child know that enables him to learn to read and to read with comprehension? Put another way, what is the nature of the knower that permits him to do this? In other words, what is his *competence?* What the child actually does after he has been called on by a teacher is his *performance*. The child's competence will in part explain his performance, an aspect of reading that is a major concern of classroom teachers. We feel that if teachers think about the question of competence and its possible answers, they will be able to select materials and methods more by reason than by rote.

The question has interested us for some time, because of a sense that the field of reading is plagued by debates over materials and methods, in professional books and periodicals and in hearings concerned with adopting textbooks. Actually, for most children, one combination of materials and methods seems about as good as the next. As a result, some authorities suggest that the differences do exist but that the teacher makes up for them in her methods.

Obviously teachers and methods are important, but we look at the child. We think that the child makes the difference. We consider him as a biological entity in the classification of man as a species, and then we review the writings and research that offer evidence to support an answer to our question.

Though we range widely, we focus on Piaget, Lenneberg, Chomsky, Vygotsky, and Underwood. Our approach is this: first we cite research studies that describe behavior as it was observed; then we turn to theoretical explanations of that behavior to get a picture of the child's competence. Against the picture of that competence we offer a series of hypotheses to account for differences in performance with various materials and methods that are quite different from one another.

At the very beginning we suggest that as long as there is no theory of competence in reading, teachers are forced to choose materials by belief and experience, or because "that's what everybody does." It follows that a theory of competence will enable teachers to be more precise in selecting materials and methods to match the competence of children. We do not state, but could, that since children are developing, the competence of one differs from that of another at any moment in time, and that genuine individualization must take competence into account.

By exploring this question of competence, we hope to develop enlightened teachers. The study we undertook is interdisciplinary, and we hope that it serves teachers well by pulling together in one place a lot of information that will give them practical help in the classroom. For instance, it seems quite plausible to us that the explanation of why certain methods work better than others will help teachers remember the methods themselves. But the book is neither a "how-to" tome nor a hopscotch across materials. Instead it attempts to be an interdisciplinary synthesis.

Finally, we caution the reader about this book: it is not an end, but a beginning. Almost every month since we completed the manuscript, an important new article or book has appeared containing information that should be considered by people concerned with reading instruction. We sincerely hope that with this book as a foundation, the reader will seek and explore those articles and books.

Justin Fishbein
Robert Emans

a question of competence

In a very general way, it must be obvious that the more we know about a child's mind and his language the better we are able to instruct him in further language skills, like reading and writing.

Jean Berko Gleason
Language Development in Early Childhood

reading instruction
past, present, and future

Teachers have used—and still use—many different instructional strategies to teach children to read. In colonial times they used the *New England Primer*;[1] this book taught the alphabet and simple religious rhymes. As the new nation was expanding westward, many used *Noah Webster's American Spelling Book*,[2] which taught a "standard of pronunciation," the alphabet, nonsense syllables, and word families such as "big, dig, fig, gig, pig, wig." Short moralistic selections were presented after the skills portion. Webster and, a few years later, William Holmes McGuffey used diacritical marks—tiny numerals over letters—to indicate to the children the sound represented by a letter. *McGuffey's Eclectic Readers*[3] also taught the alphabet first, but then the method was up to the teacher. It could be the alphabet method, the phonic method, or the word method. Probably some teachers used a combination of these. In the alphabet method, children named the letters of a word, then said the whole word; in the phonic method, children sounded out a word, then said it as a whole (for example, "ruh-a-tuh," then "rat"); in the word method, children looked at a printed word repeatedly and said it repeatedly. All these methods were aimed at enabling children to associate printed words with spoken words.

Between 1836 and 1920, more than 120 million McGuffey readers were sold, and since a reader was usually used by more than one child, no one can accurately estimate the number of children who used the series. It is known that, though millions of children learned to read using McGuffey, they by no means learned with the same method. Toward the turn of the century, the phonic method became increasingly popular. Next, as Gestalt psychology, dealing with configuration and structure as a physiological and psychological reality, gained eminence, the whole-word method waxed as the phonic method waned.[4]

Briefly during the 1920s many children did not read aloud as they were learning to read, but for the most part American reading instruction since 1920 has begun with the word method and added a phonic method toward the end of the first grade. The variations have been many. Possibly to enable more children to become successful, the number of words in reading programs declined until 1958, when it began to increase. Some programs use "service" words in reading instruction; these are words that are likely to be used in other school subjects and are likely to be meaningful to children. It made sense to educators to have children learn words that would be useful, just as it did during the days of the Puritans. Words such as *father*, *mother*, *girl*, and *baby*, it was argued, are more useful than words such as *exacerbate*.

Since the objective was to enable the child to get meaning from the printed page, no matter what method was used, reading programs had to cope with the problem of gaining and maintaining the child's interest. This was a difficult task in programs in which only a few hundred words were introduced during the first two years of instruction. Interest was maintained by an ingenious strategy: the words that the child was to read early in the program were included in a story told by the teacher, and accompanying pictures summed up the story in images, to remind the child of the story he had been told. To the teacher, this system seemed to have other advantages. Suppose a child was trying to read "Tom ran down the street" and could not get the word *street*. The teacher would say, "Look at the picture. Where is Tom?" Or perhaps she would remind the child of the story she had just told, and would ask, "Where is Tom running?" In this way, picture clues and context clues were used to help the child read words. The use of context also is very much like the sentence method, in which the child would memorize a sentence as a whole as a vehicle for enabling him to read words in the sentence, a technique used with the *New England Primer*. This method has been revived recently in programs employing audio-visual cards, or texts and tapes. Teachers used word configuration, too. For example, a teacher would introduce *monkey*, the only long word in a lesson, as "the long word with a tail on it. You know, a monkey has a tail on it." Then, if a child stumbled on the word, she would say, "That's the long word we had yesterday, the one with the tail on it."

Teachers also consider that maintaining interest is a problem in phonic programs, so they usually employ many games and drills. In general, phonics deals with letter-sound correspondence, singly and in whole words, but there are many different kinds of phonics. Webster's word families and diacritical markings were forms of phonics. Today reading programs termed "linguistic" present word families and use the alphabet method. And today, in some reading programs, letters are diacritically marked; children also mark long, short, and silent letters; for example, *smile* would be marked "smīlȩ."

Special orthographies such as the Initial Teaching Alphabet might be called "whole-word phonics." In part they stem from a widely held belief that the spelling of English is highly irregular and that, because of this, children have great difficulty learning to read. George Bernard Shaw was one of many prominent persons who advocated reform of the spelling system. To highlight the alleged irregularity, he cited the word *fish*, spelled "ghoti": *gh* as in *rough*, *o* as in *women*, and *ti* as in *nation*.

There also is single-sound phonics, in which children drill on sound-letter correspondences, on sounding out words, and on blending sounds into words, perhaps by saying the sounds faster and faster.

Then there is deductive phonics. In this technique, children memorize rules, generalizations, and exceptions, and then read lists of words exemplifying what they have memorized. For example, they might memorize that in a one-syllable word or stressed syllable ending with one vowel and one consonant, the final consonant is doubled before a suffix beginning with a vowel is added. Examples might be *bat-batting, hit-hitting, dig-digging, begin-beginning*.

Inductive phonics works the other way around. Children examine lists of words, identify the common spelling-sound element, and then formulate in words a rule, generalization, or exception. For example, the teacher may show the children a list of words such as *please, sneeze, boat, train,* and *day*. She may also show them *great* and *bread*. From these examples, the teacher may lead the children to infer that when two vowels appear together in a word or a stressed syllable, the first vowel usually says its name (has a long sound) and the second is usually silent. Syllables are taught, too. For example, a word or stressed syllable that ends in a vowel is open and the vowel has a long sound; a word or stressed syllable that ends in a vowel followed by a consonant is closed and the vowel has a short sound. Examples of the first are *me* and *tiny*, and of the second, *let* and *lemon*.

In recent years, it has become fashionable to test the verbal rules, generalizations, and exceptions on words in children's readers to determine the accuracy and applicability of these skill guides. Another popular pastime is to consider the rules in terms of dialect. For instance, does the *a* in *crash* have a short sound for a child from Chicago? from central Tennessee? from west Texas? Apparently teachers assume that regardless of whether the rules, generalizations, and exceptions are taught deductively or inductively, children can apply them in reading words. After all, the children do learn them, and they can read words; they can even tell the teacher which rule, generalization, or exception applies.

There are also two other methods that employ various strategies. One consists simply of teaching children to spell words and write brief stories. The children then learn to read what they have written. The teacher may use context, picture clues, and phonics to help the children read words they have never see before, or she may even use word families. A related system is the "language-experience" approach. The teacher provides an experience: perhaps she will take them on a field trip to a nearby zoo, or show them pictures or a film. The children describe the experience in words. The teacher records these on a chart or a sheet of paper. The child may provide an appropriate illustration. Then the teacher has each child read his own story. The teacher usually uses drill, context, picture clues, word families, and phonics to develop the child's ability to read words he has never seen before (word attack) and his instant recognition of words.

Now it is true that with each of the methods used since the Pilgrims landed, some children failed to learn to read. But it is equally true that regardless of the method and materials used, most children learned to read. Teachers seem to be aware of this; quite often a classroom visitor will hear a teacher say, "I use the eclectic method. There is no one way to teach children to read. I use a little of this and a little of that. Then if one program doesn't work, I know that another one will." So the teacher follows the manuals for the various reading programs and does what she is told to do, employing techniques and strategies that have come down through the ages.

In this regard, she is much like the physician in an ancient tale. One day a man consulted the doctor, complaining of a sore elbow. "Go home," said the doctor, "and bathe your elbow for half an hour in warm water." Unfortunately, on the way home the patient was distracted by a street brawl, and he couldn't recall whether the doctor had said warm water or cold water, so he asked his wife. She didn't know the answer either, so she asked her mother. "Cold water!" was the emphatic reply. The man did as his mother-in-law commanded and, sure enough, the pain went away. A few days later he saw the doctor again and said, "Say, Doc, I've really got to thank you. I bathed my elbow in cold water just as you said, and the pain's all gone." "I didn't say cold water," said the doctor. "I said warm water." Then the man told the doctor what had happened and that his mother-in-law had said cold water. "That's funny," mused the medico. "My mother-in-law says warm water."

The methods are different; they are ancient; and they all work. Psychologists are unable to observe directly the workings of the mind; they must rely on collected samples of behavior to infer what goes on during the learning process. Just as no one knows for certain the nature of God or the order of Nature, no one knows for certain the nature of man's mind or the structure of his intellect. Perhaps it is for this reason that religion and reading instruction have so much in common. In both there is great attention to ceremony and ritual. In both there is extraordinary fervor. In the past, this fervor and emotionalism led the followers of opposing "true" faiths to war upon one another; likewise, sincere but conflicting faiths in one or another reading method have resulted in awesome word wars. And just as man uses religion to explain himself in the scheme of things, he may also look upon a particular method of reading instruction and a particular theory of behavior as a means of explaining what goes on in the classroom and of justifying his role as a teacher. Knowing very little about the nature of the reading process, he is much like the physician who was mystified as he examined a patient and was unable to diagnose the ailment. "Have you ever had this before?"

asked the doctor. "Yes," said the patient. "Well, you've got it again," the doctor concluded.

A century ago a physician faced with such a situation would choose a treatment that had proved successful under similar circumstances. In those days, too, a wide variety of nostrums and patent remedies were available for the unwary and ill-informed populace. In the last half-century, however, the march of medical research has vastly expanded man's knowledge of his own body, and this new knowledge has in turn led to advances in the art of medical practice.

Possibly, similar advances in the behavioral sciences will lead to improvements in the art of teaching, especially the teaching of reading. The classroom teacher is almost exclusively concerned with identifying the most effective materials and methods. Arthur I. Gates expressed his concern about this situation. Consider his remarks:[5]

The extensive studies of Barton and Wilder[6] under the auspices of the Carnegie Corporation leave no doubt that scientific work in our field is at a low ebb. It is low in quantity—too few persons of high competence are devoting their time fully or even mainly to basal research. It is too limited to the more obvious, the more practical problems. It is restricted too much in range; it does not show sufficient activity in many promising lines now developing within sociology, anthropology, experimental psychology, biochemistry, statistics, and other new types of scientific approach such as systems analysis.

Change and Challenge in American Education,[7] a 115-page book written by James E. Russell, Secretary of the Educational Policies Commission, presents the main idea so well that I shall quote from it.

We may hope that specialists in educational research can find ways to alter their efforts in a rather profound way. The present thrust of most research consists in trying out someone's favorite ideas for reform and improvement. I have no resistance to most people's pet ideas. I also like to see the kind of research that tests whether phonics is better than sight-reading and what effect class size has on learning. I think too that educational television, team teaching, and programed learning can be useful.... But the notion that all these peripheral actions can add up to profound improvement or change strikes me as fanciful.

When our theoretical base is as incomplete as it is, ... suggested solutions proliferate on the fringes. What we need is to know more of the mind, its structure and operation, and the forces and factors that influence it. I do not expect to find these insights ... in programed instruction, or in any fortuitous combination of advances on the periphery. We must plunge into the central question.

One could wish that educators were highly mobilized on this front, but they are not. Although some years ago educational researchers of national reputation were involved, more recently there has been little education research at this level.... This advance must come and come soon.

... Next I wish to convince you that truths (facts and principles) most significant for reading shine out of basal, scientific research, even that done in an apparently remote region, for example, on the antics of animals, and by an investigator who wasn't thinking about reading at the time. Indeed, I shall start out by declaring that a study of animals was responsible for the greatest revolution in the teaching of reading ever made.

The animals demonstrated the major principles involved in learning to read in 1898.[8] Their demonstrations got to us only because Edward L. Thorndike introduced for the first time a revolutionary method of study—the scientific method. His famous puzzle boxes enabled him to see the main features of learning and problem solving because the activities of cat, rat, and monkey were slower, more visible, and less subtle than those of children learning to read. Later when Thorndike studied reading he realized that when a child or adult tries to read a passage he is faced by the same confusion of possibilities; and he tackles the problem as does a cat or rat, with all the knowledge, skill, insight, and reasoning ability at his command. This idea made explicit in an article entitled "Reading as Reasoning" published in 1917[9] was so fundamental, so far-reaching, that it resulted in a great number of improvements in teaching reading. The idea that reading is as complex, varied, and subtle as thinking itself has been the basis of our thinking about reading and learning to read for a half-century, and it has confronted us with a myriad of practical problems which puzzle us even today.

Let me tell you now about another tremendous contribution to the teaching of reading made by a study of animals, especially Pavlov the pig. Pavlov the pig went to school with Pavlov the professor more than a half-century ago in Russia.[10] He was the most popular pig in school. He learned quickly. Every day he led the singing. He was always healthy and hungry, but even when he reached the dinner table first he didn't make a hog of himself.

Then one day Professor Pavlov introduced reading. He taught the pig that by pushing a lever when a circle appeared above it he would get some food, and if he pushed the lever when a square was shown, he would get an electric shock. Then the Professor began to introduce figures (that is, words) which resembled both the circle and the square in various degrees, such as the outline of a rounded bar of soap or the heel of a man's shoe. As the choices became harder, Pavlov the pig made more and more mistakes. He began to get jumpy and snappy. His singing began to go off key, and eventually he had a real nervous breakdown. Pavlov the pig really was the first reading disability ever studied in a genuinely scientific clinic. Apparently when a pig suffers a reading disability, it hits him hard. It took over a year of hospital care to restore Pavlov to normalcy. Of course you must realize the pig suffered severe penalties for missing words. A mistake deprived him of food and subjected him to annoying electric shocks.

The majority of psychologists would probably say that the cause of Pavlov's breakdown was frustration resulting from efforts to learn something that is too difficult. And most of us might have continued to believe that mere difficulty did the damage, were it not for another study made on animals. Liddell[11] found that an animal did not become disorganized even when failures were frequent if—and I quote—"some freedom for evasion and procrastination is possible." What heresy is this? Possibly the pig's trouble was that it didn't know how to swear. It just had no way of saying "the devil take this miserable business. I've had enough of it."

Not one of Liddell's animals broke down when an adequate avenue for escape—a way to save face—was provided. Here is an important principle for teachers of reading that might not have been discovered outside of the pigpen, so to speak. Indeed studies of animals, beginning with those by Pavlov and Thorndike, have contributed greatly to our present information about motivation in reading and other human activities.

Studies of animals as well as of human beings have shown also that the significance of learning experiences varies, along with other things, with the character of the times—with the social and physical environment. Anthropologists and sociologists have also contributed greatly to our understanding of the influence of our environment on reading. We now know that to improve the teaching of reading the teacher should study all phases of each child's life and have a background of valid information to use in interpreting these data. . . . Basal research, however, often reveals practical principles and throws doubt on practical policies which many of us might otherwise assume to be sound.

For example, a belief long held by many is that the greater the number of sensory channels employed to feed information to a learner the better he will learn. Thus instead of having him merely see the word, you have him also sound it, write it, type it, you show a pictorial illustration of it, use it in a story, and so on. Let one sense be facilitated by another. Indeed many persons now warmly recommend a "combined method," one which uses many resources. Thus the classroom is filled with every available kind of book, workbook, phonic system, sound motion picture, teaching machine, TV lessons, and so on. Sometimes it seems that everything a teacher can get hold of is tossed into the hopper and ground into mincemeat, which she then seasons with additional suggestions as it is passed out.

A series of recent studies done not by us reading researchers but mainly in the psychological laboratory cast doubt on these policies. Robert Travers in his recent address as President of the Educational Psychology Division of the American Psychological Association summed up his review of many studies by saying, " . . . flooding the learner with information and stressing realism are likely to provide poor learning. Some schools do this, as if in the hope that the more information is available the more the learner will absorb. But the fact is that the learner has a limited ability for utilizing information, can generally utilize information from only one source at a time, and has a limited storage capacity. . . . What is needed are principles which will indicate how information can be most effectively compressed and simplified . . ." not expanded and elaborated.[12]

When new investigations like these threaten old convictions we must not be discouraged. Upsets like these are the inevitable and desirable fruits of scientific progress. The time to worry is not when we encounter changes and uncertainties but self-satisfied agreement among our experts. A state of agreement usually means merely that progress has come to a halt. . . .

The effects of . . . scholarly work . . . are sufficient to enable us to make many practical improvements now. For example, the basal reader outfits are still so fragmentary, incomplete, and difficult to use as to require a great deal of really shrewd additional work by a teacher to handle many children individually with them. These books are poor not because we do not know enough to make better ones but because everyone has assumed that we cannot afford better ones. Well, we can. And we should now be making materials that are more detailed, more comprehensive, and built deliberately for individual instruction as well as group activities. They may comprise many more packets, and in general bear little physical resemblance to the present reader-workbook outfits. . . .

I want to tell you about another problem of greatest significance in reading research which some animals recently called to our attention. Psychologist Robert Rosenthal[13] divided a large group of rats into two groups equivalent in ability to run certain mazes. To one-half of his graduate student assistants he turned over one group of rats, which were said to be "rat geniuses." The other assistants got the equivalent group but they were described as "stupid rats." The assistants went to work teaching equivalent rats by prescribed, identical methods to run an identical maze. What happened? The "genius" rats learned noticeably better than the "stupid" ones.

This little study radiates with a host of implications of great importance. I am sure I do not as yet see them all, but one seems clear. The differences seem to be due to something these teachers did differently while trying to teach in exactly the same way. Things they did differently are very subtle but they cry out that the role of the teachers is an overwhelmingly important factor in the learning situation even when the pupils are rats utterly blind to most of the things, such as the meaning of spoken words, which the teacher habitually uses.

This study demonstrates the unreliability, known for some time on the basis of other evidence, of the typical control group method widely used in education. Most of the control group studies of reading methods, especially those made during these recent years of turmoil and tempest, have yielded data which are mainly useless, indeed often misleading. So-called experiments or "demonstrations" of methods or materials which have been given great publicity are the worst offenders. They are loaded dice.

Only very extensive studies carried out for many years in many neutral schools by neutral teachers supervised by genuinely competent and neutral investigators in comparison with many other procedures will reveal reliably the relative merits of the various programs. We can afford them. We have simply got to have them. Few of us, I am sorry to say, have been trained to the level of expertness in the new science. A fine start in this direction has been made by the Federal Department of Health, Education, and Welfare in launching under the supervision of Donald Durrell, Guy Bond, Theodore Clymer, and others some large-scale studies of first-grade reading. . . .

My long professional life has convinced me that, except for sheer intelligence, the greatest professional asset is a gay heart. The leaders in educational science I have known were extremely gay men and women. They were dedicated to their work, because they found it full of thrilling challenges. I now regard the deadly ever-serious scientist with some suspicion. He is almost sure to be a bore. When one of these persons has me cornered, my mind is likely to wing off to a sweet vision. It is the vision of my dog. When I get home I shall give him the signal that means, "Let's go for a walk in the woods." He will appear to go mad with joy. All over the place he will explode into geysers of gaiety. Is it not one of the wonders of the world that this beautiful, incredibly lively animal will seem to be filled with ecstasy at the prospect of taking a walk with me—with me, poor dull clod that I am, stumbling along at a snail's pace, insensitive to the thrills of forest smells and sounds that make him tingle with heavenly delight. Is this dog's rapture the outcome of a magic fountain of acquired gaiety or the culmination of inheritances of ages of sensitivity to the thrills of venturing into the realm of mystery? Both contribute, I think; each enlivens the other. And so I express the hope that all of you will discover the excitement of adventures in the hunting grounds which the profession and science of education provide.

SUMMARY

Historically, many different approaches to reading instruction have been used in classrooms. Some have emphasized whole words as beginning units, others phonics; some meaning, some silent reading, some oral reading. Some have added diacritical markings; others have changed the alphabet. Some have used nonsense words; others have used word families. Regardless of the method used, or the emphasis in instruction, most children do learn to read.

Arthur Gates states that much research in reading has been too limited to obvious components of the reading situation: by merely comparing apparent or visible variables, such research has done little to improve the instruction of children. What is needed, Gates believes, is an emphasis on basic, theoretical issues. Gates cites research, much of it on animals, in which the investigator was not studying about reading per se, but which has nevertheless had a profound influence on the teaching of reading. He presents research by men such as Thorndike, Pavlov, and Rosenthal as examples. Thorndike's work on cats, rats, and monkeys led him to conclude that reading is a highly complex reasoning process. Pavlov studied a pig learning a readinglike behavior and found out what happens to pigs when learning becomes difficult. Studying rats, Rosenthal illustrated that the often adopted control-group method used to study the teaching of reading may result in misleading evidence because of the subtle unintended differences in the way study and control groups are treated.

Because children already do learn to read even though quite different methods of instruction are in practice, and because improvements in helping children to learn have come about as a result of basic, theoretical research rather than from superficial changes in methods, we must look carefully into the science of education. Gates refers to the science of education as a hunting ground. Those of us who wish to improve reading instruction must venture into the hunting ground which, in this case, is the reading situation. The terrain will be rough, but the scenery is magnificent.

Fortunately, we have a compass for our guide, although all of its points are not clear. One of the points is the child and how he learns. Another is language: its nature and how it is acquired. A third point is instruction; its place on the compass is especially unclear. At times, in our exploration of the learning-to-read process, we may appear to be lost. But let us assume the attitude of the hunter who claimed he had never been lost. Bewildered for days, yes, but never lost.

NOTES FOR CHAPTER 1

1. *The New England Primer*, with an introduction by Paul Leicester Ford (New York: Teachers College, Columbia Univ., 1962).
2. *Noah Webster's American Spelling Book*, with an introductory essay by Henry Steele Commager (New York: Teachers College, Columbia Univ., 1962).
3. *McGuffey's Eclectic Primer*, rev. ed. (New York: American Book Co.; copyright 1881 by Van Antwerp, Bragg & Co.; copyright 1896 by American Book Co.; copyright 1909 by Henry H. Vail).
4. One of the most interesting accounts of the McGuffey readers is contained in Mark Sullivan's *Our Times: The United States, 1900–1925*, vol. 2, *America Finding Herself* (New York: Scribner, 1927), pp. 7–48.
5. Arthur I. Gates, "What We Should Be Doing Soon," *Invitational Addresses 1965*, International Reading Assn., Newark, Del., pp. 3–15, 17.
6. Allen H. Barton and David E. Wilder, "Research and Practice in the Teaching of Reading: A Progress Report," in Matthew B. Miles, *Innovation in Education* (New York: Teachers College, Columbia Univ., 1965), pp. 361–98.
7. James E. Russell, *Change and Challenge in American Education* (Boston: Houghton Mifflin, 1965). 115 pp.
8. Edward L. Thorndike, "Animal Intelligence," *Psychological Review Monograph Supplement* 2, 4 (1898). 109 pp.
9. Edward L. Thorndike, "Reading as Reasoning: A Study of Mistakes in Paragraph Reading," *Journal of Educational Psycholoy* 4 (June 1917), 323–32.
10. Gardner Murphy, *An Historical Introduction to Modern Psychology*, Chapter 16, "Behaviorism" (New York: Harcourt, Brace, 1929), pp. 263–78. Pavlov's earlier studies did not cover all of the details, some of which were selected from later writings of other authors in order to give a fuller picture of the findings.
11. Howard S. Liddell, et al., "The Comparative Physiology of the Conditioned Motor Reflex," *Comparative Psychology Monographs* 2, 1 (December 1934), 1–89.
12. Robert M. W. Travers, "Transmission of Information to Human Receivers," *Educational Psychologist* 2, 1 (December 1964), 1–5.
13. Robert Rosentahal, et al., "The Effect of Experimenter Bias on the Performance of the Albino Rat," *Behavioral Science* 8, 3 (July 1963), 183–89.

2

the mental realities of reading

Not surprisingly, the large-scale studies of first-grade reading to which Professor Gates referred led to the conclusion that each of twenty-seven different reading programs worked; that is, in each program children learned to read. There was not any "best" method; the teacher's instructional practices were identified as the source of differences in student scores on various objective, standardized measurement instruments.

Said Russell G. Stauffer, editor of *The Reading Teacher,* in an editorial:[1]

I have become acutely aware of one tidy generalization—there is no one method of teaching reading.

Regardless of the criterion used there is no one method and this is so in spite of the tragic consequences of the internal dynamism that some so-called methods have sought to advance—tragically, eccentrically and captivatingly. Every method described used words, and phonics, and pictures, and comprehension, and teachers. True, they frequently used them differently, but they used them. There was no phonics method that was pure or uncontaminated, if you wish, by other methods. There was no one linguistic method. i.t.a. is not a method but a medium. Basal readers claim everything.

Unhappily, attention of reading specialists is still too often focused on normative performance in reading. Do children perform poorer than, as well as, or better than other children of the same age and grade? What method was used? Which textbooks? Sometimes attention is focused on the sociological characteristics of the child. For instance, he is termed "disadvantaged," or "an inner-city member of a minority group." Or perhaps he was raised in an indulgent setting of suburbia where the average annual family income exceeds twenty thousand dollars.

But what can be said about the psychological characteristics of all children? Is it a fact, as many teachers believe, that all children learn differently, or have the differences blinded educators to the similarities?

Has concern with performance in reading diverted attention from competence in reading?

That is, have we been too preoccupied in studying the overt behavior of children learning to read and not paid enough attention to their underlying mental activities and capacities which are brought to bear on the learning-to-read situation? Noam Chomsky, a professor of linguistics at the Massachusetts Institute of Technology, makes a distinction between performance and competence in respect to language.[2]

Linguistic theory is concerned primarily with an ideal speaker-listener, in a completely homogeneous speech-community, who knows its language perfectly and is unaffected by such grammatically irrelevant conditions as memory limitations, distractions, shifts of attention and interest, and errors (random or characteristic) in applying his knowledge of the language in actual performance. This seems to me to have been the position of the founders of modern general linguistics, and no cogent reason for modifying it has been offered. To study actual linguistic performance, we must consider the interaction of a variety of factors, of which the underlying competence of the speaker-hearer is only one. In this respect, study of language is no different from empirical investigation of other complex phenomena.

We thus make a fundamental distinction between *competence* (the speaker-hearer's knowledge of his language) and *performance* (the actual use of language in concrete situations). Only under the idealization set forth in the preceding paragraph is performance a direct reflection of competence. In actual fact, it could not directly reflect competence. A record of natural speech will show numerous false starts, deviations from rules, changes of plan in mid-course, and so on. The problem for the linguist, as well as for the child learning the language, is to determine from the data of performance the underlying system of rules that has been mastered by the speaker-hearer and that he puts to use in actual performance. Hence, in the technical sense, linguistic theory is mentalistic, since it is concerned with discovering a mental reality underlying actual behavior.... Observed use of language or hypothesized dispositions to respond, habits, and so on, may provide evidence as to the nature of this mental reality, but surely cannot constitute the actual subject matter of linguistics, if this is to be a serious discipline.

Paraphrasing Chomsky[3] and transposing his remarks to the reading situation, one might ask, "What is the mental reality underlying the actual behavior of reading?" He cites a problem that strikes at the heart of education. In the field of reading, despite differences in methods and historical time, children have learned to read. What must be the competence of these learners?

Moreover, to paraphrase Chomsky once again, any significant theory of learning must account for the fact that the mature user of a particular skill is able to employ it creatively; that is, he can solve mathematical problems he was not taught to solve, after performing a finite number of problems in, say, addition, subtraction, multiplication, or division. He can correctly spell words he was not taught to spell after being taught to spell a finite number of certain words. How does one account for this? How does one account for the mature person's ability to correctly read words and sentences he was never taught to read? The terms *power* and *transfer* are descriptive to the extent that both attest to the creative process; neither one, however, offers insight into the competence of the learner. Here's how Chomsky notes the problem in relation to language:[4]

The central fact to which any significant linguistic theory must address itself is this: a mature speaker can produce a new sentence of his language on the appropriate occasion, and other speakers can understand it immediately, though it is equally new to them. Most of our linguistic experience, both as speakers and hearers, is with new sentences; once we have mastered a language, the class of sentences with which we can operate fluently and without difficulty or hesitation is so vast that for all practical purposes (and, obviously, for all theoretical purposes), we may regard it as infinite. Normal mastery of a language involves not only the ability to understand immediately an indefinite number of entirely new sentences, but also the ability to identify deviant sentences and, on occasion, to impose an interpretation on them. . . .

It is evident that rote recall is a factor of minute importance in ordinary use of language, that "a minimum of the sentences which we utter is learnt by heart as such—that most of them, on the contrary, are composed on the spur of the moment," and that "one of the fundamental errors of the old science of language was to deal with all human utterances, as long as they remain constant to the common usage, as with something merely reproduced by memory" (Paul, 1886, 97–98).[5] In this remark, it is only the reference to "the old science of language" that is subject to qualification. In fact, the realization that this "creative" aspect of language is its essential characteristic can be traced back at least to the seventeenth century. Thus we find the Cartesian view that man alone is more than mere automatism, and that it is the possession of true language that is the primary indicator of this (see Descartes, *Discourse on Method,* Part V), developed by a follower along these lines (Cordemoy, 1668):[6] "If the organs . . . had a certain settled order among them [i.e., if man were a 'language-producing engine' such as, for example an artificial speaking machine, rocks that produce an echo, or, to a confirmed Cartesian like Cordemoy, a parrot],[7] they could never change it, so that when the first voice were heard, those that were wont to follow it would needs be heard also . . . whereas the words which I hear utter'd by Bodies, made like mine, have almost never the same sequel . . . to speak, is not to repeat the same words, which have struck the ear, but to utter others to their purpose and suitable to them. . . ." In any event, whatever the antiquity of this insight may be, it is clear that a theory of language that neglects this "creative" aspect is of only marginal interest.

On the basis of a limited experience with the data of speech, each normal human has developed for himself a thorough competence in his native language.

A theory concerning the creative aspect of language must account for certain interesting abilities of the ideal speaker-hearer. The ideal speaker-hearer, for instance, can provide more than one interpretation for sentences such as "Pigeons are roosting on the bank," "Editors are boring people," "They told the police to stop rioting," and "My wife drove the car into the garage."

Similarly, consider the sentences cited by Katz and Fodor:[8] "Our store sells alligator shoes," and "Our store sells horse shoes." The ideal speaker-hearer knows that the shoes are not made for the alligator or out of the horse. How? A theory of language must account for a speaker's ability to say sentences such as these even though he has never said them before, and to understand them even though he has never heard them before.

Chomsky, commenting on the relation between language acquisition and learning capacity, gives additional insight into a theory of language. He asserts:[9]

A concern with perception and acquisition of language has played a significant role in determining the course of development of linguistic theory, as it should if this theory is ever to have broader scientific significance. But I have tried to show that the basic point of view regarding both perception and acquisition has been much too particularistic and concrete. It has failed totally to come to grips with the "creative" aspect of language use, that is, the ability to form and understand previously unheard sentences. It has, in general, failed to appreciate the degree of internal organization and the intricacy of the system of abstract structures that has been mastered by the learner, and that is brought to bear in understanding, or even identifying, utterances.

Evidence . . . suggests that each natural language is a simple and highly systematic realization of a complex and intricate underlying form with highly special and unique properties. To the extent that this observation can be substantiated, it suggests that the structure of the grammar internalized by the learner may be, to a presently quite unexpected degree, a reflection of the general character of his learning capacity rather than the particular course of his experience. It seems not unlikely that the organism brings, as its contribution to acquisition of a particular language, a highly restrictive characterization of a class of generative systems (potential theories) from which the grammar of its language is selected on the basis of the presented linguistic data.

And in *Language and Mind*, Chomsky observes:[10]

I have tried to suggest that the study of language may very well, as was traditionally supposed, provide a remarkably favorable perspective for the study of human mental processes. The creative aspect of language use, when investigated with care and respect for the facts, shows that current notions of habit and generalization, as determinants of behavior or knowledge, are quite inadequate. The abstractness of linguistic structure reinforces this conclusion, and it suggests further that in both perception and learning the mind plays an active role in determining the character of the acquired knowledge. The empirical study of linguistic universals has led to the formulation of highly restrictive and, I believe, quite plausible hypotheses concerning the possible variety of human languages, hypotheses that contribute to the attempt to develop a theory of acquisition of knowledge that gives due place to intrinsic mental activity. It seems to me, then, that the study of language should occupy a central place in general psychology.

Surely the classical questions of language and mind receive no final solution, or even the hint of a final solution, from the work that is being actively pursued today. Nevertheless, these problems can be formulated in new ways and seen in a new light. For the first time in many years, it seems to me, there is some real opportunity for substantial progress in the study of the contribution of the mind to perception and the innate basis for acquisition of knowledge. Still, in many respects, we have not made the first approach to a real answer to the classical problems. For example, the central problems relating to the creative aspect of language use remain as inaccessible as they have always been. And the study of universal semantics, surely crucial to the full investigation of language structure, has barely advanced since the medieval period. Many other critical areas might be mentioned where progress has been slow or nonexistent. Real progress has been made in the study of the mechanisms of language, the formal principles that make possible the creative aspect of language use and that determine the phonetic form and semantic content of utterances. Our understanding of these mechanisms, though only fragmentary, does seem to me to have real implications for the study of human psychology. By pursuing the kinds of research that now seem feasible and by focusing attention on certain problems that are now accessible to study, we may be able to spell out in some detail the elaborate and abstract computations that determine, in part, the nature of percepts and the character of the knowledge that we can acquire—the highly specific ways of interpreting phenomena that are, in large measure, beyond our consciousness and control and that may be unique to man.

Suppose, now, that our discussion is to discover how the capacity and the performance of reading written language is developed. We see that reading theorists are also concerned with a theory of language. In reading, the individual must take account of the relation between written and spoken language. A theory of reading attempts to specify the components of the reading situation that make it possible to read and understand words and sentences in many contexts. Also, any theory of reading that neglects the creative aspects of reading—that is, the reader's ability to read words and sentences he has never read before—is of only marginal interest.

Chomsky's conceptual scheme is moving linguistics away from simply recording and classifying language to theories of its perception, acquisition and use. Thus Chomsky's work is of central importance in discovering a valid foundation for developing a theory of reading.

SUMMARY

We started our discussion in this chapter by pointing out again that children learn to read regardless of teaching methods. Since this is true, the child must have innate characteristics that dispose him to learn to read. Much of the focus of this book is on this capacity of the child. We propose that studying how we learn to speak will prepare us for a more comprehensive understanding of how we learn to read—both because reading is learned and because reading is a language-related activity and dependent on thinking processes. We will be concerned with the earliest steps of language learning as well as the complexity and extent of mental development needed to enable us to speak and understand sentences we have never heard before. We will be searching for an understanding of the earliest steps of beginning to read so as to understand the nature of this learning and how it proceeds. We wish to understand how, as mature readers, we eventually become able to read and understand material we have never read before.

In the next few chapters we will examine some of the research that has been performed and the foundations for the development of theory in respect to language. In chapters 3 and 4 we learn that all children acquire language in much the same way. A description is given of how children learn their language in the early stages. Chapter 5 explores man's capacity for language and presents theoretical explanations to account for the behavior cited in chapters 3 and 4. In chapter 6 Chomsky's ideas involving how sentences are understood are explored. In chapter 7 the relation between oral and written language is studied. With chapter 8 we begin our discussion of how the mind works. This discussion is continued throughout chapters 9, 10, 11, and 12. The last two chapters are devoted to instruction.

NOTES FOR CHAPTER 2

1. Russell G. Stauffer, "Some Tidy Generalization," *The Reading Teacher* 20 (October 1966), 4.
2. Noam Chomsky, *Aspects of a Theory of Syntax* (Cambridge: MIT Press, 1965), pp. 3–4.
3. Noam Chomsky, "The Formal Nature of Language," in *Biological Foundations of Language*, edited by Eric Lenneberg (New York: Wiley, 1967), p. 398.
4. Noam Chomsky, *Current Issues in Linguistic Theory* (The Hague: Mouton, 1964), pp. 7–9.
5. H. Paul, *Prinzipien der Sprachgeschichte*, 2d ed. (1886). Translated into English. Longmans, Green, and Co., London, 1890.
6. G. Cordemoy, *A philosophical discourse concerning speech, conformable to the Cartesian principles.* Translated from the French, 1668.
7. The bracketed material is by Chomsky.
8. Jerrold J. Katz and Jerry A. Fodor, "The Structure of a Semantic Theory," *Language* 39 (1963), 170–210.
9. Noam Chomsky, *Current Issues in Linguistic Theory*, pp. 111–13.
10. Noam Chomsky, *Language and Mind* (New York: Harcourt, Brace & World, 1968), pp. 84–85.

3

the child's first steps in language

As far as researchers can tell, according to Jean Berko Gleason,[1] children in Cambridge, Mass., and Berkeley, Calif., learn to talk in much the same way. This makes the investigators feel fairly certain that the results of the studies of language acquisition indicate the general nature of language acquisition for all children learning English.

Considering how much there is to learn, it is amazing how quickly children learn to speak. During their first year, babies spend much time listening to adults talk. They also make all sorts of strange sounds. Since babies do not know ahead of time what language they are going to grow up speaking, it is not surprising that they come equipped and ready to learn any of the world's languages and during their first few months apparently babble all the sounds of all the languages from Arapesh to Zulu.

Wick R. Miller adds this:[2]

The newborn child does not, of course, have language. Until about six months of age, he is at what is sometimes called the cooing stage. Sounds consist of crying, gurgling, and the like. While we can probably say the sounds are human in character—that is, restricted to human infants—they do not appear to be any more different than might be expected among infants of different species of animals. At around six months of age we find the babbling stage. The vocal behavior is not language, but the infant has control over the sounds he makes, as evidenced by repetitions of the same syllable. Further, the sounds are those found in languages. Some of the sounds, however, are not to be found in the language he hears, and others will be difficult to learn and will appear late.

Actually, notes Eric H. Lenneberg, "there are two distinct types of vocalization," according to naturalistic and acoustic studies, and "each has its own developmental history." He continues:[3]

The first type includes all sounds related to crying. It is present at birth (and potentially present even before the end of normal gestation). It undergoes modification during childhood and then persists throughout life. These sounds as well as other sounds more immediately related to vegetative functions seem to be quite divorced from the developmental history of the second type of vocalization, namely all of those sounds which eventually merge into the acoustic production of speech.

This second type of sound emerges only after about the sixth to eighth week. It begins with brief, little cooing sounds that fairly regularly follow the smiling response. It has the characteristics of a reflex that may be elicited by a specific stimulus, namely a nodding object resembling a face in the visual field of the baby (Spitz and Wolf, 1946),[4] (Lenneberg, Rebelsky, and Nichols, 1965).[5] Cooing sounds are obtained most easily and indiscriminately, however, between the tenth and thirteenth week; after this age, the visual and social stimuli become more and more differentiated. Soon it is necessary that the face be a familiar one in order to elicit smiling and cooing. . . .

The cooing sounds that begin to appear toward the end of the second month are acoustically fairly distinct from crying sounds. Their duration is characteristically about half a second, and energy is distributed over the frequency spectrum in a way that soon reminds us of vowel formants. This impression is reinforced because cooing contrasts with crying in that it shows resonance modulation almost at once in addition to fundamental frequency modulation. In other words, during cooing, some articulatory organs are moving (mostly tongue), whereas during crying they tend to be held relatively still.

Although cooing sounds are "vowel-like," we must guard against describing them in terms of specific speech sounds of English, for example. They are neither acoustically, nor motorically, nor functionally *speech sounds*. For instance, their acoustic onset differs from the more common vocalic onset in Germanic languages by having either no glottal stop at the beginning or an overaspirated glottal stop such as never occurs in standard English. Early vocalizations seem to be different motorically from adult speech sounds, because the articulating organs move somewhat erratically and discoordinately.

By about six months the cooing sounds become more differentiated into vocalic and consonantal components. New articulatory modulations appear.

Jean Berko Gleason[6] notes that

toward the first birthday, a change takes place. The nonsense the baby has been uttering begins to sound like strangely familiar nonsense. In an English speaking community, the baby begins to utter English sound syllables with English-sounding intonation. The sounds of Russian or Urdu are no longer to be heard. Around their first birthday many babies manage to produce a word their parents think they recognize. The babies make do with one-word utterances for several months; then, when they get to about eighteen months old—and these are strictly normative statements—most babies begin to put two words together into a minimal sentence. By this I mean that the intonational contours are those of a sentence and not just two words said one right after the other in isolation. He does not say "Daddy. Shoe." He says "Daddy shoe," and it is clear even without the possessive *s* that he is referring to his father's shoe and that the two words are to go together.

In the year and a half that intervenes between his first two-word utterance at eighteen months and his third birthday, the child learns all the essentials of English grammar. By the age of thirty-six months, many children can produce all of the major English sentence types up to about ten words in length. And by the time a child enters school, his knowledge of English is so vast and complex that no one has yet been able to program the most sophisticated computer to turn out the sentences that any five-year-old can produce with ease and assurance.

Miller cites overt evidence dealing with two aspects of the acquisition of language at about the time the child is a year old:[7]

(1) phonology, or the sound system, and (2) words, or vocabulary items. Phonology and vocabulary items are learned largely independently of each other. The child

does not learn individual sounds in individual words, nor does he learn individual sounds. Instead, he learns phonological contrasts, beginning with that between consonant and vowel. The consonant is usually a stop and usually a front consonant such as /p/. The vowel is usually a low vowel such as /a/. Next he may contrast front and back consonants, such as labial versus dental, to give him the two consonants /p/ and /t/. Then the contrast between stop and fricative multiplies by two the number of consonants, giving two labials (/p/ and /f/) and two dentals (/t/ and /s/). Next he may learn to contrast voiced and voiceless consonants, yielding four voiced consonants (/b/, /v/, /d/, /z/) that contrast with their voiceless counterparts (/p/, /f/, /t/, /s/). The same process is to be observed with the vowels. With a relatively small number of contrasts, the child is able to learn the larger number of sounds in his language. By three and a half or four years of age, the normal child has learned all or almost all of the phonological system. Though he still makes occasional mistakes, these represent mistakes within his own linguistic system, not things that he has not yet learned. By seven or eight, mistakes are about as common as in adult speech. If they are more frequent, the child is in need of speech therapy.

Since the child is learning contrasts, not sounds belonging to individual vocabulary items, a newly learned contrast will be applied to all vocabulary items, both new and old, for which that contrast is appropriate. Thus imitation cannot play an important role in learning the phonology. The child learns features that cannot be directly imitated.

Some children develop contrasts that are not to be found in the language they are learning. For example, English speaking children will sometimes have no final nasal consonants but will develop a contrast between nasal and nonnasal vowels. The nasal vowels will be used in words that end in nasal consonants in English, and the nonnasal vowels will be used elsewhere. Such contrasts are always temporary and are lost as soon as the appropriate adult contrast is learned.

The patterns of language development exhibited by each child are idiosyncratic, and it is therefore necessary, in studying the phonological development, to study individual systems and individual cases. But there is some sequencing and some order across children: contrasts between labial and dental (e.g., /p/ and /t/) almost always occur before contrast between velar (e.g., /k/) and other consonants; contrasts between high and low vowels are found before contrasts between front and back vowels; contrasts between umlauted and nonumlauted vowels for French and German speaking children tend to be late; and so on. There is also a very marked tendency for contrasts that are universal or nearly so in natural languages to occur early, and those that are found in only a minority of languages to be late.

Lenneberg points out that before the child says his first words, he imposes intonation patterns upon babbling; that is, the child seems to babble statements, questions, and so forth. The child, Lenneberg adds, is responding to whole patterns, not to small segments. An ordering of previously random sounds begins to emerge in the child's speech.

Meanwhile, the child must be able to equate his own sound patterns with those of adults, and equating patterns seems to occupy the child's attention for about a year. In fact, Lenneberg suggests that the infant's lack of concern for phonetic accuracy reflects "a fundamental principle in language acquisition: what is acquired are patterns and structure, not constituent elements."

As for the semantic aspects of one-word utterances, at first the word is overgeneralized; it may cover many objects and situations; subsequently it becomes differentiated. But Lenneberg suggests that phonological rules, involving intonation patterns and sequences of universal phonetic features, may very well give rise to grammar. The next few pages include some of Lenneberg's writing, which explains his thinking in more detail.[8]

The first feature of natural language to be discernible in a child's babbling is contour of intonation. Short sound sequences are produced that may have neither any determinable meaning nor definable phoneme structure, but they can be proffered with recognizable intonation such as occurs in questions, exclamations, or affirmations. The linguistic development of utterances does not seem to begin by a composition of individual, independently movable items but as a whole tonal pattern. With further development, this whole becomes differentiated into component parts; primitive phonemes appear which consist of very large classes of sounds that contrast with each other. R. Jakobson (1942)[9] was the first to point this out clearly.

Such development seems reasonable enough if we consider the mechanisms of sound-making in man. The vocal tract is an instrument in which a dozen or more (the number is somewhat arbitrary) different adjustments may be made. A given speech sound results from selecting just one set of adjustments. During the pre-language stage, movements are made erratically, and thus the ever-changing quality of the sounds is like the flux of patterns in a kaleidoscope. Gradually the child gains control over the fine execution of these movements, apparently over the laryngeal adjustments first, although there seems to be considerable individual variation in the order of these developmental events.

Perceptually, the child reacts also to whole patterns rather than to small segments, and so the intonation pattern of a sentence is the more immediate input rather than individual phonemes. Order is introduced into the uncontrolled variation of sound-producing movements by a succession of refinements in skills in making various adjustments and combinations of adjustments. The mass of random sounds begin to be lined up into some fundamental classes that contrast with one another in terms of articulatory mechanisms, roughly corresponding to some of the distinctive features described by Jakobson, Fant and Halle (1963).[10]

There is little regularity from child to child in the order of emergence of specific functional phoneme-units. . . . The important point is that the first words are not composed of acoustically invariant speech sounds. Instead there are equivalence classes of sounds, and each class functions as a primitive phoneme. The actual sound that is uttered at a specific instant is merely one of many possible sounds out of its given class.

The structure of contrasting sound-classes becomes more and more complex, and the differentiation takes place along articulatory dimensions until the complete distinctive feature matrix is established. Although it is true that the development is one of gradual phoneme-differentiation, it does not follow that the child *only* learns the distinctions that are phonemic in the language surrounding him. There are many phonetic niceties, styles, or mannerisms that are also acquired and that are irrelevant to the phonemic structure. Interestingly enough, these are usually late developments and may still be in a process of formation at eight or ten years of age.

Between the twelfth and eighteenth months the toddler is heard to utter unmistakable single words. There is evidence that at first these words serve quite a different function from that of mature speech. The difference is on all levels: phonological, syntactic, and semantic. The acoustic shape is merely a crude replica of the adult word, and it is only by means of our capacity to see pattern similarities that we can recognize the child's word. This is common enough knowledge. But perhaps it has not been stressed sufficiently that it is not merely the adult who must be able to equate the child's utterance to an English word; the child must have similar skills in pattern recognition and equation. For almost a whole year children are satisfied with general pattern similarity and dispense, so to speak, with segment by segment phonetic identity. Surely this has to do with their initial clumsiness and thus with maturational factors.

If this were not so, we might expect that many children would choose a different strategy toward language acquisition, namely, first to perfect their phonetic skills and only when they can reproduce a word with phonetic perfection, go on with syntax and semantics. This is what parrots do and, in fact, it is the usual strategy of teachers who want to train nonspeaking children (the retarded or the deaf) or animals to speak. It is also the strategy that most adults adopt in learning or teaching a second language. Therefore, the infant's initial lack of concern for phonetic accuracy is by no means a trivial or logically necessary phenomenon. It points to a fundamental principle in language acquisition: what is acquired are patterns and structure, not constituent elements.

There are also dramatic deviations in the realm of semantics during the first stage of single words. This is true of reference as well as of meaning. At the beginning, a word such as *daddy* covers a different and wider range of objects than later. There is overgeneralization. However, at no time does the multitude of reference relationships and the multilevel overlap of synonymy, homonymy, metonymy or the names of particulars as against the names of generalities, of aspects, qualities or objects to which the language-learning child is exposed from the beginning cause a chaotic use of words. The reference classes of objects in the beginner's language are merely less differentiated than in adult language, but from the start there is something which we might call an "understandable logic" to the word-object relationship. It is as if the child did *in principle* the same as adults do, only on a more general level.

It has already been pointed out that meaning is intimately related to syntax, because the meaning of the sentence is never equivalent to an unordered summation of the reference of words contained in the sentence.

A short elaboration on a certain aspect of the grammatical structure of adult utterances is necessary here. Is it correct to say that the unit of discourse is the *sentence*? Two objections are often raised in this connection. First, in adult speech we frequently hear single words uttered; in what respect are these sentences? Second, the transcripts of conversations always show drastic infringements upon grammar; can we call these distortions "sentences"?

Take the first point. Someone may hold out an opened pack of cigarettes and ask, *"Smoke?"* or a person may answer the question "Do you smoke?" by means of the one-word utterance *"Yes!"* or the question "Which one of these boys was seen to smoke?" by *"Johnnie!"* and so on. Countless other examples are possible. In every instance, we are clearly dealing with ellipsis. The single word utterances are only interpretable by virtue of the listener's ability to supplement the omitted parts of the sentence. The first instance is interpreted as the sentence, "Do you smoke?", the second as "I smoke" (or, "I do smoke"; hence "Yes, I do smoke."); and the third as "Johnnie has been seen to smoke." There may, in some instances, be ambiguity because not enough context is given to enable the listener to place the single word into the intended sentence. But generally it is correct to say that the meaning of words is uninterpretable in social commerce unless we have enough clues with which to construct a sentence for that word.

The second point is factually correct: utterances heard in colloquial English (or any language, for that matter) do not conform to what we know to be correct grammar. We must make here a distinction. There are indeed utterances that are totally "ungrammatical," but they are also uninterpretable—we do not know what the speaker was trying to say. On the other hand, much more often we do know what the speaker wanted to say even though his utterances are clearly ungrammatical. This may be because he omitted part of the sentence or because a sentence is begun as if it were to end in one way but is actually concluded by using the second half of a different type of construction. (Several variations of this are possible.) Our capacity to understand such semisentences can only be due to a facility to supplement the omitted part of incomplete sentences. Thus, the interpretation of semisentences is not simpler than the understanding of grammatical sentences but actually requires a special ability: to supplement the missing parts of a partially concealed pattern (analogous to pattern-completion in visual perception). If a sentence is remodeled under certain circumstances [Osgood (1957)[11] cites the example, "Garlic I taste!"], this is not necessarily a sign that syntax may be abandoned at will but rather of the existence of possible rules of correspondence that do not ordinarily enter into the writing of normative grammars. The rule of correspondence in this case relates the form of the "Garlic" sentence to the form of such sentences as "I taste garlic!" The example cited is not necessarily an instance of agrammatism but merely that of an admissible rule. That the types of such rules are limited (or that the rules have a psychological reality) is seen in the fact that the words in this sentence cannot be permutated in *all* possible ways.

In the light of this discussion, how do we explain the onset of language development where it is a universal finding that children begin with one-word utterances? Does this mean that the observations on adult language are false? or that they are irrelevant? I do not believe that either is the case. To the contrary, if we assume that the child's first single word utterances are, in fact, very primitive, undifferentiated forms of sentences, and that these utterances actually incorporate the germs of grammar, a number of phenomena may be explained.

There is a period at which an infant may have a repertoire of up to 50 words including such items as *daddy, here, milk, up, baby,* etc. He will utter any one of these words in isolation and they may mean: Daddy, come here; Daddy went by-by; I want to be picked up; thanks, no milk; more milk, please; etc. But even though the child's memory is sufficient to know all of the 50 words, and even though he hears such phrases as *here is your milk, shall daddy take you by-by,* etc., he will neither join together any two words he knows nor can he be induced to do so upon request. This cannot be explained by assuming that he makes himself better understood this way; or that the reference of the words (that is, the association with the object) is still too narrow and fixed; or that he has no need for putting words together; or that he cannot vocalize for that long a period of time; or that this is due to poorly developed general memory. All of these assumptions are refutable by observations. Nor would any of these assumptions make it clear why the child suddenly and spontaneously *does* begin to join words into two-element phrases.

The assumption that the early single word utterances are primitive syntactic units—in a sense primitive sentences—finds support in the following considerations. Semantically, and in terms of communication, the single words seem to function in the same way that sentences come to function later on: they cover a complete proposition; for instance, they may stand for a statement such as *Daddy is coming down the street.* Phonologically they may be operated upon by a given rule, much the way a whole string of symbols is operated upon later on; for example, one of a variety of intonation patterns influences the utterance—such as declarative, interrogative, or hortative pitch-contours. It is reasonable to assume that the formal processes that regulate the perception and production of sounds are essentially the same as those that enter into syntax and that the one-word stage is simply a transitional stage during which the rules are extended from the interaction of articulatory movements to the interaction of larger language units, namely morphemes and words, and that the eventual acquisition and mastery of grammar has its origin right at the beginning of language development; otherwise we would have to assume that some day the child "discovers" grammar and makes an effort to learn this phenomenon, which seems farfetched.

SUMMARY

Contrary to an often-stated belief, the child does not learn his language through parrotlike imitation. Instead he possesses, because he is human, certain innate capacities for developing a language. As we have seen, the infant can produce spontaneously most, if not all, of the various sounds of all the languages of the world. In chapter 4 we will see that he has the capacity to learn an almost endless array of vocabulary items and the necessary sentence structures characteristic of a given language. The child discovers and matches his language capacities in relation to the language he hears in his environment, discarding those rudiments which are not supported in his language encounters. Thus language is developed through an interaction between the spontaneous abilities of the child and his language environment. It would seem that the child's innate learning capacities must also be available to him and be suitably adaptable for his use in learning to read. He must be given the opportunity to interact with his environment in such a way as to foster this ability.

NOTES FOR CHAPTER 3

1. Jean Berko Gleason, "Language Development in Early Childhood," in *Oral Language and Reading*, edited by James Walden (Champaign, Ill.: National Council of Teachers of English, 1969), p. 16.
2. Wick R. Miller, "Language Acquisition and Reading," in *Oral Language and Reading*, p. 32.
3. Eric H. Lenneberg, *Biological Foundations of Language* (New York: Wiley, 1967), pp. 276–77.
4. R. A. Spitz and K. M. Wolf, "The Smiling Response: A Contribution to the Ontogenesis of Social Relations," *Genet. Psychol. Monogr.* 34 (1946), 57–125.
5. Eric H. Lenneberg, F. G. Rebelsky, and I. A. Nichols, "The Vocalizations of Infants Born to Deaf and to Hearing Parents," *Vita Humana (Human Development)* 8 (1965), 23–37.
6. Gleason, pp. 16–17.
7. Miller, pp. 32–33.
8. Lenneberg, pp. 279–83.
9. R. Jakobson, "Kindersprache, Aphasie und allgemeine Lautgesetze," *Uppsala Universitets Aarsskrift*, 1942.
10. R. Jakobson, C. G. Fant, and M. Halle, *Preliminaries to Speech Analysis: The Distinctive Features and Their Correlates*, 2d ed. (Cambridge: MIT Press, 1963).
11. C. E. Osgood, "Motivational Dynamics of Language Behavior," in *Nebraska Symposium on Motivation*, edited by M. R. Jones (Lincoln: Univ. of Nebraska Press, 1957).

4

the child masters his grammar

Since the one-word stage is merely transitional to the handling of larger language units—words and morphemes—let us now examine evidence dealing with the child's acquisition of grammar. This grammar, according to Gleason,[1]

is usually divided into morphology and syntax, morphology having to do with the smallest units of meaning, which are called morphemes. Most short words like *dog* or *cat* or *chair* consist of one morpheme. A word like *bookkeepers* is four morphemes long, *book* and *keep,* which can stand alone as single English words, *-er* which means "agent" or "one who does something," and the final *-s* which means "more than one." Both *-er* and *-s* are called bound morphemes because they only occur attached, or bound, to another word. English uses bound morphemes to convey meanings of plurality, possession, and verb tense, and we all know a set of rules, even though it is not conscious, that states when they may be used, and in what form.

English, as you know, does not rely heavily on special word endings, or morphology, to get across its meanings. Instead, the burden of the message is carried by the way in which words are arranged into sentences, the syntax. In "The farmer loves the girl," how do we know who loves and who is loved? We know it is the farmer who loves because "farmer" comes before the verb, and there is a strong English syntactic rule that says that the actor comes before the verb and the acted upon comes after the verb. . . . Word order is so important in English that when it becomes reversed, as it is in the passive, it becomes very hard to learn. If, for instance, you show first graders two pictures, one of a cat chasing a dog and the other of a dog chasing a cat, and tell them to point to the picture called "the cat is chased by the dog," only about half will respond correctly. They ignore the little words that signal the passive and pay attention to the word order. The processes by which speakers sort words into classes and the rules for the combination of members of the classes are now being worked out for adult and child speakers, but the work is far from complete.

John B. Carroll, an educational psychologist, offers a similar view of syntax:[2]

A sentence can be likened to a computer program; in fact, that is precisely what it is: a set of directions for the human thinking machine. The hearer or the reader of a sentence constructs its meaning by following the "directions" it provides in terms of the concepts and conceptual relationships it evokes, also utilizing whatever further information he may have concerning the situation in which he hears it. This process may be called *interpretation*.

Following Carroll's metaphor, the newborn infant may possess an extraordinary computer, but which program can he interpret, and where does the programming stem from? A study by Roger Brown and Ursula Bellugi describes the child's acquisition of syntax. Note that, as Lenneberg suggested, "one major aspect of the development of general structure in child speech is a progressive differentiation in the usage of words and therefore a progressive differentiation of syntactic classes." The authors also hint at possible biological foundations of the process.

THREE PROCESSES IN THE CHILD'S ACQUISITION OF SYNTAX[3]

Some time in the second six months of life most children say a first intelligible word. A few months later most children are saying many words and some children go about the house all day long naming things (*table, doggie, ball,* etc.) and actions (*play, see, drop,* etc.) and an occasional quality (*blue, broke, bad,* etc.). At about eighteen months children are likely to begin constructing two-word utterances; such a one, for instance, as *Push car.*

A construction such as *Push car* is not just two single-word utterances spoken in a certain order. As single-word utterances (they are sometimes called holophrases) both *push* and *car* would have primary stress and terminal intonation contours. When they are two words programmed as a single utterance the primary stress would fall on *car* and so would the highest level of pitch. *Push* would be subordinated to *car* by a lesser stress and a lower pitch; the unity of the whole would appear in the absence of a terminal contour between words and the presence of such a contour at the end of the full sequence.

By the age of thirty-six months some children are so advanced in the construction process as to produce all of the major varieties of English simple sentences up to a length of ten or twelve words. For several years we have been studying the development of English syntax, of the sentence-constructing process, in children between eighteen and thirty-six months of age. Most recently we have made a longitudinal study of a boy and girl whom we shall call Adam and Eve. We began work with Adam and Eve in October of 1962 when Adam was twenty-seven months old and Eve eighteen months old. The two children were selected from some thirty whom we considered. They were selected primarily because their speech was exceptionally intelligible and because they talked a lot. We wanted to make it as easy as possible to transcribe accurately large quantities of child speech. Adam and Eve are the children of highly educated parents; the fathers were graduate students at Harvard and the mothers are both college graduates. Both Adam and Eve were single children when we began the study. These facts must be remembered in generalizing the outcomes of the research.

While Adam is nine months older than Eve, his speech was only a little more advanced in October of 1962. The best single index of the level of speech development is the average length of utterance and in October, 1962, Adam's average was 1.84 morphemes and Eve's was 1.40 morphemes. The two children stayed fairly close together in the year that followed; in the records for the thirty-eighth week Adam's average was 3.55 and Eve's 3.27. The processes we shall describe appeared in both children.

Every second week we visited each child for at least two hours and made a tape recording of everything said by the child as well as of everything said to the child. The mother was always present and most of the speech to the child is hers. Both mother and child became very accustomed to our presence and learned to continue their usual routine with us as the observers.

One of us always made a written transcription, on the scene, of the speech of mother and child with notes about important actions and objects of attention. From this transcription and the tape a final transcription was made and these transcriptions constitute the primary data of the study. For many purposes we require a "distributional analysis" of the speech of the child. To this end the child's utterances in a given transcription were cross classified and relisted under such headings as: "A + noun"; "Noun + verb"; "Verbs in the past"; "Utterances containing the pronoun *it*," etc. The categorized utterances expose the syntactic regularities of the child's speech.

Each week we met as a research seminar, with students of the psychology of language,[4] to discuss the state of the construction process in one of the two children as of that date. In these discussions small experiments were often suggested, experiments that had to be done within a few days if they were to be informative. At one time, for instance, we were uncertain whether Adam understood the semantic difference between putting a noun in subject position and putting it in object position. Consequently one of us paid an extra visit to Adam equipped with some toys. "Adam," we said, "show us the duck pushing the boat." And, when he had done so: "Now show us the boat pushing the duck."

Another week we noticed that Adam would sometimes pluralize nouns when they should have been pluralized and sometimes would not. We wondered if he could make grammatical judgments about the plural, if he could distinguish a correct form from an incorrect form. "Adam," we asked, "which is right, 'two shoes' or 'two shoe'?" His answer on that occasion, produced with explosive enthusiasm, was "Pop goes the weasel!" The two-year-old child does not make a perfectly docile experimental subject.

The dialogue between mother and child does not read like a transcribed dialogue between two adults. Table 1 offers a sample section from an early transcribed record. It has some interesting properties. The conversation is, in the first place, very much in the here and now. From the child there is no speech of the sort that Bloomfield called "displaced," speech about other times and other places. Adam's utterances in the early months were largely a coding of contemporaneous events and impulses. The mother's speech differs from the speech that adults use to one another in many ways. Her sentences are short and simple; for the most part they are the kinds of sentences that Adam will produce a year later.

Perhaps because they are short, the sentences of the mother are perfectly grammatical. The sentences adults use to one another, perhaps because they are longer and more complex, are very often not grammatical, not well formed. Here for instance is a rather representative example produced at a conference of psychologists and linguists: "As far as I know, no one yet has done the in a way obvious now and interesting problem of doing a in a sense a structural frequency study of the alternative syntactical in a given language, say, like English, the alternative possible structures, and how what their hierarchical probability of occurrence structure is."[5] It seems unlikely that a child could learn the patterns of English syntax from such speech. His introduction to English ordinarily comes in the form of a simplified, repetitive, and idealized dialect. It may be that such an introduction is necessary for the acquisition of syntax to be possible but we do not know that.

In the course of the brief interchange of Table 1 Adam imitates his mother in saying: "There go one" immediately after she says "There goes one." The imitation is not perfect; Adam omits the inflection on the verb. His imitation is a reduction in that it omits something from the original. This kind of imitation with reduction is extremely common in the records of Adam and Eve and it is the first process we shall discuss.

IMITATION AND REDUCTION

Table 2 presents some model sentences spoken by the mothers and the imitations produced by Adam and Eve. These were selected from hundreds in the records in order to illustrate some general propositions. The first thing to notice is that the imitations preserve the word order of the model sentences. To be sure, words in the model are often missing from the imitation but the words preserved are in the order of the original. This is a fact that is so familiar and somehow reasonable that we did not at once recognize it as an empirical outcome rather than as a natural necessity. But of course it is not a necessity; the outcome could have been otherwise. For example, words could have been said back in the reverse of their original order, the most recent first. The preservation of order suggests that the model sentence is processed by the child as a total construction rather than as a list of words.

TABLE 1

A Section from Adam's First Record

ADAM	MOTHER
See truck, Mommy.	
See truck.	
	Did you see the truck?
No I see truck.	
	No, you didn't see it?
	There goes one.
There go one.	
	Yes, there goes one.
See a truck.	
See truck, Mommy.	
See truck.	
Truck.	
Put truck, Mommy.	
	Put the truck where?
Put truck window.	
	I think that one's too large to go in the window.

In English the order of words in a sentence is an important grammatical signal. Order is used to distinguish among subject, direct object, and indirect object and it is one of the marks of imperative and interrogative constructions. The fact that the child's first sentences preserve the word order of their models partially accounts for the ability of an adult to "understand" these sentences and so to feel that he is in communication with the child. It is conceivable that the child "intends" the meanings coded by his word orders and that, when he preserves

TABLE 2
Some Imitations Produced by Adam and Eve

MODEL UTTERANCE	CHILD'S IMITATION
Tank car	*Tank car*
Wait a minute	*Wait a minute*
Daddy's briefcase	*Daddy briefcase*
Fraser will be unhappy	*Fraser unhappy*
He's going out	*He go out*
That's an old-time train	*Old-time train*
It's not the same dog as Pepper	*Dog Pepper*
No, you can't write on Mr. Cromer's shoe	*Write Cromer shoe*

the order of an adult sentence, he does so because he wants to say what the order says. It is also possible that he preserves word order just because his brain works that way and that he has no comprehension of the semantic contrasts involved. In some languages word order is not an important grammatical signal. In Latin, for instance, "Agricola amat puellam" has the same meaning as "Puellam amat agricola" and subject-object relations are signalled by case endings. We would be interested to know whether children who are exposed to languages that do not utilize word order as a major syntactic signal, preserve order as reliably as do children exposed to English.

The second thing to notice in Table 2 is the fact that when the models increase in length there is not a corresponding increase in the imitation. The imitations stay in the range of two to four morphemes which was the range characteristic of the children at this time. The children were operating under some constraint of length or span. This is not a limitation of vocabulary; the children knew hundreds of words. Neither is it a constraint of immediate memory. We infer this from the fact that the average length of utterances produced spontaneously, where immediate memory is not involved, is about the same as the average length of utterances produced as immediate imitations. The constraint is a limitation on the length of utterance the children are able to program or plan.[6] This kind of narrow span limitation in children is characteristic of most or all of their intellectual operations. The limitation grows less restrictive with age as a consequence, probably, of both neurological growth and of practice, but of course it is never lifted altogether.

A constraint on length compels the imitating child to omit some words or morphemes from the mother's longer sentences. Which forms are retained and which omitted? The selection is not random but highly systematic. Forms retained in the examples of Table 2 include: *Daddy, Fraser, Pepper,* and *Cromer; tank car, minute, briefcase, train, dog,* and *shoe; wait, go,* and *write; unhappy* and *old-time.* For the most part they are nouns, verbs, and adjectives, though there are exceptions, as witness the initial pronoun *He* and the preposition *out* and the indefinite article *a.* Forms omitted in the samples of Table 2 include: the possessive inflection *-s,* the modal auxiliary *will,* the contraction of the auxiliary verb *is,* the progressive inflection *-ing,* the preposition *on,* the articles *the* and *an,* and the modal auxiliary *can.* It is possible to make a general characterization of the forms likely to be retained that distinguishes them as a total class from the forms likely to be omitted.

Forms likely to be retained are nouns and verbs and, less often, adjectives, and these are the three large and "open" parts-of-speech in English. The number of forms in any one of these parts-of-speech is extremely large and always growing. Words belonging to these classes are sometimes called "contentives" because they have semantic content. Forms likely to be omitted are inflections, auxiliary verbs, articles, prepositions, and conjunctions. These forms belong to syntactic classes that are small and closed. Any one class has few members and new members are not readily added. The omitted forms are the ones that linguists sometimes call "functors," their grammatical *functions* being more obvious than their semantic content.

Why should young children omit functors and retain contentives? There is more than one plausible answer. Nouns, verbs, and adjectives are words that make reference. One can conceive of teaching the meanings of these words by speaking them, one at a time, and pointing at things or actions or qualities. And of course parents do exactly that. These are the kinds of words that children have been encouraged to practice speaking one at a time. The child arrives at the age of sentence construction with a stock of well-practiced nouns, verbs, and adjectives. Is it not likely then that this prior practice causes him to retain the contentives from model sentences too long to be reproduced in full, that the child imitates those forms in the speech he hears which are already well developed in him as individual habits? There is probably some truth in this explanation but it is not the only determinant since children will often select for retention contentives that are relatively unfamiliar to them.

We adults sometimes operate under a constraint on length and the curious fact is that the English we produce in these circumstances bears a formal resemblance to the English produced by two-year-old children. When words cost money there is a premium on brevity or to put it otherwise, a constraint on length. The result is "telegraphic" English and telegraphic English is an English of nouns, verbs, and adjectives. One does not send a cable reading: "My car has broken down and I have lost my wallet; send money to me at the American Express in Paris" but rather "Car broken down; wallet lost; send money American Express Paris." The telegram omits: *my, has, and, I, have, my, to, me, at, the, in*. All of these are functors. We make the same kind of telegraphic reduction when time or fatigue constrain us to be brief, as witness any set of notes taken at a fast-moving lecture.

A telegraphic transformation of English generally communicates very well. It does so because it retains the high-information words and drops the low-information words. We are using "information" in the sense of the mathematical theory of communication. The information carried by a word is inversely related to the chances of guessing it from context. From a given string of content words, missing functors can often be guessed but the message "my has and I have my to me at the in" will not serve to get money to Paris. Perhaps children are able to make a communication analysis of adult speech and so adapt in an optimal way to their limitation of span. There is, however, another way in which the adaptive outcome might be achieved.

If you say aloud the model sentences of Table 2 you will find that you place the heavier stresses, the primary and secondary stresses in the sentences, on contentives rather than on functors. In fact the heavier stresses fall, for the most part, on the words the child retains. We first realized that this was the case when we found that in transcribing tapes, the words of the mother that we could hear most clearly were usually the words that the child reproduced. We had trouble hearing the weakly stressed functors and, of course, the child usually failed to reproduce them. Differential stress may then be the cause of the child's differential retention. The outcome is a maximally informative reduction but the cause of this outcome need not be the making of an information analysis. The outcome may be an incidental consequence of the fact that English is a well-designed language that places its heavier stresses where they are needed, on contentives that cannot easily be guessed from context.

We are fairly sure that differential stress is one of the determinants of the child's telegraphic productions. For one thing, stress will also account for the way in which children reproduce polysyllabic words when the total is too much for them. Adam, for instance, gave us *'pression* for *expression* and Eve gave us *'raff* for *giraffe;* the more heavily-stressed syllables were the ones retained. In addition we have tried the effect of placing heavy stresses on functors which do not ordinarily receive such stresses. To Adam we said: "You say what I say" and then, speaking in a normal way at first: "The doggie will bite." Adam gave back: "Doggie bite." Then we stressed the auxiliary: "The doggie *will* bite" and, after a few trials, Adam made attempts at reproducing that auxiliary. A science fiction experiment comes to mind. If there were parents who stressed functors rather than contentives would they have children whose speech was a kind of "reciprocal telegraphic" made up of articles, prepositions, conjunctions, auxiliaries, and the like? Such children would be out of touch with the community as real children are not.

It may be that all the factors we have mentioned play some part in determining the child's selective imitations: the reference-making function of contentives, the fact that they are practiced as single words, the fact that they cannot be guessed from context, and the heavy stresses they receive. There are also other possible factors: for example, the left-to-right, earlier-to-later position of words in a sentence, but these make too long a story to tell here.[7] Whatever the causes, the first utterances produced as imitations of adult sentences are highly systematic reductions of their models. Furthermore, the telegraphic properties of these imitations appear also in the child's spontaneously produced utterances. When his speech is not modeled on an immediately prior adult sentence, it observes the same limitation on length and the same predilection for contentives as when it is modeled on an immediately prior sentence.

IMITATION WITH EXPANSION

In the course of the brief conversation set down in Table 1, Adam's mother at one point imitates Adam. The boy says: "There go one" and mother responds: "Yes, there goes one." She does not exactly reproduce the model sentence of the child but instead adds something to it or expands it. What she adds is a functor, the inflection for third-person on the verb, the very form that Adam had omitted when he imitated his mother.

One of the first things we noticed when we began to study child speech several years ago was the frequency with which adults imitated children. Indeed they seemed to imitate more often than did the children themselves. We later came to realize that adult imitations are seldom exact reproductions; they are usually expansions. The mothers of Adam and Eve responded to the speech of their children with expansions about thirty per cent of the time. We did it ourselves when we talked with the children. Indeed we found it very difficult to withhold expansions. A reduced or incomplete English sentence seems to constrain the English-speaking adult to expand it into the nearest properly formed complete sentence. Table 3 lists a few sample expansions from the hundreds in the records.

The first thing worthy of attention in the expansions of Table 3 is the fact that the words spoken by the mother preserve the order of the words in the child's sentences. To be sure, words and inflections are added but they are fitted in—before, and after, and between the words the child used; they are not generally permitted to disturb the order of the child's words. It is as if these latter were taken as constants by the mother, constants to which some sentence had to be fitted. She acts as if she were assuming that the child means everything he says, all the words and also their order, but as if he might also mean more than he says. From the mother's point of view an expansion is a kind of communication check; it says in effect: "Is this what you mean?"

TABLE 3

Expansions of Child Speech Produced by Mothers

CHILD	MOTHER
Baby highchair	*Baby is in the highchair*
Mommy eggnog	*Mommy had her eggnog*
Eve lunch	*Eve is having lunch*
Mommy sandwich	*Mommy'll have a sandwich*
Sat wall	*He sat on the wall*
Throw Daddy	*Throw it to Daddy*
Pick glove	*Pick the glove up*

The second thing to notice about Table 3 is the character of the forms added to the child's utterances. They include the auxiliaries *is* and *will;* the prepositions *in, on, to,* and *up;* the verb forms *is, have, had,* and *having;* the articles *a* and *the;* the pronouns *her, he,* and *it.* For the most part, the words added are functors and functors are of course the words that the child omits in his reductions.

The interaction between mother and child is, much of the time, a cycle of reductions and expansions. There are two transformations involved. The reduction transformation has an almost completely specifiable and so a mechanical character. One could program a machine to do it with the following instructions: "Retain contentives (or stressed forms) in the order given up to some limit of length." The expansion accomplished by Adam's mother when she added the third-person inflection to the verb and said "There goes one" is also a completely specifiable transformation. The instructions would read: "Retain the forms given in the order given and supply obligatory grammatical forms." To be sure this mother-machine would have to be supplied with the obligatory rules of English grammar but that could be done. However, the sentence "There goes one" is atypical in that it only adds a compulsory and redundant inflection. The expansions of Table 3 all add forms that are not grammatically compulsory or redundant and these expansions cannot be mechanically generated by grammatical rules alone.

In Table 3 the topmost four utterances produced by the child are all of the same grammatical type; all four consist of a proper noun followed by a common noun. However, the four are expanded in quite different ways. In particular the form of the verb changes; it is in the first case in the simple present tense; in the second case the simple past; in the third case the present progressive; in the last case the simple future. All of these are perfectly grammatical but they are different. The second set of child utterances is formally uniform in that each one consists of a verb followed by a noun. The expansions are again all grammatical but quite unlike, especially with regard to the preposition supplied. In general, then, there are radical changes in the mother's expansions when there are no changes in the formal character of the utterances expanded. It follows that the expansions cannot be produced simply by making grammatically compulsory additions to the child's utterances.

How does a mother decide on the correct expansion of one of her child's utterances? Consider the utterance "Eve lunch." So far as grammar is concerned this utterance could be appropriately expanded in any of a number of ways: "Eve is having lunch"; "Eve had lunch"; "Eve will have lunch"; "Eve's lunch," etc. On the occcasion when Eve produced the utterance, however, one expansion seemed more appropriate than any other. It was then the noon hour, Eve was sitting at the table with a plate of food before her, and her spoon and fingers were busy. In these circumstances "Eve lunch" had to mean "Eve is having lunch." A little later when the plate had been stacked in the sink and Eve was getting down from her chair the utterance "Eve lunch" would have suggested the expansion "Eve has had her lunch." Most expansions are not only responsive to the child's words but also to the circumstances attending their utterance.

What kind of instructions will generate the mother's expansions? The following are approximately correct: "Retain the words given in the order given and add those functors that will result in a well-formed simple sentence that is appropriate to the circumstances." These are not instructions that any machine could follow. A machine could act on the instructions only if it were provided with detailed specifications for judging appropriateness and no such specifications can, at present, be written. They exist, however, in implicit form in the brains of mothers and in the brains of all English-speaking adults and so judgments of appropriateness can be made by such adults.

The expansion encodes aspects of reality that are not coded by the child's telegraphic utterance. Functors have meaning but it is meaning that accrues to them in context rather than in isolation. The meanings that are added by functors seem to be nothing less than the basic terms in which we construe reality: the time of an action, whether it is ongoing or completed, whether it is presently relevant or not; the concept of possession and such relational concepts as are coded by *in, on, up, down,* and the like; the difference between a particular instance of a class ("Has anybody seen *the* paper?") and any instance of a class ("Has anybody seen *a* paper?"); the difference between extended substances given shape and size by an "accidental" container (*sand, water, syrup,* etc.) and countable "things" having a characteristic fixed shape and size (*a cup, a man, a tree,* etc). It seems to us that a mother in expanding speech may be teaching more than grammar; she may be teaching something like a world-view.

As yet it has not been demonstrated that expansions are *necessary* for learning either grammar or a construction of reality. It has not even been demonstrated that expansions contribute to such learning. All we know is that some parents do expand and their children do learn. It is perfectly possible, however, that children can and do learn simply from hearing their parents or others make well-formed sentences in connection with various nonverbal circumstances. It may not be necessary or even helpful for these sentences to be expansions of utterances of the child. Only experiments contrasting expansion training with simple exposure to English will settle the matter. We hope to do such experiments.

There are, of course, reasons for expecting the expansion transformation to be an effective tutorial technique. By adding something to the words the child has just produced one confirms his response insofar as it is appropriate. In addition one takes him somewhat beyond that response but not greatly beyond it. One encodes additional meanings at a moment when he is most likely to be attending to the cues that can teach that meaning.

INDUCTION OF THE LATENT STRUCTURE

Adam, in the course of the conversation with his mother set down in Table 1, produced one utterance for which no adult is likely ever to have provided an exact model: "No I see truck." His mother elects to expand it as "No, you didn't see it" and this expansion suggests that the child might have created the utterance by reducing an adult model containing the form *didn't*. However, the mother's expansion in this case does some violence to Adam's original version. He did not say *no* as his mother said it, with primary stress and final contour; Adam's *no* had secondary stress and no final contour. It is not easy to imagine an adult model for this utterance. It seems more likely that the utterance was created by Adam as part of a continuing effort to discover the general rules for constructing English negatives.

In Table 4 we have listed some utterances produced by Adam or Eve for which it is difficult to imagine any adult model. It is unlikely that any adult said any of these to Adam or Eve since they are very simple utterances and yet definitely ungrammatical. In addition it is difficult, by adding functors alone, to build any of them up to simple grammatical sentences. Consequently it does not seem likely that these utterances are reductions of adult originals. It is more likely that they are mistakes which externalize the child's search for the regularities of English syntax.

We have long realized that the occurrence of certain kinds of errors on the level of morphology (or word construction) reveals the child's effort to induce regularities from speech. So long as a child speaks correctly, or at any rate so long as he speaks as correctly as the adults he hears, there is no way to tell whether he is simply repeating what he has heard or whether he is actually constructing. However, when he says something like "I digged a hole" we can often be sure that he is constructing. We can be sure because it is unlikely that he would have heard *digged* from anyone and because we can see how, in processing words he had heard, he might have come by *digged*. It looks like an overgeneralization of the regular past inflection. The inductive operations of the child's mind are externalized in such a creation. Overgeneralizations on the level of syntax (or sentence construction) are more difficult to identify because there are so many ways of adding functors so as to build up conceivable models. But this is difficult to do for the examples of Table 4 and for several hundred other utterances in our records.

The processes of imitation and expansion are not sufficient to account for the degree of linguistic competence that children regularly acquire. These processes alone cannot teach more than the sum total of sentences that speakers of English have either modeled for a child to imitate or built up from a child's reductions. However, a child's linguistic competence extends far beyond this sum total of sentences. All children are able to understand and construct sentences they have never heard but which are nevertheless well-formed, well-formed in terms of general rules that are implicit in the sentences the child has heard. Somehow, then, every child processes the speech to which he is exposed so as to induce from it a latent structure. This latent rule structure is so general that a child can spin out its implications all his life long. It is both semantic and syntactic. The discovery of latent structure is the greatest of the processes involved in language acquisition and the most difficult to understand. We will provide an example of how the analysis can proceed by discussing the evolution in child speech of noun phrases.

TABLE 4

Utterances Not Likely to Be Imitations

My Cromer suitcase	*You naughty are*
Two foot	*Why it can't turn off?*
A bags	*Put on it*
A scissor	*Cowboy did fighting me*
A this truck	*Put a gas in*

A noun phrase in adult English includes a noun but also more than a noun. One variety consists of a noun with assorted modifiers: *The girl; The pretty girl; That pretty girl; My girl,* etc. All of these are constructions which have the same syntactic privileges as do nouns alone. One can use a noun phrase in isolation to name or request something; one can use it in sentences, in subject position or in object position or in predicate nominative position. All of these are slots that nouns alone can also fill. A larger construction having the same syntactic privileges as its "head" word is called in linguistics an "endocentric" construction and noun phrases are endocentric constructions.

For both Adam and Eve, in the early records, noun phrases usually occur as total independent utterances rather than as components of sentences. Table 5 presents an assortment of such utterances at Time 1. They consist in each case of some sort of modifier, just one, preceding a noun. The modifiers, or as they

TABLE 5

Noun Phrases in Isolation
and Rule for Generating Noun Phrases at Time 1

A coat	*More coffee*
*A celery**	*More nut**
*A Becky**	*Two sock**
*A hands**	*Two shoes*
The top	*Two tinker-toy**
My Mommy	*Big boat*
That Adam	*Poor man*
My stool	*Little top*
That knee	*Dirty knee*

$$NP \rightarrow M + N$$

M → *a, big, dirty, little, more, my, poor, that, the, two.*

N → *Adam, Becky, boot, coat, coffee, knee, man, Mommy, nut, sock, stool, tinker-toy, top,* and very many others.

* Ungrammatical for an adult.

are sometimes called, the "pivot" words, are a much smaller class than the noun class. Three students of child speech have independently discovered that this kind of construction is extremely common when children first begin to combine words.[8] [9] [10]

It is possible to generalize the cases of Table 5 into a simple implicit rule. The rule symbolized in Table 5 reads: "In order to form a noun phrase of this type, select first one word from the small class of modifiers and select, second, one word from the large class of nouns." This is a "generative" rule by which we mean it is a program that would actually serve to build constructions of the type in question. It is offered as a model of the mental mechanism by which Adam and Eve generated such utterances. Furthermore, judging from our work with other children and from the reports of Braine and of Miller and Ervin, the model describes a mechanism present in many children when their average utterance is approximately two morphemes long.

We have found that even in our earliest records the M + N construction is sometimes used as a component of larger constructions. For instance, Eve said: "Fix a Lassie" and "Turn the page" and "A horsie stuck" and Adam even said: "Adam wear a shirt." There are, at first, only a handful of these larger constructions but there are very many constructions in which h single nouns occur in subject or in object position.

Let us look again at the utterances of Table 5 and the rule generalizing them. The class M does not correspond with any syntactic class of adult English. In the class M are articles, a possessive pronoun, a cardinal number, a demonstrative adjective or pronoun, a quantifier, and some descriptive adjectives—a mixed bag indeed. For adult English these words cannot belong to the same syntactic class because they have very different privileges of occurrence in sentences. For the children the words do seem to function as one class having the common privilege of occurrence before nouns.

If the initial words of the utterances in Table 5 are treated as one class M then many utterances are generated which an adult speaker would judge to be ungrammatical. Consider the indefinite article *a*. Adults use it only to modify common count nouns in the singular such as *coat, dog, cup,* etc. We would not say *a celery,* or *a cereal,* or *a dirt; celery, cereal,* and *dirt* are mass nouns. We would not say *a Becky* or *a Jimmy; Becky* and *Jimmy* are proper nouns. We would not say *a hands* or *a shoes; hands* and *shoes* are plural nouns. Adam and Eve, at first, did form ungrammatical combinations such as these.

The numeral *two* we use only with count nouns in the plural. We would not say *two sock* since *sock* is singular, nor *two water* since *water* is a mass noun. The word *more* we use before count nouns in the plural *(more nuts)* or mass nouns in the singular *(more coffee)*. Adam and Eve made a number of combinations involving *two* or *more* that we would not make.

Given the initial very undiscriminating use of words in the class M it follows that one dimension of development must be a progressive differentiation of privileges, which means the division of M into smaller classes. There must also be subdivision of the noun class (N) for the reason that the privileges of occurrence of various kinds of modifiers must be described in terms of such sub-varieties of N as the common noun and proper noun, the count noun and mass noun. There must eventually emerge a distinction between nouns singular and nouns plural since this distinction figures in the privileges of occurrence of the several sorts of modifiers.

Sixteen weeks after our first records from Adam and Eve (Time 2), the differentiation process had begun. By this time there were distributional reasons for separating out articles *(a, the)* from demonstrative pronouns *(this, that)* and both of these from the residual class of modifiers. Some of the evidence for this conclusion appears in Table 6. In general one syntactic class is distinguished from another when the members of one class have combinational privileges not enjoyed by the members of the other. Consider, for example, the reasons for distinguishing articles (Art) from modifiers in general (M). Both articles and modifiers appeared in front of nouns in two-word utterances. However, in three-word utterances that were made up from the total pool of words and that had a noun in final position, the privileges of *a* and *the* were different from the privileges of all other modifiers. The articles occurred in initial position followed by a member of class M other than an article. No other modifier occurred in this first position; notice the "Not obtained" examples of Table 6A. If the children had produced utterances like those (for example, *blue a flower, your a car)* there would have been no difference in the privileges of occurrence of articles and modifiers and therefore no reason to separate out articles.

TABLE 6

Subdivision of the Modifier Class

A. PRIVILEGES PECULIAR TO ARTICLES	
OBTAINED	NOT OBTAINED
A blue flower	*Blue a flower*
A nice nap	*Nice a nap*
A your car	*Your a car*
A my pencil	*My a pencil*

B. PRIVILEGES PECULIAR TO DEMONSTRATIVE PRONOUNS	
OBTAINED	NOT OBTAINED
That my cup	*My that cup*
That a horse	*A that horse*
That a blue flower	*A that blue flower*
	Blue a that flower

The record of Adam is especially instructive. He created such notably ungrammatical combinations as "a your car" and "a my pencil." It is very unlikely that adults provided models for these. They argue strongly that Adam regarded all the words in the residual M class as syntactic equivalents and so generated these very odd utterances in which possessive pronouns appear where descriptive adjectives would be more acceptable.

Table 6 also presents some of the evidence for distinguishing demonstrative pronouns (Dem) from articles and modifiers (Table 6B). The pronouns occurred first and ahead of articles in three- and four-word utterances—a position that neither articles nor modifiers ever filled. The sentences with demonstrative pronouns are recognizable as reductions which omit the copular verb *is.* Such sentences are not noun phrases in adult English and ultimately they will not function as noun phrases in the speech of the children, but for the present they are not distinguishable distributionally from noun phrases.

Recall now the generative formula of Table 5 which constructs noun phrases by simply placing a modifier (M) before a noun (N). The differentiation of privileges illustrated in Table 6, and the syntactic classes this evidence motivates us to create, complicate the formula for generating noun phrases. In Table 7 we have written a single general formula for producing all noun phrases at Time 2 $[$NP $\rightarrow$ (Dem) + (Art) + (M) + N$]$ and also the numerous more specific rules which are summarized by the general formula.

TABLE 7

Rules for Generating Noun Phrases at Time 2

$NP_1 \rightarrow Dem + Art + M + N$	$NP \rightarrow (Dem) + (Art) + (M) + N$
$NP_2 \rightarrow Art + M + N$	
$NP_3 \rightarrow Dem + M + N$	
$NP_4 \rightarrow Art + N$	( ) means class within
$NP_5 \rightarrow M + N$	parentheses is optional
$NP_6 \rightarrow Dem + N$	
$NP_7 \rightarrow Dem + Art + N$	

By the time of the thirteenth transcription, twenty-six weeks after we began our study, privileges of occurrence were much more finely differentiated and syntactic classes were consequently more numerous. From the distributional evidence we judged that Adam had made five classes of his original class M: articles, descriptive adjectives, possessive pronouns, demonstrative pronouns, and a residual class of modifiers. The generative rules of Table 7 had become inadequate; there were no longer, for instance, any combinations like "A your car." Eve had the same set except that she used two residual classes of modifiers. In addition nouns had begun to subdivide for both children. The usage of proper nouns had become clearly distinct from the usage of count nouns. For Eve the evidence justified separating count nouns from mass nouns, but for Adam it still did not. Both children by this time were frequently pluralizing nouns but as yet their syntactic control of the singular-plural distinction was imperfect.

In summary, one major aspect of the development of general structure in child speech is a progressive differentiation in the usage of words and therefore a progressive differentiation of syntactic classes. At the same time, however, there is an integrative process at work. From the first, an occasional noun phrase occurred as a component of some larger construction. At first these noun phrases were just two words long and the range of positions in which they could occur was small. With time the noun phrases grew longer, were more frequently used, and were used in a greater range of positions. The noun phrase structure as a whole, in all the permissible combinations of modifiers and nouns, was assuming the combinational privileges enjoyed by nouns in isolation.

In Table 8 we have set down some of the sentence positions in which both nouns and noun phrases occurred in the speech of Adam and Eve. It is the close match between the positions of nouns alone and of nouns with modifiers in the speech of Adam and Eve that justifies us in calling the longer constructions noun phrases. These longer constructions are, as they should be, endocentric; the head word alone has the same syntactic privileges as the head word with its modifiers. The continuing failure to find in noun phrase positions whole constructions of the type

"That a blue flower" signals the fact that these constructions are telegraphic versions of predicate nominative sentences omitting the verb form *is*. Examples of the kind of construction not obtained are: "That (that a blue flower)"; "Where (that a blue flower)?"

TABLE 8

Some Privileges of the Noun Phrase

NOUN POSITIONS	NOUN PHRASE POSITIONS
That (flower)	*That (a blue flower)*
Where (ball) go?	*Where (the puzzle) go?*
Adam write (penguin)	*Doggie eat (the breakfast)*
(Horsie) stop	*(A horsie) crying*
Put (hat) on	*Put (the red hat) on*

For adults the noun phrase is a subwhole of the sentence, what linguists call an "immediate constituent." The noun phrase has a kind of psychological unity. There are signs that the noun phrase was also an immediate constituent for Adam and Eve. Consider the sentence using the separable verb *put on*. The noun phrase in "Put the red hat on" is, as a whole, fitted in between the verb and the particle even as is the noun alone in "Put hat on." What is more, however, the location of pauses in the longer sentence, on several occasions, suggested the psychological organization: "Put ... the red hat ... on" rather than "Put the red ... hat on" or "Put the ... red hat on." In addition to this evidence the use of pronouns suggests that the noun phrase is a psychological unit.

The unity of noun phrases in adult English is evidenced, in the first place, by the syntactic equivalence between such phrases and nouns alone. It is evidenced, in the second place, by the fact that pronouns are able to substitute for total noun phrases. In our immediately preceding sentence the pronoun "It" stands for the rather involved construction from the first sentence of this paragraph: "The unity of noun phrases in adult English." The words called "pronouns" in English would more aptly be called "pro-noun-phrases" since it is the phrase rather than the noun which they usually replace. One does not replace "unity" with "it" and say "The *it* of noun phrases in adult English." In the speech of Adam and Eve, too, the pronoun came to function as a replacement for the noun phrase. Some of the clearer cases appear in Table 9.

Adam characteristically externalizes more of his learning than does Eve and his record is especially instructive in connection with the learning of pronouns. In his first eight records, the first sixteen weeks of the study, Adam quite often produced sentences containing both the pronoun and the noun or noun phrase that the pronoun should have replaced. One can here see the equivalence in the process of establishment. First the substitute is produced and then, as if in explication, the form or forms that will eventually be replaced by the substitute. Adam spoke out his pronoun antecedents as chronological consequents. This is additional evidence of the unity of the noun phrase since the noun phrases *my ladder* and *cowboy boot* are linked with *it* in Adam's speech in just the same way as the nouns *ladder* and *ball*.

TABLE 9

Pronouns Replacing Nouns or Noun Phrases and Pronouns
Produced Together with Nouns or Noun Phrases

NOUN PHRASES REPLACED BY PRONOUNS	PRONOUNS AND NOUN PHRASES IN SAME UTTERANCES
Hit ball	*Mommy get it ladder*
Get it	*Mommy get it my ladder*
Ball go?	
Go get it	*Saw it ball*
	Miss it garage
Made it	*I miss it cowboy boot*
Made a ship	*I Adam drive that*
Fix a tricycle	*I Adam drive*
Fix it	*I Adam don't*

We have described three processes involved in the child's acquisition of syntax. It is clear that the last of these, the induction of latent structure, is by far the most complex. It looks as if this last process will put a serious strain on any learning theory thus far conceived by psychology. The very intricate simultaneous differentiation and integration that constitutes the evolution of the noun phrase is more reminiscent of the biological development of an embryo than it is of the acquisition of a conditioned reflex.

Susan Ervin-Tripp suggests that classes and rules are developed by analogy. However, as the child listens to adults and to himself, there are gradual changes in the child's generalizations and analogies dealing with language, from unrefined generalizations to valid rules for language production.

IMITATION AND STRUCTURAL CHANGE IN CHILDREN'S LANGUAGE[11]

We all know that children's grammar converges on the norm for the community in which they live. How does this happen? One source might be through adult correction of errors and through operant conditioning reinforced by the responses of others. This is probably a relatively weak source of change in first language learning. We know, for instance, that children learn certain grammatical structures which nobody taught them explicitly, and we also know that often teachers try hard to eradicate some of them. All over the world children learn grammatical patterns whether or not anyone corrects their speech, and there have been cases in which children who were believed for years to be mute have been found employing relatively mature grammatical patterns. A second source of change is maturation. Young children cannot learn grammatical and semantic concepts of a certain degree of complexity, and they produce sentences limited in length. Gvozdev (1961),[12] in a book on child language development in Russian, has presented evidence that, when grammatical complexity is held constant, semantic difficulty is related to the age of acquisition of certain grammatical patterns. For instance, the conditional is learned late. Recent work by Roger W. Brown and his group supports this view.

But maturation cannot account for the content of language nor for the particular structures acquired. A third factor affecting language development might be comprehension. We know that, typically, recognition precedes production. We know that people can understand many more words than they ever use. The number of cues for recognition is less than the information needed for accurate production, and in recognition we can often profit from redundancy.

Fraser, Bellugi, and Brown (1963)[13] have recently found that children's imitation of grammatical contrasts regularly surpassed their comprehension, which in turn was superior to their freely generated speech. For instance, they would choose the right picture, or repeat "The sheep are jumping," or "The sheep is jumping," more often than they could speak the right name when a picture was pointed out.

The children in this study were asked to imitate. The real test as to whether imitation is significant as a source of progress in grammar should be based on spontaneous imitations, for children may imitate selectively.

The material to be reported here is merely suggestive. It consists of a study of only five children.[14] It is unique in that I have the advantage of working from careful descriptive grammars for each of the children about whom I shall report. The crucial test is this: Are imitated utterances grammatically different from free utterances? If they are different, are they more advanced grammatically?

Ideally, one would write independent grammars for the imitated sentences and for the freely generated sentences and compare the grammatical rules. Since the number of imitations was far too small, grammatical rules were written only for the free sentences, and then the imitations were tested for their consistency with these rules. This method loads the dice against the similarity of the imitations to the free sentences.

First I shall describe what I mean by a grammar, then define what I mean by imitation, and finally test the hypothesis of similarity.

We collected 250 sentences of two words or more from Donnie (Table 1). At this time, when he was 2 years and 2 months old, his mother reported that he had just begun to put words together. The rule described here accounts for 198 of Donnie's sentences.

Another 16 sentences followed another rule, producing "what's that" and "what's this." There were 35 sentences which could be described by neither rule.

You will see that the following sentences were grammatically consistent:

Blanket water.	Oh, there's a bed.
Bow-wow dog.	Oh, car.
Here big truck.	Oh, dear, the truck.
Where go the car?	Where's a big choochoo car?

We could not account for 7 per cent of Donnie's sentences by any simple rules. These included the following:

Where the more bead?	Here's it go.
Naughty Donnie.	Here's it goes.
Go get the truck.	What the choochoo car?
Go bye-bye Daddy.	

Three months later, Donnie's grammar had changed (Table 2). Some of the sentences that we could not account for at the earlier stage have now become

TABLE 1

Sentence-Generating Rule for Donnie, Age 2:2

OPTIONAL CLASSES[a]						REQUIRED CLASS
1	2	3	4	5	6	7
goodness	*here(s)*	*go* [b]	*a*	*big*	*bead*	*bead(s)*
oh	*there(s)*				*blanket*	*blanket*
oh oh	*where(s)*		*the*		*bow-wow*	*bow-wow*
oh dear					*car*	*car(s)*
					choochoo	*choochoo*
see	*this*				*Daddy*	*Daddy*
whee	*that(s)*				*kiddy-car*	*kiddy-car*
					ring	*ring*
					truck	*truck(s)*
					water	*water*
					etc.	*etc.*

[a] Classes 1 to 6, selected in that order, may precede 7.
[b] "This" and "that(s)" never precede "go."

more frequent and stable. We now find it necessary to set up a phrase rule for a nominal phrase, which you see in Table 2. Although all the regular sentences at the younger age contained at least one nominal, there are now more frequent sentences without a nominal phrase (Table 3). We can conveniently divide Donnie's sentences into four types at this age. The largest number, 173, were declarative sentences like "there's a bus," "there's a green," "here's a broken," and "there's all-gone." Ninety-six were nominal sentences like "big yellow," "oh, broken," "yellow broken," or "monkey broken." Another 76 contained "go" or "goes" as

TABLE 2

Nominal Phrase-Generating Rule For Donnie, Age 2:5

	OPTIONAL CLASSES [a]			REQUIRED CLASS
	1	2	3	4
	a	*red*	*all-gone*	*all-gone*
	the	*big*	*ball*	*ball*
		more	*bead*	*bead (s)*
NOMINAL			*broken*	*broken*
			bye-bye	*bye-bye*
			choochoo	*choochoo*
			green	*green*
			monkey	*monkey*
			truck	*truck*
			yellow	*yellow*
			etc.	*etc.*

[a] Classes 1 to 3, in that order, may precede 4.

in "car go broken," "goes the bubbles," and "there's it go." There were 20 sentences with "have-it," meaning "I want it." For example, "there beads, have-it" and "where the choochoo, have-it."

TABLE 3

Sentence-Generating Rule For Donnie, Age 2:5

1	2	3 [a]	4	5	6
oh boy	there (s)	it			
hi	where (s)	all	go	NOMINAL	have-it [c]
no	here (s)		goes		
don't	that (s) [b]				
etc.	this is [b]	NOMINAL			

[a] Multiword sentences contain at least one item from columns 3 to 6, with order as in the sequence of columns.

[b] That (s) and this (is) never precede columns 4 to 6.

[c] Columns 4 and 6 are mutually exclusive.

These are inductive or descriptive rules or grammars. Alternative descriptions might do as well: our criteria were brevity and completeness. We can test a grammar of an adult language by asking speakers if test sentences are acceptable; with so-called dead, literary languages we can cross-check different sources. With children, our descriptions must be more tentative. For these two-year-olds we found that between 77 and 80 per cent of the sentences could be described by our grammars.

Now we turn to the central issue. Are the spontaneous imitations of these children governed by the same rules as their freely generated sentences? To illustrate, here are some examples of Donnie's imitations at 2:5. You will find the first three are consistent, the last two are not.

This is a round ring.	This ring.
Where does it go?	Where's it go?
Is Donnie all-gone?	Donnie all-gone.
Is it a bus?	It a bus.
Is it broken?	Is broken?

We have confined this study only to overt, immediate repetitions. We have excluded imitations in which there were changes, as in "Liz is naughty," "He's naughty." We found that adult conversations are heavily threaded with such partial imitations and also that they are hard to separate from answers to questions. Judges might easily disagree in judging which were imitations. We kept the clear-cut cases, including exact repetitions, which were few, echoes of the final few words in sentences, and repetitions with words omitted. There were few cases of repetitions with changes in word order. Omissions bulked large in our cases of imitation. These tended to be concentrated on the unstressed segments of sentences, on articles, prepositions, auxiliaries, pronouns, and suffixes. For instance: "I'll make a cup for her to drink" produced "cup drink"; "Mr. Miller will try," "Miller try"; "Put the strap under her chin," "Strap chin." Thus the imitations had three characteristics: they selected the most recent and most emphasized words, and they preserved the word order.

When the imitations have been isolated, the next step is to identify the grammatically consistent sentences. These were of two types. Some used vocabulary that we had included in describing the grammars. As I have said, our rules included lists of words according to classes, or by positions they could occupy. Some of the imitated sentences included new words that were not on these lists. Any speech sample is selective in vocabulary, and since we were interested in structure and not vocabulary, we arbitrarily included as grammatical any sentences containing a single new word by treating these words as "deuces wild." That is to say, any new word could be assigned to a class so as to make a grammatical sentence. The same rule was used on the residual sentences which were freely generated. Some of these sentences were called ungrammatical simply because they included grammatically ambiguous words.

We used exactly the same rule of procedure for the imitated sentences and for the free sentences in deciding whether the sentence fit the structural rules or not. We made liberal, but equally liberal, provision for accepting new vocabulary in both samples. Thus we can see whether the rules of word arrangement were the same in the two samples (Table 4).

TABLE 4

Grammatical Novelty of Imitations

	PERCENTAGE IMITATED	PERCENTAGE GRAMMATICALLY CONSISTENT	
		FREELY GENERATED	IMITATED
Susan (1:10)	7	83	79
Christy (2:0)	5	91	92
Donnie (2:2)	6	93	100
Lisa (2:3)	15	83	65
Holly (2:4)	20	88	68 [a]
Donnie (2:5)	8	91	94
Donnie (2:10)	7	92	91

[a] $X^2 = 9.4$

For all the children except one, Holly, the sentences in both samples were equally predictable from both rules. Donnie was studied at three ages, and there was no change with age in the consistency of his imitated sentences.

But what about Holly? We must move to our second question with her: Were the imitated sentences grammatically more advanced than the free ones, or simply more inconsistent? We shall use three criteria in judging the grammatical maturity of these sentences. These criteria are based on the changes that characterized the children's speech in the months following those we are considering. First, sentence length increased with age. Donnie's sentences at the three ages considered had an average length of 2.2, 2.4, and 2.7 words. Secondly, there is an increase in certain grammatical markers with age, including an increase in the use of articles and pronouns. Finally, there is an increase in adult-like sentence constructions consisting of imperative-plus-object, or subject-verb-object, or subject-verb-plus-adjective, or subject-verb-particle. Examples are "hold it," "he took it," "that's hot," and "they came over."

Using these three criteria, we examined all of Holly's residual sentences, both imitated and free, that did *not* fit the rules of arrangement we had called her grammar. The average length of the free sentences was three words, of the imitated sentences, two words. There were grammatical markers such as articles and pronouns in 62 per cent of the free sentences, and in 28 per cent of the imitated sentences. Half of the free sentences and a third of the imitated sentences were structurally complete, from an adult standpoint. There were no subject-verb-object imitated sentences, but there were six subject-verb-object free sentences, such as "I want play game" and "I don't see Heather car," Heather being Holly's sister.

We are left with a question about why Holly was so different from the other children. It was something of a *tour de force* to write a grammar for Holly. One class, identified as a class by the fact that its members occupied initial position in sentences, included "this-one," "see," "want," and "there." Another heterogeneous class, identified only by the fact that it followed the words just described, included "around," "pull," "raining," "book," and "two." No other child had such a bizarre system, if system it was. Probably Holly's imitations did not fit this system because these were not in fact rules governing her speech. Donnie's rules were far more simple, consistent, and pervasive. It is possible that the high percentage of imitations produced by Holly is related to the fluidity of her grammar. But if it is so, then her imitations were a disturbing rather than a productive factor in her grammatical development.

If we can rely at all on this sample of five children, there is an inescapable conclusion. Imitations under the optimal conditions, those of immediate recall, are not grammatically progressive. We cannot look to overt imitation as a source for the rapid progress children make in grammatical skill in these early years.

A word of caution. I have *not* said that imitation is never important in language learning. In comprehension covert imitation may be important. Possibly imitation aids in the acquisition of vocabulary or of phonetic mastery. Perhaps overt imitation is indispensable in the special conditions of classroom language learning. All I have said is that there is not a shred of evidence supporting a view that progress toward adult norms of grammar arises merely from practice in overt imitation of adult sentences.

FITTING THEORIES TO FACTS

One may take several different approaches in accounting for child language development. We have already touched on one: the imitative view. According to this conceptualization the child makes errors and introduces abbreviations in his effort to approximate sentences he hears. Development is thought to consist of gradual elimination of such random errors.

This point of view is implied in the studies of grammatical development which have counted grammatical errors, omissions, and sentence length as criteria for developmental level. A second view assumes that children have sets of rules like those of adults, since they can understand adults, but that in speaking they have a combination of editing rules and random production errors. Development consists in eliminating the omissions and redundancies arising from these editing rules. A third view would assume that development can be described as the evolution of a series of linguistic systems increasing in complexity, with changes in behavior reflecting changes in the child's syntactical rules.

The data reported below have been collected in a collaborative study with Wick Miller, in which frequent texts were collected from seven monolingual oldest children, and monthly systematic tests were conducted on 24 children, during a period approximately from age 2 to 4.

In English plural inflection, the contrast *dogs* vs. *dog* might be learned as if the two words were unrelated, separate items of vocabulary. Each would be learned by imitation and by association with the appropriate semantic discrimination.

Yet imitation will not account for the behavior of adults speaking English. If an adult hears a new word, say, the name of a new tool, such as a *mindon*, he will surely call two of them *mindons*, a word he has never heard. We might say that he has formed a new word by analogy. Such analogic extensions are not explainable as simple generalization, because they occur when both the referent and the word itself are new and clearly distinguishable from previously known words. We found that children formed new plurals in this way when they were between 2 and 3 years old.

We tested children systematically by showing them objects, first singly and then in pairs, and asking for a description. These tests were conducted at monthly intervals. Some of the things we asked about were familiar, such as "boys" and "oranges." Others were new objects, called such things as a *bik, pud,* or *bunge.*

If the child learns the plural first in terms of separate items of vocabulary, we would expect him to employ the plural suffix with some consistency with familiar words before he generalized to new words. In fact, this is just what happened. For nearly all the children, there was a time gap between the time when a familiar plural was used and the time when an analogous new word was given a plural. Thus, between the time when the child contrasted *block* and *blocks* and the time when he said that two things called *bik* were *biks,* there was a small but reliable gap of about two weeks. For *car* and *boy* and the analogous *kie,* the gap was about six weeks. For other words the gap was greater. In all cases—*pud, bik, kie, tass,* and *bunge*—the new contrast appeared later than the contrasts the children had heard.

We would expect that this extension to new forms also would occur for the irregular plurals. All of the children, over the period we studied them, regularized the plural for *foot* and *man.* They said *man-mans,* and *foot-foots* or *feet-feets.* Most preferred *foot-foots.* Very few of the children fluctuated between *foot* and *feet,* so although the word *feet* must have been heard by the children, we can clearly see a regularizing influence. If imitation alone were at work, we would have expected fluctuation between *foot* and *feet.*

There was a difference in the time of acquisition depending on form. The English plural form is quite regular and has few exceptions. Its form is governed by certain sound rules. Thus we have *mat* and *mats,* but *match* and *matches.* We can describe this difference by saying that words ending in sibilants, such as *horse, buzz, match, judge, marsh,* or *rouge,* add a vowel plus *s.* Children at this age frequently do not distinguish these sounds phonetically—orange may be pronounced unpredictably as *orinch, orinz, orins, orinsh* by the same child. The children all shared the problem of adding *s* to words ending in sibilant sounds. What they did was omit a plural contrast for these words. The usual pattern in the earlier grammars was distinction of singular and plural except for words ending in sibilants, which had the same forms for singular and plural. Occasionally we would have analogies which removed the sibilant, as in singular *bun* plural *buns* for *bunges,* and singular *bok* plural *boks* for *boxes.*

At some point each child produced the regular plural for one of these sibilant words. Quite often, when this happened, the plural for other earlier forms changed. Thus when *box-boxes* first was given, we found such forms as *foot-footses,* or *hand-handses.* Another pattern sometimes appeared. When *tass-tasses* came in, we found *foot-footiz* or *bik-bikiz.*

These changes occurred with children who had previously used the *-s* plural regularly, for *foot, bik,* and *hand.* Why did these words change? If we examine the whole range of plurals employed at one of these points in time, we might describe the system as involving two plural forms vacillating unpredictably from *-s* to *-iz*. Alternatively, *-s* or *-iz* were both in unpredictable variation. Surely, at this point, it is clear that the child is employing some common response, whatever you may call it, in using all of these plural forms. A linguist would say the child had a plural morpheme with two allomorphs in free variation. How can a psychologist translate this behavior into terms familiar to him? This is most certainly not behavior learned by accumulated imitation. It is transitory, lasting at most two months, and then is resolved into a system of conditioned variation like that of adults.

There are two pieces of evidence here which will not fit a theory that inflection develops through imitation of familiar forms and extension by generalization to new items. One is the fact that *foot* and *feet* do not fluctuate as much as imitation of adults would lead us to expect. The other is that even highly practiced, familiar plurals may be temporarily changed in form by overgeneralization of new patterns. Both these data suggest that analogy in the production of sentences is a very important process and may outweigh the imitation of familiar forms.

Analogy is a familiar process to linguists. Formal similarity is the basis for the construct they call a morpheme. Yet overlaid on the child's systematic analogic forms, or morphemic patterns, we have a gradual accumulation of successful imitations which do not fit the stabilized pattern of the child, in such instances as *oranges* and *boxes*. Eventually these result in a change in the system, which becomes evident in the errors, from the adult standpoint, and in the analogic extensions to nonsense words. The conditioned allomorphs in the adult system—the different plurals in *mats* and *matches*—were imitated one by one at first. Then they produced random fluctuation between the two forms, and later stable responses conditioned by the same features in the phonetic environment as the adult plurals.

Now let us turn to past tense inflection. Our best data are from the group of seven children from whom we collected extensive texts in interviews over a period of time. It is, of course, much harder to elicit a contrast in tense than one in plurality. The semantic cues are less controllable. For this reason we relied on less systematic methods of testing. Now it happens that the English tense system has analogies to the system of plurals. Like the plurals, it has both a regular pattern and irregular forms. There is *walk-walked,* and there is *go-went.* As with the plurals, the specific phonemic pattern depends on the particular final phoneme of the simple verb—we have *pack-packed* and *pat-patted,* when a vowel is added in the suffix. As with plurals, the children used forms that indicated the difficulty of the pattern of adding a vowel—forms such as *toasteded.*

The major formal difference in English between plural inflection of nouns and tense inflection of verbs is the great frequency of irregular (or strong) verbs, whereas irregular nouns are relatively few. It was a surprise to me, in examining verb frequency tables for the children we studied, to find that verbs with regular inflection were few and infrequent in our earliest texts. Therefore, tense inflection begins with the *irregular* forms.

I looked for the first case of extension of the regular past tense suffix which could not have been imitated—for instance *buyed, comed, doed.* The odd, and to me astonishing, thing is that these extensions occurred in some cases before the child had produced *any* other regular past tense forms according to our sample. In some cases the other past tense forms consisted of only one or two words of dubious significance as past tense signals.

Relatively rare was the extension of irregular patterns—though we did find *tooken.* With plurals we had found that extension to new instances followed considerable practice with the regular pattern. Of course, our texts must underestimate the frequency of regular verbs, since they are small samples, but the regularity with which we found such extensions occurring quite early suggests that it takes relatively few instances and little practice to produce analogic extension. Another interpretation is that such extensions can occur with little or no actual contrasts in the child's speech; he may base them on the variety of types employing the regular contrast in the language of the adult. That is, if he can comprehend the contrast in the adult language he may on that basis be led to produce analogous forms.

With plurals, the regular patterns were learned and extended first; children did not waver between *foot-feet* and *foot-foots* but employed *foot-foots* normally. With the irregular past tense forms, the children learned the unique, irregular contrasts as separate items of vocabulary first. Sometimes they were separate even contextually, as in the child who said *it came off* and *it came unfastened,* but *come over here* and *come right back.* Next, the children produced analogic past tense forms for these highly frequent words. At the same period in which a child said *did,* he might say *doed;* at the same age at which he said *broke,* he might say *breaked,* and so on. We do not know if there were correlated linguistic or semantic differences between these two versions of the past tense forms. At any event, these productive analogies occurred before we had evidence of practice on the familiar forms from which the analogies presumably stemmed. Whatever its basis in practice, it seems clear that the regularizing or analogizing tendency is very strong.

The learning of syntax is even more difficult to explain. Let us go back before the age of two. In the earliest examples we have obtained, we find that there are consistencies of order between words. A very simple system might be one that produces sentences like *all-gone candy, candy up-there, all-gone book, read book,* and *book read.* Another said *snap on, snap off, fix on.* Notice that these sentences could not all be produced by simple abbreviation of adult sentences. Many of the children's sentences are such imitations, but some have a word order that cannot be explained by simple imitation. Children talk a great deal and they hear a great deal. It is improbable that they could produce the great variety of sentences they do produce from memorized strings of words.

When we introduced words to a child in controlled sentences, he put them into new and appropriate sentences. When told of a nonsense object *that's a po,* or *this is a po,* the child said *here's a po, where's a po, there's a po, the po go up there,* and *poz go up there.* When told *I'm gonna sib the toy,* he later said *I sib 'em* indicating the appropriate gesture. Yet the form *wem,* in *this is a wem bead,* was not extended. Thus a noun form was productively utilized in many new contexts, a verb form in one, and an adjective form in none. However slight, at least here is an indication of an analogic extension at the syntactic level.

One explanation which has been offered by several different observers of young children, for instance, Braine (1963),[15] Brown and Fraser (1963),[16] and Miller and Ervin (1964),[17] is that these early systems indicate the beginnings of syntactic classes.

How do such classes develop? Two features of classes have been noted to account for the development of regularities. In children's language, there is greater semantic consistency than in adult language. Brown (1957)[18] has shown that by nursery school age children identify verbs with action, nouns with things. Perhaps groupings into classes of words that can occur in the same place in sentences rest at least partly on semantic similarities. Another feature is that in all these grammars there are some positions where only a few words can occur, but that these words are very frequent. Thus one child started many of her sentences with *thats*. Another ended many of her sentences with *on* or *off*. The words that can occur following *thats* constitute a class, in the same sense that nouns are identified as following *the* for adults. This is not the only way we recognize nouns, but it is almost as useful as a suffix in marking the class. How do we know that these words "go together" in a class for the child? We find that the recorded bedtime monologues of a child described by Weir (1962)[19] were filled with instances of words substituting for each other: *what color blanket, what color mop, what color glass; there is the light, here is the light, where is the light*. Such practice, like the second-language drill in the classroom, could make some words equivalent counters in the game of rearrangement we call language. Thus, both meaning and high frequency of certain linguistic environments seem important in the evolution of syntactic classes.

Clearly, we have evidence that children are creative at the very beginnings of sentence formation. They imitate a great deal, but they also produce sentences which have both regularity and systematic difference from adult patterns. At the same time, within these classes there are always statistical tendencies toward finer differentiations.

As my last example, I will take the grammatical features called transformations by Chomsky (1957).[20] A good instance is the rule for the purely syntactical use of *do* in English. This word appears in a variety of sentence types: in elliptical forms, such as *yes, they do*, in emphatic forms such as *they do like it*, in questions such as *do they like it?* and in negatives as in *they don't like it*. According to Chomsky's analysis, these uses of *do* are analogous and can be described by a single set of related rules in the grammar of adult English.

Let us see how children employ *do*. In the negative, a simple rule for the contrast of affirmative and negative would be simply to add *no* or *not* in a specified place: *He's going* vs. *he's not going; he has shoes* vs. *he has no shoes*. Another procedure would be to contrast *is* with *isn't*, *can* with *can't*, and so on. In both cases, the contrast of affirmative and negative rests on a simple addition or change, analogous to the morphological change for tense or for the plural. Neither rule presents new problems.

Some children had several co-existing negative signals. During the time period, one child had the following: (1) *any* in possession sentences, such as *Joe has any sock* and *all the children has any shirt on;* (2) *not* in descriptions and declaratives, such as *Not Polly;* (3) *don't* in most verb sentences, such as *Don't eat that,* and *I don't like that*. Note that all these utterances can be described in very simple terms without the use of more complex constructs than those needed to account for inflection, or simple syntactic classes.

But as the child acquires verb inflection, more complex rules develop. We say *he goes*, but we do not usually say *he goes not*. Simple addition of *not* is inadequate. We say *he doesn't go*. In the contrast *he can go* vs. *he can't go* there is only one difference. In the contrast *he goes* vs. *he doesn't go* there are two: the addition of the word *don't* in appropriate number and tense, and the difference between *go* and *goes*.

Usually children use *don't* quite early as a negative signal, but as inflections began we found sentences like *Joe doesn't likes it* and *it doesn't fits in there*. In these sentences inflections appeared, but in two places. In an analogous development, *do* appeared early in elliptical sentences as a verb substitute. Thus we find, in response to the remark *there aren't any blocks in this book,* the reply *there do,* and when Wick Miller said *I'm Joe,* the child said *no you don't, you're Wick.* Thus the child had not differentiated subclasses of words used in elliptical constructions, just as the subclasses of inflections of *do* with different number and tense did not appear until later. By age three, this child said *it goes right here, doesn't it?* and *you're named "she," aren't you?,* employing complex constructions which cannot be explained in terms of the simple semantic signals we found in *Joe has any sock.*

Chomsky has described the various uses of *do* in adult English economically as based on the same rule. Does the use of *do* appear concurrently in negatives, interrogatives, ellipsis, and emphasis? Quite clearly this is not the case. As we have seen, *don't* appears early in negatives. It is often the only negative signal. In interrogatives, the question is signaled by question words or by a rising pitch, and *do* is typically not present until months after it appears in negatives or in ellipsis. Thus we cannot infer the process of acquisition from an analysis of the structure of the adult language. Sentences that are described as generated through transformation rules in the adult grammar may be based on different, and simpler, rules in the early stages of the child's grammar. And a rule that may apply to a variety of types of sentences in the adult grammar may develop through quite separate and independent rules in the early stages of the children's grammars.

I have mentioned the development of tense and number inflection, simple syntax, and more complex syntactical processes called transformations. These have all raised certain similar problems of explanation.

In adult language, it has been found necessary to postulate such constructs as morpheme classes, syntactic classes, and grammatical rules. It is not inevitable that similar constructs need be employed in accounting for the earliest stages of language acquisition.

Three different theories of child language development were described earlier. The imitation view assumed that the child imitates adult sentences and gradually eliminates abbreviations and errors as he grows older. A second view assumes that children comprehend adult rules but make random errors in speaking. A third view sees language in children as involving successive systems, with increasing complexity.

In their simplest forms all these positions seem wrong. Let us review the evidence. We found that spontaneous imitations were syntactically similar to or simpler than nonimitations. In examining plural inflection, we saw that indiscriminate imitation would lead us to predict free variation of *foot* and *feet,* but, in fact, one form was usually preferred, and the plural contrast was based on analogic extension. We found it necessary to postulate a plural morpheme to account for the sudden and transitory appearance of forms like *bockis* and *feetsiz.* With verbs, mere frequency of use of a contrast was less important than the variety of types employing it, suggesting again the need for conditions giving rise to a past-tense morpheme, with varied environments for a particular form, before analogic extension can occur.

In children's early syntax, the data are still ambiguous, for it is hard to elicit and identify extensions to new cases. On the one hand, sentences like *fix on, all-gone puzzle, I not got red hair,* and *once I made a nothing pie* clearly involve processes of analogic extension. Here we see at least rudimentary classes. On the other hand, in any system we devised, there were indications of incipient subdivision, of statistical irregularities in the direction of the adult model, prior to shifts in the system.

In the use of *do* we found that the adult rule applies equally to the negative, interrogative, elliptical, and emphatic sentence. But among children *do* did not appear at the same time in these types of sentences. The pattern of development, and the rules that might describe usage at a particular point in time, differed for these different sentence types and differed for different children. Yet there were rules; errors were not random.

In all these cases, we find that children seem to be disposed to create linguistic systems. We have not examined the speech of twins, but it seems likely that we would find there a rich source of systematic creation of constructions. It is hard to conceive that children could, by the age of four, produce the extraordinarily complex and original sentences we hear from them if they were not actively, by analogic extensions, forming classes and rules.

At the same time we cannot wholly accept the third position presented—that of idiosyncratic systems. In every instance of systematic change I have examined, there has been some evidence of fluctuation, some evidence of greater similarity to adult speech than one would expect on the basis of the system alone. In addition, in the early stages of some complex rules—such as the use of *do*—we found that there were phases that seemed to rest on rudimentary acquisition of vocabulary. The use of *don't* as an undifferentiated negative signal could be so described.

The shift from one system to another may be initiated from several sources. One is the comprehension of adult speech, another is imitation. The relation of imitation to comprehension has barely been faced in discussions of child language, yet these two must account for the accretion of instances which eventuate in systematic changes.

In language, unlike other intellectual processes, the child can monitor his output through the same channel by which he receives the speech of others. If he knows how—if he can make discriminations and remember models—he can compare his own speech to that of others. Thus, language development involves at least three processes.

It is obvious that there is continual expansion in the comprehension of adult speech. Perhaps comprehension requires some ability to anticipate and hence, at a covert level, involves some of the same behavior that occurs in speech production. But this practice in comprehension alone is not sufficient to bring overt speech into conformity with understood speech. Consider again the phenomenon of so-called twin languages, for instance, or the language skills of second-generation immigrants who have never spoken the parents' first language but understand it, or of second-language learners who persistently make certain errors of syntax after years of second-language dominance, or of some children of immigrants who understand their age peers but speak the English of their parents. More than comprehension is involved.

Another process is the imitation of particular instances by children. What is entailed in hearing and imitation we do not know at this point. The fact that phrases may be uttered long after they are heard, without overt practice, suggests that our study of immediate, spontaneous imitation concerns only a fraction of actual imitation-derived utterances. Yet unless these utterances constitute a systematically simpler sample of all imitated utterances, it is obvious from our analysis of them that syntactical development at least cannot rest on imitation.

The third process is the building by analogy of classes and rules, a process which we infer from the child's consistent production of sentences he could not have heard. Of the three approaches which I offered earlier, I would suggest that the third is closest to the truth, but that the accrual of gradual changes under the influence of listening to adults lies at the base of the generalizations and analogies formed by the child. Any system of analysis which omits either the idiosyncratically structured and rule-governed features of children's language or the gradual changes within these rules is contradicted by evidence from all levels of the linguistic behavior of children.

Ervin-Tripp's observation about classes and analogies also seems valid when one considers the way children acquire the English morphological system. Research evidence on this topic led Gleason to conclude that the process involves more than imitation:[21]

Earlier, when we talked about the plural morpheme in English, we said it is *-s*, as in *bookkeepers*. We tend to think of it as *-s* because that is the way we write it. But, if we listen to the sound we make when we pluralize a noun, we find that it is not always the same. The sound the plural makes depends on the last spoken sound in the singular form. If the noun ends in a vowel or a voiced consonant like *b*, *d*, or *g*, we add a /-z/ sound, as in *bags*, *heads*, or *days*. If the noun ends with an unvoiced consonant like *p*, *t*, or *k*, we add a real /-s/ sound, as in *hats* or *racks*. And if the noun ends in an /-s/ or /-z/ or related sibilant sound, we add an /-əz/ sound, as in *watches* or *wishes*. Although this is the kind of rule that the descriptive linguist might write for English, we all know it too. We do not have to learn the plural of every new word as a separate item. If a new word comes into English, we can form the plural automatically. When the word *bazooka* came into English, we all knew that the plural was *bazookas* with a /-z/ and not *bazookass* with an /-s/ sound. It is clear that at some stage in our lives we learned to pick and apply, without even thinking about it, the right plural ending for any given noun.

The regular past tense in English has parallel forms. We think of the past as adding *-ed*, because that is the way we spell it. Actually, like the regular plural, it has three forms, which depend on the last sound of the verb. We add a plain /-d/ sound after vowels and voiced consonants except /-d/, as in *played* or *lived*. We add a /-t/ after voiceless sounds except /-t/, as in *hopped* or *lacked*; after verbs that end in a /-t/ or a /-d/ we add an /-əd/ sound as in *melted* or *handed*.

Other inflexional forms we all know in English are the possessive *(John's hat)*, which follows the same rules as the plural, the progressive tense made with an *-ing (going, doing)*, the third person of the verb *(he hits, he plays, she watches)* and the comparison of adjectives, like *big, bigger, biggest*.

Adults know these rules, but clearly we have not always known them. There has to be some period of life during which we acquire them. We also know many other rules of morphology—that the *un-* in *unhappy, unbreakable,* and similar words means "not," that the *-er* ending in *teacher* or *listener* means something like "one who does the thing just mentioned." We can add a *-y* to a noun to make an adjective, like *meaty* from *meat*. We have a veritable arsenal of bound morphemes at our disposal. They can be used to form new words or to figure out the likely meaning of new words we meet.

What we wanted to find out was whether or not children operate with any rules at all and, if they did, to what extent the children's rules were the same as adult morphological rules. It was quite possible that children simply learn everything by rote memory and so have no rules. By this model, the only way a child could know that the plural of *dog* is *dogs* is if someone told him so, and so on for the plural of every noun and the past tense of every verb. For a number of reasons, this seemed unlikely.

One reason that we believe that children have rules is the kind of errors they make. We have all heard children say things like "I digged a hole" or "some mouses were there" or "the bell ringed." These errors are, of course, simply regular forms, and the child is wrong only because English is inconsistent and has a lot of irregular words. If he says *mouses* or *digged,* it must be because at some level he thinks he knows how to make a singular noun into a plural noun and a present tense verb into a past tense verb. Unfortunately the irregularities that abound in English keep spoiling his theories. His tendency to make errors like this at least gives us a clue to what is going on in his own inner organization of English. If anyone thinks that a child simply imitates this type of production from other children, we can point to experimental evidence and to much rarer words that the child has clearly made up all by himself.

In one experiment with first, second, and third graders,[22] we showed them pictures of mice and geese and such things and told them what they were. We would say, "This is a mouse, and now there are two mice." "What's this?" (pointing to the mouse) and the children would say, "a mouse." "And what's this?" (pointing to the two mice), and the first graders in particular answered, "two mouses," having just one second before heard the correct form. So imitation is not as simple as people think it is. You can only imitate what you can already do, using whatever is already in your repertory. That this is true becomes evident if I were to ask you to repeat after me a sentence in Arabic or Sanskrit. Only people who already know Arabic or Sanskrit can successfully imitate sentences in Arabic or Sanskrit.

We have reasonably good evidence that it is something more than imitation that leads children to produce words like *mouses,* and we have many less common words to which we can point that the child has clearly made up all by himself. My own middle child, for instance, is a sensitive soul, like all middle children. When she was about two and a half, she was feeling rather put-upon for a while, and when we asked, "Who loves you?" she would answer, "Nobody." After a little while, she cheered up and changed her mind. Now when we asked her who loved her, instead of answering, "Nobody," she said, "Yesbody." I am sure that the creation *yesbody* by analogy with *nobody* was her very own word.

Another example I might cite from our own family is a question our present three-year-old, Cindy, asked about a month ago. She said to me, "Mommy, what do giraffes eat?" Summoning up all the jungle lore at my command, I answered, "Well, they eat leaves, mostly." She paused a moment and then asked, "And what do they eat lessly?" She wanted to know what the next most common item in their diet was, after leaves, and so formed an adverb based on less. Unfortunately there is no English adverb that fills that slot.

Collecting children's errors is both delightful and instructive, but it would take a very long time to get enough data in this way to make any really positive statement about how children learn English. It does tell us that at an early age they are able to manipulate meaningful parts of words in order to make new words with new meanings.

In order to gain systematic knowledge about the English morphological system, we were able to devise an experimental approach. First, to get an idea of what to test for, we looked at children's actual vocabulary. We could not very well expect children to form the comparison of adjectives in an experiment if they had no real comparative adjectives in their own vocabulary, for instance. Accordingly, we examined the 1000 most frequent words in the first graders' vocabulary. We found that they had all of the regular inflexional forms like the plural of nouns, the past tense of verbs, and so on. We also found some adjectives ending in -y like *healthy,* a number of words ending in -er like *teacher,* and a number of compound nouns like *blackboard.*

Now that we knew what items were in the children's vocabulary, we had an idea of what sort of rules we might expect them to know. How could we test their ability to apply the rules of English morphology to new words? If we asked them for the plural of *dog,* and they told us *dogs,* it would not prove they had any rules. They might have memorized the form *dogs.* We had to be sure the words were new words. So we made up some words. We made a lot of pictures of nonsense animals and people doing strange things, and we made up some words to go with them. For the plural ending in a /-z/ sound, for instance, we made a picture of one bird-like animal and then of two. We would first point to the single animal and say, "This is a Wug." Then, pointing at the two animals, "Now there is another one. There are two of them. There are two ———," and the subjects were expected to fill in *Wugs.* In this experiment we tested a group of adults, to make sure that adults do indeed respond as we thought they would, and eighty nursery school and first grade boys and girls. We could be sure that the nonsense words were new words, and that if the children supplied the right endings they knew more than the individual words in their vocabulary—they had to know general rules enabling them to deal with new words. If knowledge of English consisted of no more than the storing up of many memorized utterances, the child might be expected to refuse to answer, on the grounds that he had never heard of a Wug and could not give the plural since no one had ever told him what it was.

This was decidedly not the case. All the children answered the questions with a great deal of conviction. Their answers were not always the same as those of our group of adults, but they were consistent and orderly answers. Boys and girls answered in just the same way, and, although the first graders were a little more like the adults in their answers than the preschoolers were, the types of answers given by both groups of children were very much the same.

To test the plural endings we have in *dogs,* a /-z/, *racks,* an /-s/, and *watches,* an /-əz/, we used nonsense creatures called a *Wug,* a *Bick,* and a *Gutch.* The children did by far the best with the /-z/ sound of *dogs,* or *Wugs,* which is the most common. They could also add an /-s/ sound to make one *Bick* into two *Bicks.* But when it came to the less common /-əz/ sound of *watches* or *glasses,* they added nothing at all. They said, "One Gutch. Two Gutch." And "One Tass. Two Tass." They had real words like *glass* in their vocabularies and could tell us it was "two glasses," but when we showed them a picture of an animal called a *Tass,* they said that two of them were "Two Tass." They did not yet generalize the rule for adding /-əz/ to words ending in /-s/ even though they had a model for it in their own speech. Their rule for the plural was, "To make a plural, add /-s/ or /-z/ unless the word already ends in an /-s/ or /-z/ or related sound, in which case add nothing at all."

With the past tense we found a very similar situation. We showed our subjects a picture of a man with a strange thing on his head, and said, "This is a man who knows how to *Spow.* He is Spowing. He did the same thing yesterday. What did he do yesterday? Yesterday he ———." And most of them supplied the common

/-d/ ending and said that yesterday he "Spowed." They could also tell us that a man who is "Ricking" today "Ricked" yesterday, with a final /-t/ sound. But then we showed them a man who knows how to *Mot*. They said that yesterday he "Mot." Adults, of course, say, "he Motted," but the children did not add the /-əd/ sound to new words ending in /-t/ or /-d/, even though they could tell us that in our picture of an ice cube turning into a puddle the ice cube had "melted," with the /-əd/ ending. Their rule for the past tense was, "To make a verb into a past tense verb, add /-t/ or /-d/, unless the verb stem already ends in /-t/ or /-d/, in which case add nothing at all." The children's rules for the past tense and the plural were very similar simplifications of the adult rules. The third person of the verb and the possessive were formed like the plural.

We also tried some irregular forms. There is, for instance, a group of verbs in English like *sing, cling, bring,* and *ring*. They are nearly all irregular in the past; there are almost no one-syllable verbs ending with *-ing* that are regular. So we made a picture of a man jumping on a thing and said, "This is a man who knows how to Gling. He is Glinging. He did the same thing yesterday. What did he do yesterday? Yesterday he ———." Adults are really torn when they hear something like this. Our adult subjects said that yesterday he "Glang" or "Glung," or even "Glought." Of course, some of them said he "Glinged," and that is what all the children said. Their rules were always regular and consistent and based on the most general and frequent cases in English.

We also tried to find out if children could make new words patterned on *teacher* with the *-er* ending. So we showed them a picture of a man balancing a thing on his nose and said, "This is a man who knows how to Zib. What is he doing? He is ———." And they said "Zibbing," which showed that they know how to form the present progressive tense. Next we asked, "What would you call a man whose job is to Zib?" Every adult said that a man whose job is to Zib is a "Zibber." The children tended to call him a "Zibman" or a "Zibbingman," putting together two free morphemes into a compound word rather than adding a suffix. Of course, since we do have words like *cleaning lady* in English, *Zibbing man* is not such a bad choice, but it was only made by children. When we showed pictures of a big Wug and a tiny Wug and asked our subjects what they would call a tiny Wug, the adults again used suffixes made of bound morphemes, and the children made up compound nouns of two free morphemes. Adults said a tiny Wug was a "Wuglet," a "Wugling," even a "Wugette," and of course a "Wuggie." Children said it was a "baby Wug."

Besides imitation, another possibility is that somehow, when the child says two-word sentences, he has memorized adult sentences but has left out grammatical elements and unstressed words. Miller explains why this is not so:[23]

First, there are always some that do not follow adult patterns (e.g., *Book read* or *A water*). Further analysis normally shows that such sentences fit into the pattern exhibited in other sentences used by the child and are thus true creations of the child's linguistic system, not part of a stock of memorized and abbreviated sentences. Second, if one examines the sentences used by an individual child and ignores their adult counterparts, a very clear pattern emerges for the majority of sentences. A few words, which can be called "pivot words," are of high frequency and typically occur in a particular position in the sentence. The remainder consist of all other vocabulary items and are of low frequency. Thus a typical pivot system might consist of *this, that, one, the, other* in initial position, and the remainder—words that can be classified in the adult system as nouns, verbs, and adjectives—in final position. As the child grows older, the pivot class and remainder class become divided into subclasses. This is, of course, the genesis of word classes in child languages.

It is important to note that pivot structure is observable only if individual cases are examined, because children differ in what they place in pivot and remainder classes. But there are certain patterns that recur frequently. Demonstratives, articles, modifiers such as *other,* and the verbs *want* and *see* are common as initial pivots. The locatives *here* and *there* are used by some children as initial pivots, by others as final pivots. Usually, but not always, the pivot and remainder classes will at least partially match adult classes—and when they do not, they are usually short-lived.

After the pivot system, there is a period of very rapid grammatical development starting at two or two and a half years of age and lasting for about a year or a year and a half. When this period is over, the bulk of the grammatical system has been learned. We find the introduction of grammatical words such as modal auxiliaries, prepositions, conjunctions, and the like, inflectional suffixes such as the plural for nouns and tense for verbs, and complex grammatical operations which allow for the formation of questions, negatives, infinitives, manipulation of indirect objects, and the like.

Brown and Fraser (1964)[42] have shown that sentence length is a useful index of grammatical development. When the child starts to use such grammatical words as articles, modals, conjunctions, and prepositions, telegraphic speech wanes and sentence length increases. It is important to note that sentence length is an index and *only* an index of grammatical development. It cannot indicate, for example, when articles or auxiliaries enter the child's grammatical system. And the index in fact disguises some grammatical developments that result in shorter sentences. For example, a linguistically appropriate answer to "When did John go?" could either be "John went yesterday" or simply "Yesterday." If the second type of answer is given, a short sentence results. Children must have a fairly complex grammar before they are able to correctly interpret questions and give short answers of this type. We do not find them until the telegraphic stage is past or on the way out.

In a study by Ervin-Tripp and myself, we kept track of sentence fragments that contained *not*. We found that such sentences did not appear until the child's grammar had the appropriate rules for full negative sentences. Two examples from a child at two years, seven months, will illustrate this type of sentence fragment. In response to the question "Does she walk yet?" the child answered "No, not yet." A second example: "She's not through eating?" "Not through." These sentence fragments are quite different from the earlier abbreviated sentences of telegraphic speech.

The development of three related sentence types is particularly revealing. The first is the yes-no question, in which the subject and part of the verb phrase trade places: "He can go" becomes "Can he go?" In the second type, negative sentences, the grammatical word "not" is inserted in the appropriate place within the verb phrase: "He can go" becomes "He cannot go" (with *cannot* normally contracted to *can't).* In the third type, verbal ellipsis, most of the verb phrase is deleted: "He can go" becomes simply "He can." In certain contexts these three types of sentences must include an inserted *do*: "He went" becomes "Did he go?" "He did not go" (usually contracted to "He didn't go"), and "He did."

Children do not have elliptical sentences until the appropriate rule for verbal ellipsis is learned. This is not surprising because these sentences are of no special semantic importance; they are useful only in reducing redundancy. But the two other types are different. The child asks questions and forms negatives before he has learned the adult rules. The technique for early questions seems to be universal: a sentence with rising intonation is used. Thus "He go?" is used in place of "Can he go?" or "Did he go?" Negatives, however, are variable. One common pattern is to use *don't* before the verb and to make no adjustments for tense, e.g., "He don't want milk." Some children use *no* or *not*: "He no want milk" or "He not want milk." Other children have less common patterns or various combinations of those listed above.

The early negative sentences illustrate again the child's search for grammatical rules, or even his invention of them. There are similarities across children, but we do not find identical patterns of development.

When the child learns the appropriate rules for questions, negatives, and elliptical sentences, the grammatical patterns are normally learned relatively slowly for one type and then extend very rapidly to the other two. Most commonly the negative will be learned first, followed by questions and elliptical sentences in quick succession, but this order of acquisition is not invariable. Ervin-Tripp and I observed one child who first learned the patterns for modal questions. Certain modals such as *could* were learned and used only in inverted position: "Could I have the dish?" or "Could you make this one?" Later the child learned to use the modals in both inverted and normal order, then to form questions with the appropriate form of *do*. Soon after this, the full range of patterns was found with negatives and elliptical sentences. Again, though there are similarities across children, each child develops his own system.

It is obvious to anyone who has listened to small children that they are mimics. There is wide individual variability, but almost all children imitate at least a little, and, for a few, imitations comprise almost half of the sentences. Thus it would seem that imitation must play an important role in the child's linguistic development; but what is that role? There has been some recent work on imitation, reported in the literature by Brown and Fraser (1964)[42] and Ervin (1964).[11] We find that imitated sentences of young children have exactly the same character as non-imitated sentences: sentences are abbreviated, grammatical words are left out, and sentences have the telegraphic style typical of children's speech. The omissions reflect those aspects of grammar not yet mastered by the child. In short, imitated sentences are not grammatically different from the child's freely composed sentences. They are not grammatically progressive and thus cannot be forerunners of grammatical change in the child's linguistic system.

If this is true for imitated sentences, it is true *a fortiori* for memorized sentences. Such sentences are not common, seeming so to the adult because they are repeated by the child and especially noted by the fond parent. But either the child knows the underlying grammar of the sentence and hence can learn nothing by it, or else he does not know the underlying grammar, does not understand the sentence, and cannot profit from it. Memorizing sentences is of no use to the child because he must learn the language, the set of grammatical rules that underlies the infinite set of sentences that he must learn to produce, interpret, and understand. And grammatical rules are abstract and formal operations that cannot be directly obtained from memorized or imitated sentences. These sentences are the result of the grammatical operations, not the operations themselves.

So again, what is the role of imitation in the child's linguistic development? This is an easy question to answer: I don't know. But I can offer a suggestion. It allows the child to practice the grammatical rules he has already acquired but which are not yet firmly established. The child must run through the grammatical rules to interpret or understand the sentences. By repeating and imitating, the child is given an opportunity to run through the rules again.

Repetition and imitation, Miller suggests, allow the child to practice the rules. Earlier, Ervin-Tripp suggested that this is similar to second-language drill in the classroom, but that perhaps it has another function: the formation of classes.

Consider, then, the recorded conversation of Anthony Weir, who was two and a half when his mother, the late Ruth Weir, recorded his bedtime speech when he was alone in his crib at night. Mrs. Weir reported the child's remarks in *Language in the Crib*.[19] Ursula Bellugi reviewed the book and commented on the "soliloquies":[24]

This may be a rather common phenomenon, but has been largely ignored as an area of research interest until the present time. It is perfectly conceivable that these soliloquies could be monotonous repetitions, or gibberish, or memorized routines, or lists, or numbers, or random fragments of utterances. As such they would be quite unrevealing to the student of language acquisition. Instead, as one reads through the soliloquies themselves, it becomes obvious that they are none of these. They are in places impressively similar to workbook exercises for foreign students who want to learn English. Parts of the monologues look like selection of a grammatical pattern and then substitution in one slot of the grammatical frame—a well-established device for teaching English to foreigners. Consider the following sets of data:

Noun substitutions	*Noun-phrase substitutions*
What color	There's a hat
What color blanket	There's another
What color mop	There's hat
What color glass	There's another hat

Adjective substitutions	*Verb substitutions*
Big Bob	Listen to microphone
Little Bob	Go to microphone
Big and little	
Little Bobby	
Little Nancy	
Big Nancy	

There are also sets of consecutive utterances in which the substitutions are pronominal, either for a noun or noun-phrase, or for another pronoun. Notice the following:

| Take the monkey | Don't take it off |
| Take it | Don't take the glasses off |

Stop it	I go up there
Stop the ball	I go
Stop it	She go up there

There are enough such sets in the data that they do not seem to be random productions, but can be considered as pronomial substitution exercises. Other practice sets in the data seem striking: the child produces minimal phonetic pairs in succession, corrects his pronunciation, builds up utterances out of constituents, makes occasional grammatical corrections, and so forth.

The interesting fact about [the] data and results seems to me to be that they often corroborate current observations of children's daytime speech. The data match in many respects speech collected from children who are going about their normal daily activities and interacting with other people in the process. Just to cite one example, the data reported here on pronomial substitutions is remarkably parallel to that presented in the Brown and Bellugi paper.

Writing in *Childhood Education,* Courtney B. Cazden summarized studies of the acquisition of syntax and explained that when a child acquires a grammar, he acquires a set of rules:[25]

When we say that a child has learned his native language by the time he enters first grade, what do we mean he has learned? A set of sentences from which he chooses the right one when he wants to say something? The *meaning* of a set of sentences from which he chooses the right interpretation for the sentences he hears? Even if the sets of sentences and interpretations were enormous, the result would still be inadequate. Outside of a small and unimportant list of greetings like *Good morning* and clichés like *My, it's hot today*, few sentences are spoken or heard more than once. Any speaker, child or adult, is continuously saying and comprehending sentences he has never heard before and will never hear or comprehend again in the same way. Creativity in expressing and understanding particular meanings in particular settings to and from particular listeners is the heart of human language ability.

The only adequate explanation for what we call "knowing a language" is that the child learns a limited set of rules. On the basis of these rules he can produce and comprehend an infinite set of sentences. Such a set of rules is called a grammar, and the study of how a child learns the structure of his native language is called the study of the child's acquisition of grammar.

When we say that a child knows a set of rules, of course we don't mean that he knows them in any conscious way. The rules are known nonconsciously, out of awareness, as a kind of tacit knowledge. This way of knowing is true for adults too. Few of us can state the rules for adding /s/ or /z/ or /iz/ sounds to form plural nouns. Yet if asked to supply the plurals for nonsense syllables such as *bik* or *wug* or *gutch* (Berko, 1958),[26] all who are native speakers of English could do so with ease. Most six-year-old children can too. We infer knowledge of the rules from what adults or children can say and understand.

Children learn the grammar of their native language gradually. Might one assume, therefore, that the stages they pass through on their way to mature knowledge could be characterized as partial versions of adult knowledge? Not so! One of the most dramatic findings of studies of child language acquisition is that these stages show striking similarities across children but equally striking deviations from adult grammar.

For example, while children are learning to form noun and verb endings, at a certain period in their development they will say *foots* instead of *feet, goed* instead of *went, mines* instead of *mine* (Cazden, 1968).[27] Children do not hear *foots* or *goed* or *mines.* These words are overgeneralizations of rules that each child is somehow extracting from the language he does hear. He hears *his, hers, ours, yours,* and *theirs;* and he hypothesizes that the first person singular should be *mines.* Human beings are pattern- or rule-discovering animals, and these over-generalizations of tacitly discovered rules are actively constructed in each child's mind as economical representations of the structure of the language he hears.

Rules for formation of sentences show the same kinds of deviations. In learning how to ask a question, children will say, *Why I can't go?*, neglecting temporarily to reverse the auxiliary and pronoun (Bellugi-Klima, in press).[28] And their answer to the often-asked question, *What are you doing?*, will temporarily be, *I am doing dancing* (Cazden, 1968).[27] If the answer to *What are you eating?* takes the form, *I am eating X,* the child hypothesizes that the answer to *What are you doing?* is, *I am doing X-ing.* Only later does he learn that answers with *doing* require the exceptional form *I am X-ing.*

The commonsense view of how children learn to speak is that they imitate the language they hear around them. In a general way, this must be true. A child in an English-speaking home grows up to speak English, not French or Hindi or some language of his own. But in the fine details of the language-learning process, imitation cannot be the whole answer, as the above examples show.

Sometimes we get even more dramatic evidence of how impervious to external alteration the child's rule system can be. Jean Berko Gleason's conversation with a four-year-old is an example (Gleason, 1967):[29]

> She said, *My teacher holded the baby rabbits and we patted them.*
> I asked, *Did you say your teacher held the baby rabbits?*
> She answered, *Yes.*
> I then asked, *What did you say she did?*
> She answered, again, *She holded the baby rabbits and we patted them.*
> *Did you say she held them tightly?* I asked.
> *No,* she answered, *she holded them loosely.*

Impressed by the confidence with which the child continued to use her own constructions despite hearing and comprehending the adult form, Gleason conducted a variation of her older test (Berko, 1958)[26] with first-, second-, and third-grade children. She asked the children to give irregular plural nouns or past tense verbs after she had supplied the correct form as she asked the question. "In the case of verbs, they were shown a bell that could ring and told that yesterday it rang; then they were asked what the bell did yesterday" (Gleason, 1967).[29] Even under these conditions, only 50 percent of the first-graders (7 out of 14) said *rang;* 6 said *ringed* and one said *rung.* Gleason concludes:[29]

> In listening to us, the children attended to the sense of what we said, and not the form. And the plurals and past tenses they offered were products of their own linguistic systems, and not imitations of us.

When sophisticated parents try deliberately to teach a child a form that does not fit his present rule system, the same filtering process occurs. The following conversation took place when a psychologist tried to correct an immaturity in her daughter's speech:[30]

C. *Nobody don't like me.*
M. *No, say "Nobody likes me."*
C. *Nobody don't like me.*
   (eight repetitions of this dialogue)
M. *No. Now listen carefully; say "Nobody likes me."*
C. *Oh! Nobody don't likes me!*

It happens that irregular verbs such as *went* and *came* are among the most common verbs in English. Children usually learn the irregular forms first, evidently as isolated vocabulary words, and later start constructing their own overgeneralizations *goed* and *comed* when they reach the stage of tacitly discovering that particular rule. Finally, they achieve the mature pattern of rule plus exceptions. Stages on the way to the child's acquisition of mature behavior may look for the moment like regressions, like new errors in terms of adult standards, and yet be significant evidence of intellectual work and linguistic progress.

With a very few pathological exceptions, all children learn to speak the language of their parents and home community. They do so with such speed and ease, at an age when other seemingly simpler learnings such as identification of colors are absent, that one wonders how the environment helps the process along. Just as the commonsense view holds that the child's process is basically imitation, so it implies that the adult's contribution is to shape the child's speech by correcting him when he is "wrong" and reinforcing him when he is "correct." Here too the commonsense view seems invalid. So far no evidence exists to show that either correction or reinforcement of the learning of grammar occurs with sufficient frequency to be a potent force. Analysis of conversations between only a few parents and children are available, but that generalization holds for them without exception.

Brown and his colleagues have found corrections of misstatements of fact but not correction of immature grammatical forms in hundreds of hours of recordings of three children—Adam, Eve, and Sarah—and their parents (Brown, Cazden and Bellugi, 1969;[31] Brown and Hanlon, 1970).[32] Horner (1968)[33] found only correction of "bad language" *(pee-pee)* in her study of conversation between parents and two three-year-old lower-class children. Finally, students recording the acquisition of language in such farflung areas of the world as India, California, and Samoa report the same lack of correction (Slobin, 1968).[34]

Reinforcement of immature constructions could be expressed in many ways. Brown et al. have looked for two kinds of reinforcement: verbal signs of approval and disapproval and differential communication effectiveness. In either case, the critical requirement for the operation of reinforcement is that the parent's utterance must be supplied contingently—supplied when the child speaks maturely and denied when he speaks in an immature fashion. Without that contingent relationship, the adult behavior cannot reinforce the child's mature utterance and make it more likely to occur again. Brown et al. examined parental response to specific constructions—such as questions—at times when the children were oscillating between mature and immature forms (as with *went* and *goed* above). They found no evidence of differential approval or of differential communication effectiveness (Brown, Cazden and Bellugi, 1969;[31] Brown and Hanlon, 1970[32]). Analyzing these same parent-child conversations, Bellugi-Klima concludes:[28]

The mother and child are concerned with daily activities, not grammatical instruction. Adam breaks something, looks for a nail to repair it with, finally throws pencils and nails around the room. He pulls his favorite animals in a toy wagon; fiddles with the television set; and tries to put together a puzzle. His mother is concerned primarily with modifying his behavior. She gives him information about the world around him and corrects facts. Neither of the two seems overtly concerned with the problems that we shall pursue so avidly: the acquisition of syntax. . . .

In modifying behavior, supplying information about the world, and correcting facts, mothers of young children do seem to use simpler language than they address to other adults. At least, this is indicated in the only study in which the mother's utterances to her child and to another adult have been compared. The utterances to her child were both shorter and simpler (Slobin, 1968).[34] Presumably, as the child's utterances become longer and more complex, so do the mother's. Other than this simplification, there is no sequencing of what the child has to learn. He is offered a cafeteria, not a carefully prescribed diet. And, seemingly impelled from within, he participates in the give-and-take of conversation as best he can from the very beginning, in the process takes what he needs to build his own language system and practices new forms to himself, often at bedtime (Weir, 1962).[35] As far as we can tell now, all that the child needs is exposure to well-formed sentences in the context of conversation that is meaningful and sufficiently personally important to command attention. Whether the child could learn as well from an exclusive diet of monologues or dialogues in which he did not participate—as he could get from television—we don't know and, for ethical reasons, may never be able to find out.

Each encounter with a sample of a class of events in the environment implies a correlate of the event in the mind. Any specific encounter with the kind of event is internally referred to some generalized form of the event in the mind. This generalized form, refined over a number of encounters, may be referred to as an abstract schema. The above discussion suggests to us the comments by Lenneberg on the significance of the child's acquisition of syntax. He suggests that there exists in the mind an abstract schema which serves as a common denominator that enables us to perceive similarities in two or more patterns which on the surface are apparently different. Each pattern is transformed from the surface—what we perceive—to its abstract schema.

Lenneberg concedes that we do not know how these transformational operations come about. It is noteworthy, however, that his view is one of gradual differentiation and elaboration. Thus, as the child's language is still developing because the necessary schemata are not adequately generalized, certain "grammatical transformations may be beyond the language-learner's capacity; he does not understand the sentence; he cannot organize the material, nor can he produce any utterance containing specific transformational relationships between the component parts."[36] In Carroll's metaphor, the learner cannot process the language data because he is not completely programmed.

FROM *Biological Foundations of Language*[36]

In the absence of systematic research on children's understanding of adult sentences, and hence of their developing "analytic equipment" for syntax, we can only make educated guesses at how grammar actually develops. The study of adult syntax makes it clear that discourse could not be understood, and that no interpretable utterances could be produced, without syntactic development *pari passu* with lexical and phonological development. Syntax is the calculus, so to speak, of functional categories, and the categories are arranged hierarchically from the all-inclusive to the particular.

The child whose language consists of nothing but single word utterances has obviously a more primitive syntactic understructure than the mature speaker. Syntactic categorization is the speaker's act of superimposing structure; he assigns given lexical terms to parts of speech. The child's syntax is primitive because all of his words have the same syntactic function: they may be used as a self-sufficient utterance. There is just one undifferentiated syntactic category, and any word heard or produced is assigned to it. If we wish to introduce Chomskian notation already at this primitive stage, we might use the equation or *rewriting instruction* as he calls it,

$$S \rightarrow W$$

which reads in this grammar a sentence S is formed by the use of any word that belongs to the class W, and all of the child's words do belong to it.

Notice that it would make no sense to ask whether the child, at this stage, knows more adjectives than nouns or whether he has any verbs. Strictly speaking, *adjectives, nouns, verbs* are modes of functioning, given a complex syntax. But since the syntactic conditions for such functioning are not yet present, we cannot ask whether the infant has verbs. We do not ask whether a fertilized human egg thinks or what the social order among chicks is before they have hatched.

The joining of two words in a single utterance is a sign that the initial global category, labeled W, is splitting up into two functionally distinct categories. The following examples, collected from Braine (1963),[37] Brown and Fraser (1963),[38] Brown and Bellugi (1964),[39] and Ervin (1964),[40] show that the two words are not random concatenations but that a functional distinction is emerging.

find it	here sock	more milk
fix it	here allgone	more nut
drink it	here is	more up
etc.	etc.	etc.

A paradigm is clearly being formed.

One of the two words has a higher frequency of occurrence and seems to be a grammatical functor, whereas the other word appears to come from a large pool of lexical items with a great variety of meanings. Braine (1963)[37] has called the functor words the *pivot* of these two-word sentences. The entire utterance seems to "turn around them."

It is not always easy to recognize the pivot of the two-word utterances, and we cannot always be sure how to characterize the sentences formally. For instance, "mommy sandwich," "baby highchair," "throw daddy," "pick glove" are all quite typical productions. At present, there are no reliable procedures to demonstrate that the two elements of these sentences belong to two different syntactic categories, although such an assumption is not unreasonable. We may have the primitive subject-predicate distinction.

The structure of these second-stage sentences might be characterized formally by diagrams such as these:

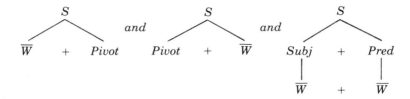

By the time he uses three-word sentences, further differentiations of categories have taken place. We now find utterances such as these:

fix a Lassie	my horsie stuck
here two sock	poor Kitty there
more nice milk	that little one

At this stage, many types of utterances are heard, and it becomes increasingly difficult to describe the child's syntactic skills by an exhaustive catalogue of phrase-markers. Instead, we endeavor to discover the principles by which these structures are recognized and produced.

The last examples cited illustrate, however, the progressive differentiation of syntactic categories. The structure of these sentences may be characterized by postulating a splitting of the earlier category W into two, namely a modifier m and a noun N. A tree diagram might look like the following:

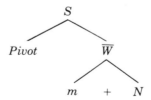

GENERAL COMMENTS ON THE GENESIS OF PHRASE-STRUCTURE, NESTED DEPENDENCIES, AND RECURSIVENESS

So far we have described how sentences (primitive or mature) are understood, that is, what the relationships are between the component elements. We have studied phrase-structure. The diagram that characterizes any particular structure is the phrase-marker. The ontogenetic development of "phrase-structuring" is a differentiation process of grammatical categories. Notice that a similar differentiation process takes place in other aspects of language: in the child's semantic development, any motor vehicle may at first be labeled by the single term *car* until the referents are subdivided, perhaps into cars and trucks, with each word still being applied to a wider range than is customary. Gradually more and more distinct semantic groups emerge until the full vocabulary is established. In phonology, we have pointed out a similar procedure. Global sound-patterns become differentiated further and further until the phonemic inventory of a natural language is present.

This differentiation process is not confined to language. In fact, it is the hallmark of *all* development. In the visual sphere, we have already mentioned how the three-months old tends to smile to a wide variety of facelike objects. Soon a painted mask is no longer reacted to in the same way as a human face. Psychologists speak here of discrimination procedures, which, in this context, are synonymous with visual differentiation. As this process advances, specific faces become differentiated into distinct visually perceived structures.

We also have parallels in motor development. The movement of the embryo of lower vertebrates consists of gross, undifferentiated movements involving the whole trunk (Carmichael, 1954).[41] Gradually a global flexion may give way to undulation and parts of the body begin to gain some autonomy. Similarly, in the human neonate we see both arms move synchronously at first, whereas independent control comes only at a later stage of differentiation of motor coordination. Thus, the differentiation process is quite universal, and the building-up of phrase structuration by differentiation of categories may be seen as a natural consequence of maturation in the field of language.

The process of differentiation, seen during ontogeny, becomes a process of specification or elaboration in the mature speaker. The string

That man thinks.

is a complete and mature sentence. We can specify or elaborate on the main elements of this sentence, a process which is formally similar to the differentiation process of categories during ontogeny. We may elaborate on *man* by saying

That old man thinks.

This expansion comes about by "applying an elaboration principle." We may apply this principle as often as we wish. For instance, we may say

That old old man thinks.

The repetitive application of the identical principle is called *recursiveness*. Obviously, the sentence may be expanded in many ways not only by reapplying the same principle just introduced, but also by applying other, similar but not identical principles of elaboration or specification. Thus we may produce a sentence

That old, old, hoary man who is well known by all who were folk-music lovers as far back as the early twenties thinks he is the great Italian opera singer Caruso.

In this sentence, elements were being differentiated progressively and/or repeatedly. As a consequence of these differentiations, the elements *man* and *thinks* have become physically separated although they continue to be related or dependent upon one another, and the same is true of other elements interposed between these two words, for instance, the words *known* and *lovers*. This phenomenon of splitting up elements by introducing other elements, which in turn may be split up, is called *nested dependencies*. Both recursiveness and nested dependencies are simply consequences of differentiation or specification.

Again there are parallels in vision, although we are dealing here with the receptive side (that is, with the understanding of structure). From tachistoscopic studies we know that it takes considerable time to "understand" a picture. The more complex the picture, the more time it takes. This can be explained by assuming that we take in only certain details or aspects at a time, say a 30 msec period; as our eyes move across the stimulus, further and further details are sent up for processing. In fact, the perception of figures may not be simply a piecing together of various fragments of the picture as a whole, but various aspects such as color, contours, contrasts, etc., take different amounts of time for perception and integration. These elements "mean nothing" in isolation. They are temporally integrated, and an interpretation is fitted to them, so to speak. This is not that there is a template stored for a specific figure, but a peculiar mode for processing the details must be presupposed. A picture that has many details is a good analogue to the complex sentence. The over-all schema is expanded and elaborated upon; as we keep gazing at the picture, there is further and further differentiation, without, however, interrupting the relational dependencies of the main structure or main elements.

We are discovering a basic process that is reflected in language as well as in many other aspects of behavior. It consists of first grasping a whole that is subsequently further differentiated, each of the specifics arriving at a different time and being subordinated to the whole by a process of temporal integration. In productive behavior a plan for the whole is differentiated into components, and the temporal integration results in ordering of movements (or thoughts). Organization of phrase-structure with the resulting phenomenon of recursiveness and nested dependencies appears as a "natural phenomenon" once we assume that a ubiquitous process is influencing a specific behavior. Nevertheless, the execution of this behavior seems to necessitate specific cognitive and thus biological adaptations.

GENERAL COMMENTS ON THE GENESIS OF TRANSFORMATIONS

Transformations have come to play a major role in the interpretation of grammar. It may be well to outline the basic ideas and to show that we are dealing also here with a very general phenomenon. . . .

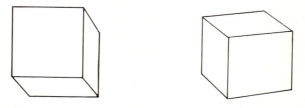

Fig. 7.7. Two physically different patterns, recognized as similar due to rules of geometrical transformations

Let us disregard words and sentences for a moment and concentrate on visual phenomena again. In Fig. 7.7 we have two patterns that are physically very different from each other, but by the application of certain rules (in this case rules of perception and transformational rules of geometry coincide), we immediately see a marked similarity between them. Conversely, Fig. 7.8 constitutes a single graphic pattern, but as we stare at it, we begin to see it representing one pattern and then another. The ambiguity of the figure is due to an alternative application of either of two available rules (again perceptual and geometric) that we have stored within ourselves: one rule imposes one interpretation; the other imposes another interpretation.

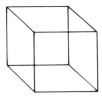

Fig. 7.8. The Necker cube illusion, which is due to alternative transformations to either of the two patterns of Fig. 7.7

Let us now look more generally at the phenomenon of similarity. All animals have the ability to group together stimulus configurations which may be physically totally different from each other; however, the animal makes an identical response to certain ones and thus treats them as if they were similar in some respect; we cannot escape the conclusion that for the animal, some similarity exists among such stimuli. Man is no different from other animals. From a wealth of ethological studies we know that species differ considerably in the specific perceptions of similarities and correspondences. For instance, a child needs no special training to see the similarity between a black-and-white photograph of a birthday cake and the physical object. Cats and dogs do not have the capacity to see that similarity or to relate this one type of stimulus configuration to this other one. It is a matter of empirical investigation to trace out the extent and the rules that allow a specific animal to relate any two stimulus configurations to each other.

So far, we do not know exactly how similarities are recognized between patterns which do not have any topological invariant qualities. For instance, why can any child recognize the similarities between the two patterns shown in Fig. 7.9? . . . Semantic labeling has nothing to do with this. All we can say is that each of the patterns in Fig. 7.9 is a member of a large and abstract category and that any member of this category has a common denominator. Since it is not necessary that there be any one common physical attribute, we may conclude that the common denominator is an *abstract schema*. This type of reasoning is familiar from philosophy since ancient time. We can see similarities whenever we can transform two or more physically given patterns into the same, common abstract schema. In this terminology, similarities are due to transformations from the physically given (surface) to abstract (deep) schemata. Thus all similarities involve transformational processes. The similarities of Fig. 7.7 are special cases because we need not assume the transformational bridge through the abstract schema; instead we might argue that the similarity is due to the geometric correspondences. However, in most instances of similarities it is necessary to assume the transformational route via the abstract schema (because of the absence of tangible invariance), and therefore it is more economical to assume that the similarity of Fig. 7.7 is merely a special case of the general phenomenon of seeing similarities.

Fig. 7.9. The patterns that are recognized as similar in some respects, although no point-to-point correspondence exists between them. (There is similarity only in deep, but none in surface, structure.)

The necessity for assuming transformations from the physically given to abstract representations or schemata is best seen in discussions of perceived similarities. The need for such an assumption is a universal one, relevant to all fields of pattern recognition, and it is not confined to theories on human perception.

It is not surprising, therefore, that when we discuss the perception of sentences, it is also necessary that we have to assume the existence of specialized transformational capacities, for instance, to account for the perceived similarities among sentences:

The dog chases the fox. ⎯ ⎰ The fox is chased by the dog.
Why does the dog chase the fox?
The chasing of the dog.
etc.

It is interesting to note that the similarity among these sentences is in some sense a special case much the way the similarity between the cubes of Fig. 7.7 was. The transformations involved in these cases have fairly easily discernible rules; they may be called concrete rules of correspondence (between one phrase-marked structure and another).

The necessity for assuming transformational procedures that mediate between the concretely given and the deep or abstract schemata goes much beyond the type of perceived similarities demonstrated in these sentences. At age four a child understands most types of sentences, and most of his utterances are interpretable in terms of syntactic structures. That is, he can recognize the structure of a given sentence which by itself is totally novel to him. If you say to him, "Did you know that the piffles fly to the curda every night?" he is liable to ask back, "Who is flying to the curda every night?" or "What are piffles and why do they fly?" or some such question, indicating his comprehension of the syntactic structure of your statement, even though the significance or meaning of the sentence is not clear to him. Thus, there is evidence that a child can recognize structural similarities in a string of words that compose a sentence even if he has never seen or heard the sentence before. Applying now the same argument used previously, we begin

to see that structural similarity between two strings of words implies the transformation of the physically given sound-patterns into an abstract schema (such
as a phrase-marker) or, in other words, grammatical structure is the name of
that class of abstract schemata by means of which we recognize structural similarity
between physically different sentences. The question of whether the string, *Colorless
green ideas sleep furiously,* is or is not a sentence is decided upon by searching
for a structural similarity between this string and classes of other strings which
belong to the set of grammatical sentences. Thus we discover that Chomsky's
sentence is similar to any one of the infinite set of sentences patterned after the
structural schema

subject predicate

or more specifically

> Subject (consisting of a noun modified by an adjective that is modified
> by an adverb) predicate (consisting of an intransitive verb modified
> by an adverb).

This is the abstract schema to which sentences such as

> Colorless green ideas sleep furiously.
> Very interesting movies run longer.
> Friendly little dogs bark loudly.
> etc.

are transformed in the course of perceiving and understanding them. We do not
have to assume, however, that the child knows the grammar consciously. A tennis
player or bicycle rider responds to and behaves in accordance with laws of physics
without being able to formulate them or to work out consciously any of the computations that his nervous system is doing for him. . . .

We may once more ask, when and how do these transformational operations
come about? This is as difficult to answer as the question of when and how the
perception of visual similarities comes about. This is the general type of phenomenon
we are dealing with. It is true that both are empirical questions, but because
they are inquiries into the modes of processing input data (which in the case
of language happen to be identical with the mode of processing neural events
underlying a specific output: discourse), they require verification techniques that
are not well-developed as yet. This is an obstacle that will be overcome sooner
or later.

As soon as we have appropriate techniques we will be able to answer these
questions more specifically. However, we can never expect to find that the basis
for perceiving similarities, or processing data transformationally, is a skill that
is suddenly acquired. The perception of similarities must be a deeply ingrained
process; it is the very nature of perceptual and even more generally, behavioral,
organization. In Lashley's example, for instance, he states that most of us learn
to write with our right hand. Nevertheless, it is possible to take a pencil into
the left hand (or between the teeth), close our eyes, and write our name upside-down.
It is possible to produce something quite legible at first try. Lashley argued that
in this case, where entirely different sets of muscles in a different part of the
body are being activated and the direction of movements is opposite to the one
we are used to, we must assume the existence of a central *(abstract)* schema for

a motor pattern by means of which we are capable of transferring the skill from right to left (or to the muscles that guide the head movements). Thus the peripheral motor patterns are transformed into a schema, and the schema again is applied to different peripheral structures; the two motor patterns are related *transformationally*.

The ontogenetic history of transformational development is also one of gradual differentiation and elaboration. The essence of transformations must go back to neonate days and may well be discernible at even more immature stages. Gradually, various types of transformations emerge—those that organize visual input, those that organize motor output, and, eventually, those that organize verbal input and output. The perception of specific types of similarities may presuppose a given degree of organization and so emerge only at a later stage and as a clear-cut milestone of development. Certain types of grammatical transformations may be beyond the language-learner's capacity; he does not understand the sentence; he cannot organize the material, nor can he produce any utterance containing specific transformational relationships between the component parts. But apart from this gradual differentiation of various transformational relationships, it can hardly be expected that transformation as a general type of process for organization is "suddenly learned."

If phrase-structure and transformations are simply special applications of general modes of organization, modes that are common to the organization of the behavior of all higher animals, why is language species-specific? There is only one possible answer. In order to achieve such special adaptation, cognitive processes must be highly adapted biologically. The slightest alteration in the peculiarities of data-acceptance, data-storage, and temporal integration apparently interferes with the proper reception and production of the peculiar patterns called sentences.

Lenneberg's comments suggest that before proceeding further with a review of research on the acquisition of language, we must explore a theory for intellectual development that is adequate to explain the acquisition of language. Such a theory ought to lead us into an examination of perceptual processes and into an exploration of the formation of concepts and word-concept relationships.

SUMMARY

We have learned in this chapter that babies are equipped to learn any language when they are born and that all children learn to speak their language in much the same way. Around six months of age the baby enters into a babbling stage in which he exercises control over the sounds he makes. About the time he reaches his first birthday he makes complex one-word utterances, which continue until about eighteen months of age. By the age of three the child has learned the essentials of English grammar. Upon entering school his knowledge of English is vast and very complex.

In respect to phonology the child learns his phonetics through exploring their contrastive nature, beginning with the difference between a vowel and a consonant. The phonological system is fairly well developed by the time he is three and a half or four years old.

In respect to intonation an infant imposes patterns upon his babbling so that he seems to babble statements, questions, and the like. In so doing, the child responds to whole patterns rather than to small segments. The whole becomes differentiated after further development.

In summary, we see that by the time the child is learning to read he already possesses a well-developed language. He learns his language through a process involving the differentiation of global units rather than a process of stringing small units together. Errors due to over-application of early tentative rules are common throughout language learning and can provide valuable insight into developing competence. This same process is used in all aspects of language learning: sounds, meanings, and sentence structure.

NOTES FOR CHAPTER 4

1. Jean Berko Gleason, "Language Development in Early Childhood," in *Oral Language and Reading,* edited by James Walden (Champaign, Ill.: National Council of Teachers of English, 1969), pp. 18–19.
2. John B. Carroll, *Language and Thought* (Englewood Cliffs, N.J.: Prentice-Hall, 1964), pp. 41–42.
3. Roger Brown and Ursula Bellugi, "Three Processes in the Child's Acquisition of Syntax," *Harvard Educational Review* 34, 2 (1964), 133–51. This investigation was supported in whole by Public Health Service Research Grant MH-7088 from the National Institute of Mental Health.
4. We are grateful for intellectual stimulation and lighthearted companionship to Dr. Jean Berko Gleason, Mr. Samuel Anderson, Mr. Colin Fraser, Dr. David McNeill, and Dr. Daniel Slobin.
5. H. Maclay and C. E. Osgood, "Hesitation Phenomena in Spontaneous English Speech," *Word* 15 (1959), 19–44.
6. Additional evidence of the constraint on sentence length may be found in R. Brown and C. Fraser, "The Acquisition of Syntax," in *Verbal Behavior and Learning,* edited by C. N. Cofer and Barbara Musgrave (New York: McGraw-Hill, 1963).
7. Brown and Fraser, ibid.
8. M. D. S. Braine, "The Ontogeny of English Phrase Structure: The First Phrase," *Language* 39 (1963), 1–13.
9. W. Miller and Susan Ervin, "The Development of Grammar in Child Language," in *The Acquisition of Language,* edited by U. Bellugi and R. Brown, Monographs of the Society for Research in Child Development, 1964.
10. Brown and Fraser, op. cit.
11. Susan M. Ervin, "Imitation and Structural Change in Children's Language," in *New Directions in the Study of Language,* edited by Eric H. Lenneberg (Cambridge: MIT Press, 1964), pp. 163–89.
12. A. N. Gvozdev, *Voprosy izucheniia detskoi rechi* [Problems in the language development of the child] (Moscow: Academy of Pedagogical Science, 1961).
13. C. Fraser, U. Bellugi, and R. Brown, "Control of Grammar in Imitation, Comprehension, and Production," *J. verb. Learn. verb. Behav.* 2 (1963), 121–35.
14. The study was conducted with the support of a grant from the National Institute of Mental Health and the facilities of the Institute for Human Development and the Institute for Human Learning at the University of California, Berkeley. The work was done in collaboration with Wick Miller, now Assistant Professor of Anthropology at the University of Utah.

15. M. D. S. Braine, "The Ontogeny of English Phrase Structure: The First Phrase," *Language* 39 (1963), 1–13.
16. R. Brown and C. Fraser, "The Acquisition of Syntax," in *Verbal Behavior and Learning,* edited by C. N. Cofer and Barbara Musgrave (New York: McGraw-Hill, 1963).
17. W. Miller and Susan Ervin, "The Development of Grammar in Child Language," in *The Acquisition of Language,* edited by U. Bellugi and R. Brown, Monographs of the Society for Research in Child Development, 1964.
18. R. Brown, "Linguistic Determination and the Part of Speech," *J. abnorm. soc. Psychol.* 55 (1957), 1–5.
19. R. H. Weir, *Language in the Crib* (The Hague: Mouton, 1962).
20. Noam Chomsky, *Syntactic Structures* (The Hague: Mouton, 1957).
21. Jean Berko Gleason, op. cit., pp. 19–25.
22. Jean Berko, "The Child's Learning of English Morphology," *Word* 14 (1958), 150–77.
23. Wick R. Miller, "Language Acquisition and Reading," in *Oral Language and Reading,* edited by James Walden (Champaign, Ill.: National Council of Teachers of English, 1969), pp. 34–39.
24. U. Bellugi, "Review of *Language in the Crib*," *Harvard Educational Review* 34 (1964), 332–34.
25. Courtney B. Cazden, "Suggestions from Studies of Early Language Acquisition," *Childhood Education* 46 (December 1969), 127–31.
26. Jean Berko, "The Child's Learning of English Morphology," *Word* 14 (1958), 150–77. Also in *Psycholinguistics*, edited by S. Saporta (New York: Holt, Rinehart & Winston, 1961), pp. 359–75.
27. Courtney B. Cazden, "The Acquisition of Noun and Verb Inflections," *Child Development* 39 (1968), 433–48.
28. U. Bellugi-Klima, *The Acquisition of the System of Negation in Children's Speech*. Unpublished manuscript.
29. Jean Berko Gleason, "Do Children Imitate?" *Proceedings of the International Conference on Oral Education of the Deaf,* June 17–24, 1967, vol. 2, pp. 1441–48.
30. D. McNeill, "Developmental Psycholinguistics," in *The Genesis of Language: A Psycholinguistic Approach,* edited by F. Smith and G. A. Miller (Cambridge: MIT Press, 1966), p. 69.
31. R. Brown, C. B. Cazden, and U. Bellugi, "The Child's Grammar from I to III," in *1967 Minnesota Symposium on Child Psychology*, edited by J. P. Hill (Minneapolis: Univ. of Minnesota Press, 1969), pp. 28–73.
32. R. Brown and C. Hanlon, *Cognition and the Development of Language*, edited by John R. Hayes (New York: Wiley, 1970).
33. V. M. Horner, "The Verbal World of the Lower-Class Three-Year-Old: A Pilot Study in Linguistic Ecology," unpublished doctoral dissertation, Univ. of Rochester, 1968.
34. D. I. Slobin, "Questions of Language Development in Cross-Cultural Perspective," paper prepared for symposium on *Language Learning in Cross-Cultural Perspectives,* Michigan State Univ., September 1968.
35. R. H. Weir, *Language in the Crib* (The Hague: Mouton, 1962).
36. Eric H. Lenneberg, *Biological Foundations of Language* (New York: Wiley, 1967), pp. 292–302.
37. M. D. S. Braine, "The Ontogeny of English Phrase Structure: The First Phrase," *Language* 39 (1963), 1–13.
38. R. Brown and C. Fraser, "The Acquisition of Syntax," in *Verbal Behavior and Learning,* edited by C. N. Cofer and Barbara Musgrave (New York: McGraw-Hill, 1963).
39. R. Brown and U. Bellugi, "Three Processes in the Child's Acquisition of Syntax," in *New Directions in the Study of Language,* edited by Eric H. Lenneberg (Cambridge: MIT Press, 1964).
40. Susan M. Ervin, "Imitation and Structural Change in Children's Language," in *New Directions in the Study of Language,* edited by Eric H. Lenneberg (Cambridge: MIT Press, 1964), pp. 163–89.
41. L. Carmichael, *Handbook of Child Psychology,* 2d ed. (New York: Wiley, 1954).
42. Roger Brown and Colin Fraser, "The Acquisition of Syntax," Monograph of the Society for Research in Child Development, no. 29 (1964), 43–74

5

man's capacity for language

Lenneberg suggests that the capacity for language acquisition is innate. It is programed into the organism; environmental conditions may release, or trigger, action patterns. Man has innate in him the propensity to utilize the environment in certain species-specific ways.

"As long as the child is surrounded at all by a speaking environment, speech will develop in an automatic way, with a rigid developmental history, a highly specific mode for generalization behavior, and a relative dependence upon the maturational history of the child." Thus in man, as in certain lower animals, "the communicating trait is the result of an *innate predisposition elicited by* environmental circumstances."[1]

In *Biological Foundations of Language,* Lenneberg states:[2]

(1) Language is the manifestation of species-specific cognitive propensities. It is the consequence of the biological peculiarities that make a human type of cognition possible.[3] The dependence of language upon human cognition is merely one instance of the general phenomenon characterized by [the premise that cognitive function is species-specific]. There is evidence that cognitive function is a more basic and primary process than language, and that the dependence-relationship of language upon cognition is incomparably stronger than vice versa.

(2) The cognitive function underlying language consists of an adaptation of a ubiquitous process (among vertebrates) of categorization and extraction of similarities. The perception and production of language may be reduced on all levels to categorization processes, including the subsuming of narrow categories under more comprehensive ones and the subdivision of comprehensive categories into more specific ones. The extraction of similarities does not only operate upon physical stimuli but also upon categories of underlying structural schemata. Words label categorization processes. . . .

(3) Certain specializations in peripheral anatomy and physiology account for some of the universal features of natural languages, but the description of these human peculiarities does not constitute an explanation for the phylogenetic development of language. During the evolutionary history of the species form, function and behavior have interacted adaptively, but none of these aspects may be regarded as the "cause" of the other. Today, mastery of language by an individual may be accomplished despite severe peripheral anomalies, indicating that cerebral function is now the determining factor for language behavior as we know it in contemporary man. This, however, does not necessarily reflect the evolutionary sequence of developmental events.

(4) The biological properties of the human form of cognition set strict limits to the range of possibilities for variations in natural languages. The forms and modes of categorization, the capacity for extracting similarities from physical stimulus configuration or from classes of deeper structural schemata, and the operating characteristics of the data-processing machinery of the brain (for example, time-limitations on the rate of input, resolution-power for the analysis of intertwined patterns such as nested dependencies, limits of storage capacities for data that must be processed simultaneously, etc.) are powerful factors that determine a peculiar type of form for language. Within the limits set, however, there are infinitely many variations possible. Thus the outer form of languages may vary with relatively great freedom, whereas the underlying type remains constant.

(5) The implication of (1) and (2) is that the existence of our cognitive processes entails a potential for language. It is a capacity for a communication system that must necessarily be of one specific type. This basic capacity develops ontogenetically in the course of physical maturation; however, certain environmental conditions also must be present to make it possible for language to unfold. Maturation brings cognitive processes to a state that we may call *language-readiness*. The organism now requires certain raw materials from which it can shape building blocks for his own language development. The situation is somewhat analogous to the relationship between nourishment and growth. The food that the growing individual takes in as architectural raw material must be chemically broken down and reconstituted before it may enter the synthesis that produces tissues and organs. The information on how the organs are to be structured does not come in the food but is latent in the individual's own cellular components. The raw material for the individual's language synthesis is the language spoken by the adults surrounding the child. The presence of the raw material seems to function like a releaser for the developmental language synthesizing process. The course of language-unfolding is quite strictly prescribed through the unique maturational path traversed by cognition, and thus we may say that language-readiness is a state of *latent language structure*. The unfolding of language is a process of *actualization* in which latent structure is transformed into *realized structure*. The actualization of latent structure to realized structure is to give the underlying cognitively determined type a concrete form.[4]

(6) The actualization process is not the same as "beginning to say things." In fact, it may be independent from certain restraints that are attending upon the capacity for making given responses. Actualization may take place even if responses are peripherally blocked; in this case actualization is demonstrable only through signs of understanding language. In cases where the proper raw material for language synthesis cannot be made available to the growing child (as in the deaf), the latent structure fails to become actualized either temporarily or permanently.

(7) The maturation of cognitive processes comes about through progressive differentiation. Physiological (and, therefore, cognitive) functions assume characteristics and specificities much the way cells and tissues do during ontogeny. Organs do not suddenly begin to function out of a state of silence, but every function in the mature individual is a derivative of embryologically earlier types of function. Although the primitive functions may often be different from the mature ones, we cannot say just when a later or derived process had its beginning. If language is an aspect of a fundamental, biologically determined process, it is not scientifically profitable to look for a *cause* of language development in the growing child just

as we do not look for a *cause* for the development of his ears. It might be more fruitful to think of maturation, including growth and the development of behavior such as language, as the traversing of highly unstable states; the disequilibrium of one leads to rearrangements that bring about new disequilibria, producing further rearrangements, and so on until relative stability, known as *maturity*, is reached. Language-readiness is an example of such a state of disequilibrium during which the mind creates a place into which the building blocks of language may fit.

(8) The disequilibrium state called language-readiness is of limited duration. It begins around two and declines with cerebral maturation in the early teens. At this time, apparently a steady state is reached, and cognitive processes are firmly structured, the capacity for primary language synthesis is lost, and cerebral reorganization of functions is no longer possible.

(9) The language potential and the *latent structure* may be assumed to be replicated in every healthy human being because they are a consequence of human-specific cognitive processes and a human-specific course of maturation. In other words, universal grammar is of a unique type, common to all men, and it is entirely the by-product of peculiar modes of cognition based upon the biological constitution of the individual. This notion of replication, which is a cornerstone of the present theory, also leads us to assume that the actualization process from latent to realized structure is universal because of replicated sequences of similar states of disequilibrium, and there is evidence for this assumption in the regularity of language-acquisition strategies. . . .

(10) Because latent structure is replicated in every child and because all languages must have an inner form of identical type (though an infinity of variations is possible), every child may learn any language with equal ease. The realized structure or outer form of the language that surrounds the growing child serves as a mold upon which the form of the child's own realized structure is modeled. This maneuver is possible only because all languages are so constructed as to conform to the stringent requirements imposed upon them by cerebral language-data processing mechanisms. Insistence upon universal, underlying identity of type in all languages may be difficult to understand in the face of differences in rules of syntax and semantic divergences. This puzzle is solved by considering the remarkable freedom allowed individual speakers to make creative and novel use of word-meanings, to reclassify words into various syntactic categories, and to take creative freedoms with rules of syntax. All aspects of outer form or realized structure are in a state of fluidity (of relatively high viscosity) indicating that it is our "mode of calculating with categories" that is universal, but the categories themselves are not fixed nor the particular choice of the many possible operations.

(11) The raw material from which the individual synthesizes building blocks for his own language development cannot be the cause of the developing structure as evidenced by the autochthonous beginnings in the infant's language acquisition. Primitive stages of language are simply too different from adult language to be regarded as a direct mirroring of the input. Nor is there any evidence that the adults surrounding the child are the causative or shaping agents that determine language onset or his course of development. . . . Purposiveness cannot, logically, be the mainspring for language development.

(12) Social settings may be required as a trigger that sets off a reaction. Perhaps a better metaphor still is the concept of resonance. In a given state of maturation, exposure to adult language behavior has an excitatory effect upon the actualization process much the way a certain frequency may have an excitatory effect upon

a specific resonator; the object begins to vibrate in the presence of the sound. In the case of language onset, the energy required for the resonance is, in a sense, supplied by the individual himself; if the trigger-analogy is preferred, we might say that he unwinds himself. The resonance analogy, on the other hand, illustrates more vividly how slight variations in the frequencies that impinge on the resonator may affect the quality or nature of the resonance; it is comparable to the child's hearing of French resulting in his speaking of French, each natural language being a selected frequency band from the limited possible frequency range that is capable of eliciting resonance. Once the critical period during which resonance may occur is outgrown, one language is firmly established, and exposure to new and different natural languages is no longer resonated to.

Thus the propagation and maintenance of language behavior in the species are not comparable to cultural tradition which is handed down from generation to generation. The individual does not serve as a passive vehicle or channel through which information is transmitted; instead, he is an autonomous unit constituted in very much the same way as other units around him, ready to behave in the same fashion as they do. His behavior is activated by social contact, and there is some superficial adaptation to the structure of their behavior, but it may be well to remember that he can only function if he can synthesize (recreate might be another word) the entire language mechanism out of the raw material available to him. The raw material is of no use unless it can be broken down as food proteins are broken down into amino-acids and built up again into the pattern of his in-dwelling latent structure. Thus, the individual is seen as functioning by virtue of his own power supply, so to speak; he constructs language by himself (provided he has the raw material to do it with), and the natural history of his development provides for mechanisms by which he will harmonize his function with that of other equally autonomously functioning individuals around him; the outer form of his language will have the outer form of the language of his native community.

(13) Even though biological constitution of the individual is an essential replica of its progenitors, there are, naturally, individual variations. In fact, there are two distinct levels that are relevant to language: in the formation of the latent structure and in the actualization process from latent to realized structure. The former may be due to variations in the operation of cognitive processes or due to variations in the maturational course; the latter is primarily due to variations in peripheral function and structures such as the vocal tract or the ears. Variations on these two levels explain the main facts about language constancies, language change, and language universals.

Chomsky cites the field of comparative ethology to support the concept of innate predispositions, and current work in experimental and physiological psychology. Consider excerpts from his book *Language and Mind*:[5]

One can cite many examples: for example, in the latter category, the work of Bower suggesting an innate basis for the perceptual constancies; studies in the Wisconsin primate laboratory on complex innate releasing mechanisms in rhesus monkeys; the work of Hubel, Barlow, and others on highly specific analyzing mechanisms in the lower cortical centers of mammals; and a number of comparable studies of lower organisms (for example, the beautiful work of Lettvin and his associates on frog vision). There is now good evidence from such investigations that perception of line, angle, motion, and other complex properties of the physical world is based on innate organization of the neural system.

In some cases at least, these built-in structures will degenerate unless appropriate stimulation takes place at an early stage in life, but although such experience is necessary to permit the innate mechanisms to function, there is no reason to believe that it has more than a marginal effect on determining how they function to organize experience. Furthermore, there is nothing to suggest that what has so far been discovered is anywhere near the limit of complexity of innate structures. The basic techniques for exploring the neural mechanisms are only a few years old, and it is impossible to predict what order of specificity and complexity will be demonstrated when they come to be extensively applied. For the present, it seems that most complex organisms have highly specific forms of sensory and perceptual organization that are associated with the *Umwelt* and the manner of life of the organism. There is little reason to doubt that what is true of lower organisms is true of humans as well. Particularly in the case of language, it is natural to expect a close relation between innate properties of the mind and features of linguistic structure; for language, after all, has no existence apart from its mental representation. Whatever properties it has must be those that are given to it by the innate mental processes of the organism that has invented it and that invests it anew with each succeeding generation along with whatever properties are associated with the conditions of its use. Once again, it seems that language should be, for this reason, a most illuminating probe with which to explore the organization of mental processes.

Turning to comparative ethology, it is interesting to note that one of its earliest motivations was the hope that through the "investigation of the a priori, of the innate working hypotheses present in subhuman organisms," it would be possible to shed light on the a priori forms of human thought. This formulation of intent is quoted from an early and little-known paper by Konrad Lorenz. Lorenz goes on to express views very much like those Peirce had expressed a generation earlier. He maintains:[8]

> One familiar with the innate modes of reaction of subhuman organisms can readily hypothesize that the a priori is due to hereditary differentiations of the central nervous system which have become characteristic of the species, producing hereditary dispositions to think in certain forms. . . . Most certainly Hume was wrong when he wanted to derive all that is a priori from that which the senses supply to experience, just as wrong as Wundt or Helmholtz who simply explain it as an abstraction from preceding experience. Adaptation of the a priori to the real world has no more originated from "experience" than adaptation of the fin of the fish to the properties of water. Just as the form of the fin is given a priori, prior to any individual negotiation of the young fish with the water, and just as it is this form that makes possible this negotiation, so it is also the case with our forms of perception and categories in their relationship to our negotiation with the real external world through experience. In the case of animals, we find limitations specific to the forms of experience possible for them. We believe we can demonstrate the closest functional and probably genetic relationship between these animal a priori's and our human a priori. Contrary to Hume, we believe, just as did Kant, that a "pure" science of innate forms of human thought, independent of all experience, is possible.

In recent discussion, models and observations derived from ethology have frequently been cited as providing biological support or at least analogue, to new approaches to the study of human intelligence. I cite these comments of Lorenz' mainly in order to show that this reference does not distort the outlook of at least some of the founders of this new domain of comparative psychology.

What seems to me important in ethology is its attempt to explore the innate properties that determine how knowledge is acquired and the character of this knowledge. Returning to this theme, we must consider a further question: How did the human mind come to acquire the innate structure that we are led to attribute to it? Not too surprisingly, Lorenz takes the position that this is simply a matter of natural selection.

Lorenz himself has recently commented on the relationship between innate propensities and learning. In an article by Joseph Alsop in *The New Yorker*, he is quoted as saying:[6]

"Nothing is truly innate except the blueprint of the genome. A baby may have a genetic blueprint for the most beautiful nose in Western Europe, but if bad diet makes the baby rachitic the blueprint will not be realized. Yet the approximate realization of the genetic blueprint is still the normal result, so it seems to me quibbling to refuse to apply the word 'innate' to behavioral and other characteristics whose blueprints are demonstrably transmitted in the germ plasm. All the same, we ethologists were mistaken in the past when we made a sharp distinction between 'innate' and 'learned.' Viewed in one light, all life is a learning process. No animal species or lower organism could survive for very long without adaptedness, and evolutionary adaptation molds each species or organism so that it fits its own environmental niche and therefore survives. This molding to fit an environment really amounts to forming an image of that particular environment within the species or organism, and one can quite properly speak of information concerning the environment being acquired by adaptation. Hence, there are really two ways of learning—genetically and by individual experience—and these two ways of learning, though different in kind, nonetheless form a continuum, as W. N. Russell has pointed out. In a good many cases, genetically transmitted information is not subject, or hardly subject, to revision or correction by individual experience. One example is the computing mechanism in a starling's nervous system which enables the bird to know the points of the compass by the sun's motion across the sky. A similar mechanism plays the primary role in the route-finding of homing pigeons. Another example is the human nervous system's computing mechanism which enables you to see that this is a pencil"—he brandished one—"whether I point it at you or hold it upright. Human optical illusions result almost invariably from false premises being fed into our innate mechanism of *Gestalt* perception. In other words humans must see everything as organized or sensible. But these nervous mechanisms into which individual learning does not enter, or hardly enters, are only part of the story. In every individual's system of fixed motor patterns and innate information there are pre-formed places where individual learning can be fitted in. The number of these pre-formed places for individual learning increases in proportion to the complexity of the organism. Hence, higher animals are capable of much individual learning, while insects have a rather limited capacity."

"To understand individual learning," Dr. Lorenz added, "you must begin with the fact that we and all the rest of animal creation start our lives with a substantial store of innate information that can be amplified by the right kind of experience. The information is put there by adaptation for just that purpose. Much of the innate information takes a rather simple plus-or-minus form, telling us, 'This feels good, that feels bad—do this again, don't do that again.' I am not speaking here, either, merely of feeling pain from a cut or satisfaction after a good meal. It's more complicated than that. For example, P. N. Richter and John Garcia have done quite fabulous experiments with rats. One was to break down the needed protein component in the rats' diet into the constituent amino acids and offer these separately. Judging by their weight gains, the rats quickly learned to take just enough of each amino acid to get the equivalent of their optimum protein requirement. And obviously, they synthesized their protein requirement so correctly—think of that!—because they felt better that way. Another experiment was to give the rats saccharin water, which they like. Nausea was then induced quite a bit later, by injections of apomorphine, or something similar. Since the saccharin water was the last thing that had entered their stomachs, the rats at once associated the nausea with the saccharin water, and they refused it thereafter. But when other kinds of discomfort were inflicted on the rats, no matter how frequent and severe, these were never associated with food or drink—the discomfort had to be the kind that bad food normally causes in order to induce this special kind of learning. Per contra, the rats could never be conditioned to go here, or avoid going there, or do the other things that operant conditioners think up, by infliction of discomforts normally caused by food. Electric shocks and the like rapidly conditioned the rats in these ways, but not nausea. You see what I mean, then, by pre-formed places for learning. It doesn't stop with 'This feels good or bad' either. In some species, for instance, the innate schoolmarm, as I call it, is also able to say, 'This sounds good.' Father James Mulligan, of St. Louis University, and one of the really able younger men, Masakazu Konishi, of Princeton University, began to wonder how songbirds learned to sing. So song sparrows were reared in isolation, in sound-proof rooms. Eventually, by a kind of trial-and-error process of lonely song, the sparrows produced rough but recognizable approximations of the standard song of their species. And when they were taken out of isolation and allowed to hear other birds—not song sparrows, though—they borrowed this additional note or that until their own songs were perfect down to the last trill. Song sparrows, therefore—but not all bird species, by any means—are demonstrably born with what you can only call a clear idea of how their song ought to sound but without the song itself. Yet they have to hear in order to be able to judge. When deafened very young, Konishi's experimental sparrows never got nearer to the true song than a kind of amorphous twittering. When deafened after they got the song right, however, Konishi's sparrows continued to perform it correctly—it had become a fully learned motor pattern. And, like countless other bird species, the sparrows also proved to have certain innate calls that were, in reality, nothing but fixed motor patterns. Even when deafened very young, they always gave the song sparrow's characteristic warning call, *trank, trank, trank,* whenever they were frightened."

Ethology may also supply a purpose for babbling, its function not being apparent. Alsop notes, too, that "as ethological research has advanced, moreover, the role of mechanism in behavior has seemed to expand continuously. Even in the higher animals, for instance, the young can be seen testing out innate motor patterns before there is any need for them."[7] Perhaps this is what the child is doing when he babbles.

A number of Lorenz's concepts are remarkably similar to those of Jean Piaget, the Swiss psychologist whose concepts we will review in more detail later. They share the concept of adaptation of an organism to its environment. Lorenz's view that molding to fit an environment really amounts to forming an image of that particular environment within the species or organism is similar to Piaget's concept of accommodation: a change in the nature of the organism to lead to adaptation. It is reminiscent, too, of Lenneberg's "abstract schemata" underlying transformations. Lorenz also notes that "one can quite properly speak of information concerning the environment being acquired by adaptation." The equivalent Piagetian concept is his theory itself: assimilation—the intake of encounters with the environment—leads to accommodation changes in the organism, which become the progressively organized and reorganized cognitive and affective structures. Thus intelligence has its roots in behavior, and behavior has its roots in the innate reflexes. Reflexes are coordinated behaviors activated in relation to environmental encounters. They thus form the understructure for subsequent organizations. Adaptation and organization, according to Piaget, is intelligence itself.

SUMMARY

As we have been reminded in this and the preceding chapter, language is a very complex activity. The child does not learn the whole of it at one time. He does, however, notice and direct his efforts to one of the discernible sub-wholes at any one time or at overlapping times. As Gestaltists might say, one aspect of the language configuration achieves "figure" proportions at one time, and another at another time, depending on the child's sensitivity to the environment. Phonemic sounds are emitted, explored through contrast, and matched to the sounds of the mother tongue and mastered so that the child can command them at will. A vast number of vocabulary items are learned in their reference context so that "names belonging to things" seem to be explored as one distinct noticeable regularity of language. Intonation, as a discernible regularity of the language complex, is also explored for its own sake. The child imposes on his babbling the intonation characteristic of his mother tongue, exploring the possible kinds of intonation characteristic of different sentence forms. Finally, with all these constituents of language wholly or partially mastered and with much skill in the "how to do it" of these components, the child begins to bring them all together as he approaches the task of communicating meanings and responding to them in the language of the people around him.

It has only been through careful recording and analysis of children's language that some insight has been gained into the process of achieving mature speech. Over time and with maturity, speech becomes more complex and more compact. Sentence length is not a sophisticated measure of mature language; but instead, the grammatical expression of interrelatedness and interdependency of ideas to convey meaning is the proper index of this maturity. Thus, as Brown and Bellugi propose, gradual changes occur in the development of language in a child from "unrefined generalizations to valid rules for language production."

Analysis of the process of language achievement shows the child actively engaged in discovering regular patterns and consistencies in word classes in the language environment. His own language productions are never random assemblies of possible utterances, but instead display organization from the beginning. What he does achieve is mastery of his mother tongue. Therefore, he reconstructs within himself the language of his immediate environment. Thus he achieves his language in interaction with the language environment. The nature of the child predisposes him to notice and to take account of regularities and patterns and to behave in reference to inner organization even when it is primitive. He also can match his later perceptions to his internal organization and reorganize for future productions, thus mastering mature speech. The organization he perceives in the language environment depends on the nature and possibilities for organization within it.

Children generally learn language in the language environment provided by their mothers. This results in a relatively restricted environment of objects and events around which the mother and child develop meanings. Also, any one mother will display consistencies in her grammar selection for the linguistic environment she provides for her child.

There is evidence to support the idea that mothers play an active role in tailoring an environment that supports language development. It is not that children learn language by imitating their mothers, for children imitate speech only in respect to their personal sentence-making bias; their imitations are not parrotlike. Mothers, in talking to their young children, speak in language only slightly higher in level than that at which the children speak spontaneously, and the mothers' speech is restricted to immediate and present events. Their speech to their children is grammatical and complete.

In general, a child's apparent imitation of adult speech displays a reduction of the imitated sentence by preserving the word order, repeating the contentives, and dropping the functors. The mother plays an important role in supporting the child's early language. Her imitations of the child's utterances are not automatic expansions to good grammar, but show judgments reflecting her knowledge of the immediate situation of the child and his intention in relation to it. Thus the mother supports and encourages the child's early language attempts by providing the kind of feedback which will indicate to the child that his attempts at communication are successful.

For the reading teacher, there are characteristics of the language-learning situation that have implications of how children learn in general and how they learn to read in particular: interaction with a limited but nevertheless patterned and meaningful part of the whole task area; early flexibility to allow the child to select that particular sub-whole or general aspect to which he is most attracted at any one time; sufficient time to fully explore the sub-wholes of the task before setting performance expectations with regard to the whole; provision of a sufficient sample displaying the desired characteristics before the child begins to perform; much planning of the situation to ensure support by feedback of the success of early attempts; a recognition of the place of errors in the mastery sequence so that errors are seen as indications of lack of mastery of the necessary concepts or as indicators that the child is operating according to some inappropriate bias. If inappropriate biases are involved, the teacher would need to provide a broader sample displaying clearly the regularities of the critical concept to be learned.

Thus the beginning reading situation should provide for a planned and regular, but restricted, sampling of the whole. This whole must encompass fully the possible sub-wholes of reading as the interactive environment in which the child begins to master the complex task of reading.

NOTES FOR CHAPTER 5

1. Eric H. Lenneberg, "The Capacity for Language Acquisition," in *The Structure of Language: Readings in the Philosophy of Language,* edited by Jerry A. Fodor and Jerrold J. Katz (Englewood Cliffs, N.J.: Prentice-Hall, 1964), p. 600.
2. Eric H. Lenneberg, *Biological Foundations of Language* (New York: Wiley, 1967), pp. 374–79.
3. It is true that this statement introduces some profound problems in the theory of evolution but our preoccupation with language should not oblige us to solve at the same time the general problems that affect all evolutionary phenomena. The emergence of celestial navigation in birds or the diving abilities of whales are no less mysterious than the emergence of a language-enabling cognition.
4. This formulation might be regarded as the biological counterpart to what grammarians have for centuries called *universal* and *particular* grammar. Latent structure is responsible for the general type of all features of universal grammar; realized structure is responsible for the peculiarities of any given statement as well as those aspects that are unique to the grammar of a given natural language.
5. Noam Chomsky, *Language and Mind* (New York: Harcourt, Brace & World, 1968), pp. 80–82.
6. Joseph Alsop, "Profiles: A Condition of Enormous Improbability," *The New Yorker,* March 8, 1969, p. 48.
7. Ibid., p. 71.
8. Konrad Lorenz, "Kants Lehre vom apriorischen in Lichte gegenwärtiger Biologie," *Blätter für Deutsche Philosophie* 15 (1941).

6

how sentences are understood

Chomsky's theory of the nature of language is probably best introduced by an example. The sentences "Jeanne is eager to photograph" and "Jeanne is difficult to photograph" appear very much alike on the surface. Both consist of a noun, the verb *is*, an adjective, and an infinitive. However, they have very different interpretations. In one sentence, Jeanne is doing the photographing; in the other, Jeanne is being photographed.

Chomsky attempts to describe how meaning is communicated through language. He states that "a fully adequate grammar must assign to each of an infinite range of sentences a structural description indicating how this sentence is understood by the ideal speaker-hearer."

He calls this a *generative* grammar if it is perfectly explicit—that is, if it provides an explicit analysis of the ideal speaker-hearer's contribution which allows him to ascribe meaning either as a speaker of the above sentences or as a listener. In Chomsky's view, a grammar describes linguistic elements and their relationships. It requires that the user identify and discriminate well-formed utterances. It will indicate the manner in which ill-formed utterances deviate from those that are well formed.[1] This grammar, according to Chomsky's theory, is a system of rules that represent the competence of the ideal speaker-hearer to understand sentences he has never heard before and say sentences he has never said before. Comments George A. Miller, chairman of the department of psychology at Rockefeller University:[2]

But what is the scientific status of a rule as an explanatory concept in psychology? It is not a law, for it can be violated, and often is. Ordinarily, one would like to define a rule as an explicit statement, couched in some formal or informal notation, that specifies the appropriate actions to take under certain well-defined circumstances. But this conception of a rule as an explicit statement is ill-suited to the situation in psycholinguistics, for it is generally the case that people who can follow the rules with amazing skill are often completely unable to provide any explicit statement of the rules they are following. If people know the rules, therefore, they must know them implicitly. The only way we know they know the rules is by inference from the fact that, under certain carefully specified circumstances, their behavior conforms to them, and from the fact that they can recognize what it means to make a mistake.

These rules of language are divided into three subsystems—syntactic, phonological, and semantic. The syntactic rules comprise one component of the grammar. The semantic and phonological rules comprise a second component, which is called *interpretative*. The syntactic component is expressed through the semantic and phonological components.

The syntactic component consists of elements called *formatives*. The formatives are of two types: lexical (for example, *the, boy*) and grammatical (for example, the possessive). In addition, the syntactic component contains "categories," which include sentences, noun phrases, and verbs, and "functions," which refer, for example, to the *subject* of a sentence as opposed to a noun phrase of a sentence. Finally, there are "structural interrelations," which refer to the rules that pair the sounds of an utterance (surface structure) with the logical relationship between concepts (deep structure). These rules are the *transformational rules* that transform surface structures to deep structures and vice versa. There is also a set of rewriting rules, which form "phrase markers" (for example, "the boy," "is going," "across the street").

Thus, as in our previous examples, "Jeanne is eager to photograph" and "Jeanne is difficult to photograph," there are two levels of structure: one that is heard or seen, and one that is abstract. The transformations intercede between the meaning and the pronunciation by means of processes which delete, add, rearrange, or combine various elements. "Strings" are produced which preserve the meaning. At the surface level additional pronunciation rules are applied and the strings become pronounced as sentences.

Let us now turn to Chomsky for further examples and elaboration.[3] Consider sentence (4): "What disturbed John was being disregarded by everyone." It "must be assigned at least two semantic representations, and ... one of these must be essentially the same as the interpretation assigned to both (9) and (10)."

(9)   Being disregarded by everyone disturbed John.
(10)   The fact that everyone disregarded John disturbed him.

Furthermore, it is clear that the semantic representation of a sentence depends on the representation of its parts, as in the parallel case of phonetic interpretation. For example, in the case of (10), it is obvious that the semantic interpretation depends, in part, on the semantic interpretation of "everyone disregarded John"; if the latter were replaced in (10) by "life seemed to pass John by," the interpretation of the whole would be changed in a fixed way. This much is transparent, and it suggests that a principle like the principle of cyclic application in phonology should hold in the semantic component.

A slightly more careful look at the problem shows that semantic interpretation must be significantly more abstract than phonological interpretation with respect to the notion of "constituent part." Thus the interpretation of "everyone disregarded John" underlies not only (10), but also (9) and (4), and in exactly the same way. But neither (4) nor (9) contains "everyone disregarded John" as a constituent part, as does (10). In other words, the deep structures underlying (9) and (10) should both be identical (or very similar) to one of two deep structures underlying (4), despite the wide divergence in surface structure and phonetic form. It follows that we cannot expect deep structure to be very close to surface structure in general.

In the case of a sentence like (6) ("John saw Bill"), there is little difference between deep and surface structure. Semantic interpretation would not be far from the mark, in this case, if it were quite parallel to phonetic interpretation. Thus the interpretation of "saw Bill" can be derived from that of "saw" and that of "Bill," and the interpretation of (6) can be determined from that of "John" and that of "saw Bill." To carry out such interpretation we must know not only the bracketing of (6) into constituents, but also the grammatical relations that are represented; that is, we must know that "Bill" is the *direct object* of "saw" and that the subject-predicate relation holds between "John" and "saw Bill" in "John saw Bill." Similarly, in the slightly more complex case of "John saw Bill leave," we must know that the subject-predicate relation holds between "John" and "saw Bill leave" and also between "Bill" and "leave."

Notice that at least in such simple cases as (6), we already have a mechanism for representing grammatical relations of just the sort that are required for semantic interpretation. Suppose that we define the relations *subject-of* as the relation holding between a noun phrase and a sentence of which it is an immediate constituent and the relation *predicate-of* as holding between a verb phrase and a sentence of which it is an immediate constituent. The subject-predicate relation can then be defined as the relation holding between the subject of a sentence and the predicate of this sentence. Thus, in these terms, "John" is the subject and "saw Bill (leave)" the predicate of "John saw Bill (leave)," and the subject-predicate relation holds between the two. In the same way, we can define the relation *direct-object* (in terms of the immediate constituency of verb and noun phrase in verb phrase) and others in a perfectly appropriate and satisfactory way. But returning now to (6), this observation implies that a *labeled bracketing* will serve as the deep structure (just as a labeled bracketing will serve as the surface structure); it contains just the information about constituency and about grammatical relations that is required for semantic interpretation.

We noted that in "John saw Bill leave" the subject-predicate relation holds between "Bill" and "leave," as well as between "John" and "saw Bill leave." If (6) or something very much like it ... is to be taken as the deep structure, with grammatical relations as previously, then the deep structure of "John saw Bill leave" will have to be something like (11) (many details omitted):

(11) [s [NP John]NP [vp [v saw]v [s [NP Bill]NP [vp [v leave]v]vp]s]vp]s

The labeled bracketing (11) expresses the subject-predicate relation between "John" and "saw Bill leave" and between "Bill" and "leave," as required.

Moving to a somewhat more complex example, the sentences (9) and (10) (as well as (4) under one interpretation) will each have to contain something like (12) in the deep structure:

(12) [s [NP everyone]NP [vp [v disregards]v [NP John]NP]vp]s

If this requirement is met, then we will be able to account for the fact that, obviously, the meaning of (4) (= "what disturbed John was being disregarded by everyone") in one interpretation and of (9) (= "being disregarded by everyone disturbed John") is determined in part by the fact that the direct-object relation holds between "disregard" and "John" and the subject-predicate relation between "everyone" and "disregards John," despite the fact that these relations are in no way indicated in the surface structure in (4) or (9).

From many such examples, we are led to the following conception of how the semantic component functions. This interpretive component of the full generative grammar applies to a deep structure and assigns to it a semantic representation, formulated in terms of the still quite obscure notions of universal semantics. The deep structure is a labeled bracketing of minimal "meaning-bearing" elements. The interpretive rules apply cyclically, determining the semantic interpretation of a phrase X of the deep structure from the semantic interpretations of the immediate constituents of X and the grammatical relation represented in this configuration of X and its parts.

A quote from Chomsky offers a suitable conclusion for the above:[4]

Thus each of the two interpretive components maps a syntactically generated structure onto a "concrete" interpretation, in one case phonetic and in the other, semantic. The grammar as a whole can thus be regarded as, ultimately, a device for pairing phonetically represented signals with semantic interpretations, this pairing being mediated through a system of abstract structures generated by the syntactic component. Thus the syntactic component must provide for each sentence (actually, for each interpretation of each sentence) a semantically interpretable *deep structure* and a phonetically interpretable surface structure, and, in the event that these are distinct, a statement of relation between these structures.

The "statement of relation" would be the appropriate transformational rules.

Why should human languages be designed like this? Perhaps, Chomsky speculates, the design rules out deep structures that are not well formed. Again, it may have something to do with man's perceptual mechanisms: sound is unrecoverable for the infant learning a language and for the adult receiving a spoken message (as opposed to writing). Transformations may facilitate speech perception by requiring a rather limited short-term memory, since a vast array of utterances can be quickly reduced to a limited set of kernels.

And what about a child who must acquire a language? Says Chomsky:[5]

The child must acquire a generative grammar of his language on the basis of a fairly restricted amount of evidence.[6] To account for this achievement, we must postulate a sufficiently rich internal structure—a sufficiently restricted theory of universal grammar that constitutes his contribution to language acquisition.

For example, it was suggested earlier that in order to account for the perception of stress contours in English, we must suppose that the user of the language is making use of the principle of cyclic application. We also noted that he could hardly have sufficient evidence for this principle. Consequently, it seems reasonable to assume that this principle is simply part of the innate schematism that he uses to interpret the limited and fragmentary evidence available to him. It is, in other words, part of universal grammar. Similarly, it is difficult to imagine what "inductive principles" might lead the child unerringly to the assumptions about deep structure and about organization of grammar that seem to be necessary if we are to account for such facts as those we have mentioned. Nor is a search for such principles particularly well-motivated. It seems reasonable to assume that these properties of English are, in reality, facts of universal grammar. If such properties are available to the child, the task of language-acquisition becomes feasible. The problem for the child is not the apparently insuperable inductive feat of arriving at a transformational generative grammar from restricted data, but rather that of discovering which of the possible languages he is being exposed to. Arguing in this way, we can arrive at conclusions about universal grammar from study of even a single language.

The child is presented with data, and he must inspect hypotheses (grammars) of a fairly restricted class to determine compatibility with this data. Having selected a grammar of the predetermined class, he will then have command of the language generated by this grammar. Thus he will know a great deal about phenomena to which he has never been exposed, and which are not "similar" or "analogous" in any well-defined sense to those to which he has been exposed. He will, for example, know the relations among the sentences, despite their novelty:

(a) I persuaded the doctor to examine John.
(b) I persuaded John to be examined by the doctor.
(a) I expected the doctor to examine John.
(b) I expected John to be examined by the doctor.

He will know what stress contours to assign to utterances, despite the novelty and lack of physical basis for these phonetic representations; and so on, for innumerable other similar cases. This disparity between knowledge and experience is perhaps the most striking fact about human language. To account for it is the central problem of linguistic theory.

A footnote to Chomsky's language-acquisition model mentioned strategies for sampling hypotheses. This same point was noted in greater detail in his "Review of B. F. Skinner's *Verbal Behavior*":[7]

The child who learns a language has in some sense constructed the grammar for himself on the basis of his observation of sentences and nonsentences (i.e., corrections by the verbal community). Study of the actual observed ability of a speaker to distinguish sentences from nonsentences, detect ambiguities, etc., apparently forces us to the conclusion that this grammar is of an extremely complex and abstract character, and that the young child has succeeded in carrying out what from the formal point of view, at least, seems to be a remarkable type of theory construction. Furthermore, this task is accomplished in an astonishingly short time, to a large extent independently of intelligence, and in a comparable way by all children. Any theory of learning must cope with these facts.

It is not easy to accept the view that a child is capable of constructing an extremely complex mechanism for generating a set of sentences, some of which he has heard, or that an adult can instantaneously determine whether (and if so, how) a particular item is generated by this mechanism, which has many of the properties of an abstract deductive theory. Yet this appears to be a fair description of the performance of the speaker, listener, and learner. If this is correct, we can predict that a direct attempt to account for the actual behavior of speaker, listener, and learner, not based on a prior understanding of the structure of grammars, will achieve very limited success. The grammar must be regarded as a component in the behavior of the speaker and listener which can only be inferred, as Lashley has put it, from the resulting physical acts. The fact that all normal children acquire essentially comparable grammars of great complexity with remarkable rapidity suggests that human beings are somehow specially designed to do this, with data-handling or "hypothesis-formulating" ability of unknown character and complexity.[8] The study of linguistic structure may ultimately lead to some significant insights into this matter. At the moment the question cannot be seriously posed, but in principle it may be possible to study the problem of determining what the built-in structure of an information-processing (hypothesis-forming) system must be to enable it to arrive at the grammar of a language from the available data in the available time. At any rate, just as the attempt to eliminate the contribution of the speaker leads to a "mentalistic" descriptive system that succeeds only in blurring important traditional distinctions, a refusal to study the contribution of the child to language learning permits only a superficial account of language acquisition, with a vast and unanalyzed contribution attributed to a step called *generalization* which in fact includes just about everything of interest in this process. If the study of language is limited in these ways, it seems inevitable that major aspects of verbal behavior will remain a mystery.

SUMMARY

In this chapter we have shown Chomsky's views on how meaning is communicated through language. A system of rules is at the disposal of the speaker of a language that makes it possible to explain how he can say sentences he has never said before and understand sentences he has never heard before. Chomsky proposes that these rules are biological givens, built into the structure of the mind and functioning implicitly in speaking and understanding what we hear. Other theorists propose that these rules are learned but that the nature of the human organism is such as to predispose the speaker to learn them. There are three subsystems of rules that function to provide human language capacity—syntactic, phonological, and semantic. The syntactic subsystem is expressed through the phonological and the semantic. The system can be viewed as consisting of two levels, one heard or seen and the other abstract. The series of implicit rules are used to go from the abstract-meaning level to the physical representation and vice versa. These are the transformations.

Human beings are especially designed to learn the rules by interacting with the language environment. Once the rules are learned, using them to process what is heard becomes almost a necessity rather than a possibility. There is no reason to believe that the rules for communicating meaning through written language are substantially different from those for communicating meaning through oral language. However, in written language there is obviously a visual component that is added to (or perhaps replaces parts of) the system of spoken language rules. The relation between oral and written language will be discussed in the next chapter.

NOTES FOR CHAPTER 6

1. Noam Chomsky, *Aspects of a Theory of Syntax* (Cambridge: MIT Press, 1965), pp. 4–5.
2. George A. Miller, "Language and Psychology," in *New Directions in the Study of Language*, edited by Eric H. Lenneberg (Cambridge: MIT Press, 1964), p. 98.
3. In Eric H. Lenneberg, *Biological Foundations of Language* (New York: Wiley, 1967), pp. 416–19.
4. Noam Chomsky, *Current Issues in Linguistic Theory* (The Hague: Mouton, 1964), pp. 9–10.
5. In Eric H. Lenneberg, *Biological Foundations of Language,* pp. 437–38.
6. Furthermore, evidence of a highly degraded sort. For example, the child's conclusions about the rules of sentence formation must be based on evidence that consists, to a large extent, of utterances that break rules, since a good deal of normal speech consists of false starts, disconnected phrases, and other deviations from idealized competence.
   The issue here is not one of "normative grammar." The point is that a person's normal speech departs from the rules of his own internalized grammar in innumerable ways, because of the many factors that interact with underlying competence to determine performance. Correspondingly, as a language learner, he acquires a grammar that characterizes much of the evidence on which it was based as deviant and anomalous.
7. Noam Chomsky, "A Review of B. F. Skinner's *Verbal Behavior,*" in *The Structure of Language: Readings in the Philosophy of Language*, edited by Jerry A. Fodor and Jerrold J. Katz (Englewood Cliffs, N.J.: Prentice-Hall, 1964), pp. 577–78. The review originally appeared in *Language* 35 (1959).
8. There is nothing essentially mysterious about this. Complex innate behavior patterns and innate "tendencies to learn in specific ways" have been carefully studied in lower organisms. Many psychologists have been inclined to believe that such biological structure will not have an important effect on acquisition of complex behavior in higher organisms, but I have not been able to find any serious justification for this attitude. Some recent studies have stressed the necessity for carefully analyzing the strategies available to the organism, regarded as a complex "information-processing system" (cf. J. S. Bruner, J. J. Goodnow, and G. A. Austin, *A Study of Thinking* [New York, 1956]; A. Newell, J. C. Shaw, and H. A. Simon, "Elements of a Theory of Human Problem Solving," *Psych. Rev.* 65 [1958], 151–66), if anything significant is to be said about the character of human learning. These may be largely innate, or developed by early learning processes about which very little is yet known. (But see Harlow, "The Formation of Learning Sets," *Psych. Rev.* 56 [1949], 51–65, and many later papers, where striking shifts in the character of learning are shown as a result of early training; also D. O. Hebb, *Organization of Behavior* [New York: Wiley, 1949], 109 ff.). They are undoubtedly quite complex. Cf. Lenneberg ["The Capacity for Language Acquisition," in Fodor and Katz, p. 579] and R. B. Lees, review of N. Chomsky's *Syntactic Structures* in *Language* 33 (1957), 406 f., for discussion of the topics mentioned in this section.

7

the relation between oral and written language

A host of specialists in reading and the language arts share a popular misbelief: they contend that English is "unphonetic." By this they seem to mean that the relation between spoken and written words is confusing. No wonder, they argue, that children have so much trouble learning to read and spell. If only our language were phonetic! They will cite, for example, the *a* in *fat, was, yacht, call, hasty, orange, liar, war, far, fare, thermal, quay, courage.* The element *ch* is regarded as confusing because it stands for *ch, sh,* and *k,* or it is silent—as in *much, machine, stomach,* and *yacht.* Consider *s* in *was, saw, beds, bets, occasion, mission, deserve,* and *conserve.* Words can sound alike but be spelled differently: *bear-bare.* And words can look alike but be pronounced differently: Tomorrow I shall *read* the sign; yesterday I *read* the sign. Letters are silent one time, as in *sign;* not silent the next time, as in *signal.*

Displaying the evidence, these specialists argue that we can ease beginning reading instruction by reforming our orthography (as in the case of the Initial Teaching Alphabet) or by reforming our spelling system: for instance, by spelling *laugh* l-a-f-f or *freight* f-r-a-t-e. In this way, there will be a more regular correspondence between letters and sounds, they contend.

Perhaps it may come as a shock to these specialists to learn from Chomsky that "conventional orthography in English is remarkably close to optimal" in the sense that "it provides just the information needed by a person who has command of the syntactic and phonological rules (up to ambiguity)."

It appears that the reason so many specialists have been confused over this issue is that they were seeking relationships between conventional orthography and the surface structure of spoken English. This is epitomized by the frequently seen assertion that written English is just "talk written down." But in fact, says Chomsky, "conventional spelling is, by and large, a highly effective system for a wide range of dialects because it corresponds to a common underlying phonological representation." Thus written language is not "talk written down," but an underlying phonological representation that can be written down. What is the nature of the underlying phonological representation?[1]

THE SOUND PATTERN OF ENGLISH

Consider a spoken utterance; it has a surface structure. Phonological rules transform the surface structure to a phonetic representation. These rules apply to words and strings of formatives which may be words, parts of words, or phrases that include words. The phonetic representation consists of a sequence of segments in which each segment specifies the presence or absence of distinctive features, such as "consonantal" or "strident." Sequences of these segments are lexical formatives (in *bedtimes, bed* and *time* are lexical formatives, for instance), and some are grammatical formatives (in *bedtimes, s* represents the grammatical formative, plural). The lexical formative has a semantic interpretation; that is, it represents a concept. Syntactic rules and transformational rules relate the surface structure to the deep structure—the logical relationships between concepts. In complex utterances, however, there may be phonological phrases that are related in part to the syntactic structure. In addition, there are readjustment rules that replace certain formatives by complexes of features. These rules modify the surface structure and relate the syntax of the utterances to its phonology. A readjustment rule, for example, would relate *sing*-plus-past to *sang.* The phonetic representation *after* applying the readjustment rules is what Chomsky terms the "phonological representation." Thus readjustment rules apply to the syntactically justified surface structure to produce the input to the phonological component.

For example, consider *consume* and *resume.* The /s/ is unvoiced in *consume* and voiced in *resume.* The relation between conventional orthography and phonological representation is evident when we consider these lists of words:

consume	resume
conserve	preserve, deserve
consist, insist, persist	resist
consign	resign, design

The /s/ of the stems *-sume, -serve, -sist,* and *-sign* is unvoiced when the prefix ends in a consonant, and voiced when the prefix ends in a vowel. An additional rule is needed to explain words such as *recite* and *recede.*

To summarize,[2] rules of syntax generate surface structures; principles of interpretation assign boundaries; readjustment rules modify the surface structure, yielding a phonological surface structure; phonological rules convert this into a phonetic representation.

Here is Chomsky's view, then, of what must be learned by a nonliterate person who is going to read:[3]

When we consider the structure of a language we are, fundamentally, concerned with a relation of sound and meaning. The rules of the language—the rules that the native speaker intuitively commands and that the linguist tries to discover and exhibit—relate certain physical signals to certain semantic interpretations; more precisely, they relate phonetic representations of sentences to their structural descriptions. Thus one level of representation that must have psychological significance, both on the perceptual and motor levels, is the level of phonetic representation; another is the level of representation that appears in structural descriptions. . . .

Consider now the character of the lexicon. . . . Each item, of course, has a unique . . . spelling—a single entry—in the lexicon. This spelling must contain all information not predictable by phonological rules (presupposing the rest of the structural description of the sentence in which the item is embedded). Thus the lexical representation of the common item of *histor-y, histor-ical, histor-ian,* or of *anxi-ous, anxi-ety,* or of *courage, courage-ous,* or of *tele+graph, tele+graph-ic, tele+graph-y,* etc., must be selected so as to contain just what is not predictable in the variant phonetic realizations of these items. . . .

Observe that a lexical representation, in this sense, provides a natural orthography for a person who knows a language. It provides just the information about words that is not predictable by phonological rule or by the syntactic rules that determine the phrasing of the sentence in which the item is embedded. It provides just the information needed by a person who has command of the syntactic and phonological rules (up to ambiguity). Conventional orthography, in English, as in every case of which I have any knowledge, is remarkably close to optimal, in this sense. For example, the spellings *histor-, anxi-, courage, telegraph* are (minor notational conventions aside) essentially what would appear in the lexicon of spoken English. Conventional orthographies tend to differ *systematically* from lexical representation only in that true irregularities (e.g., *man-men, cling-clung*) are differently represented, as is quite natural. The symbols of conventional orthography correspond to feature sets, in the underlying sound system of the spoken language.

It seems fairly well established that the level of lexical representation is highly resistant to change, and is highly persistent over time (and hence over a range of dialects). Correspondingly, one finds that conventional orthographies remain useful, with minor change, over long periods and for a wide range of dialects. . . .

We may say that the relation between conventional spelling and phonological representation is very close, and that conventional spelling is, by and large, a highly effective system for a wide range of dialects because it corresponds to a common underlying phonological representation, relatively invariant among dialects despite wide phonetic divergence. Let me emphasize again the advantages of phonological (i.e., essentially conventional orthographic) representation *for a speaker who understands the language.* . . .

In considering problems of literacy, the questions of "phoneme-grapheme correspondences" and of dialect variation naturally arise. As to the latter, this is a problem only to the extent that dialects differ on the syntactic and lexical level. Differences in phonological rules are irrelevant, since orthography corresponds to a deeper level of representation than (broad) phonetic. . . . As to the question of "phoneme-grapheme" correspondence . . . the only reasonable way to study sound-letter correspondences seems to be to utilize the fact that orthography corresponds closely to a significant level of linguistic representation—namely, phonological representation . . .—which is, furthermore, related to sound by general rules—namely, the rules of the phonological component. . . .

If this much is correct, then it would seem to follow that the rules of sound-letter correspondence need hardly be taught, particularly the most general and deepest of these rules. For these rules are in any event part of the unconscious linguistic equipment of the non-literate speaker. What he must learn (except for true ir-regularities) is simply the elementary correspondence between the underlying phonological segments of his internalized lexicon and the orthographic symbols.

Chomsky's underlying premise for the above discussion is that writing is not just talk written down. There are, however, other reasons why this is so. A number of them are cited by Vygotsky. He asserts:[4]

Communication in writing relies on the formal meanings of words and requires a much greater number of words than oral speech to convey the same ideas. It is addressed to an absent person who rarely has in mind the same subject as the writer. Therefore it must be fully deployed; syntactic differentiation is at a maximum; and expressions are used that would seem unnatural in conversation. Griboedov's "He talks like writing" refers to the droll effect of elaborate con-structions in daily speech.

In oral speech (as opposed to inner speech), adds Vygotsky,[5]

inflection reveals the psychological context within which a word is to be understood. . . . When the context is . . . clear . . . it really becomes possible to convey all thoughts, feelings, and even a whole chain of reasoning by one word.

In written speech, as tone of voice and knowledge of subject are excluded, we are obliged to use many more words, and to use them more exactly. Written speech is the most elaborate form of speech. . . .

In written speech, lacking situational and expressive support, communication must be achieved only through words and their combinations; this requires the speech activity to take complicated forms—hence the use of first drafts. The evolu-tion from draft to final copy reflects our mental process. Planning has an important part in written speech, even when we do not actually write out a draft. Usually we say to ourselves what we are going to write; this is also a draft, though in thought only. . . . This mental draft is inner speech. . . . Inner speech functions as a draft not only in written but also in oral speech. . . .

Consider both inner and oral speech in terms of their tendency toward abbreviation and predication. Inner speech always employs abbreviation and predication; oral speech does so sometimes. (Written speech never does, says Vygotsky.) This is because we know what we are thinking about; we know the subject and the situation. Marriage partners, in a conversation, may communicate in a word or so, for the same reason. Or consider a common expression of someone in an elevator as it stops at a floor: "Out, please." Passengers know the situation and the subject; few words are necessary. And the child, who is egocentric—who construes the world in terms of himself—also speaks to himself in abbreviated messages and predicates, Vygotsky suggests, because he is speaking for himself. He knows the situation. Egocentric speech—the muttering one often hears in a kin-dergarten or first-grade classroom—exists at just the time the child is about to learn to read written language.

Vygotsky asks:[6]

Why does writing come so hard to the school child that at certain periods there is a lag of as much as six or eight years between his "linguistic age" in speaking and writing?

Our investigation has shown that the development of writing does not repeat the developmental history of speaking. Written speech is a separate linguistic function, differing from oral speech in both structure and mode of functioning. Even its minimal development requires a high level of abstraction. It is speech in thought and image only, lacking the musical, expressive, intonational qualities of oral speech. In learning to write, the child must disengage himself from the sensory aspect of speech and replace words by images of words. Speech that is merely imagined and that requires symbolization of the sound image in written signs (i.e., a second degree of symbolization) naturally must be as much harder than oral speech for the child as algebra is harder than arithmetic. Our studies show that it is the abstract quality of written language that is the main stumbling block, not the underdevelopment of small muscles or any other mechanical obstacles.

Writing is also speech without an interlocutor, addressed to an absent or an imaginary person or to no one in particular—a situation new and strange to the child. Our studies show that he has little motivation to learn writing when we begin to teach it. He feels no need for it and has only a vague idea of its usefulness. In conversation, every sentence is prompted by a motive. Desire or need leads to request, question to answer, bewilderment to explanation. The changing motives of the interlocutors determine at every moment the turn oral speech will take. It does not have to be consciously directed—the dynamic situation takes care of that. The motives for writing are more abstract, more intellectualized, further removed from immediate needs. In written speech, we are obliged to create the situation, to represent it to ourselves. This demands detachment from the actual situation.

Writing also requires deliberate analytical action on the part of the child. In speaking, he is hardly conscious of the sounds he pronounces and quite unconscious of the mental operations he performs. In writing, he must take cognizance of the sound structure of each word, dissect it, and reproduce it in alphabetical symbols, which he must have studied and memorized before. In the same deliberate way, he must put words in a certain sequence to form a sentence. Written language demands conscious work because its relationship to inner speech is different from that of oral speech: The latter precedes inner speech in the course of development, while written speech follows inner speech and presupposes its existence (the act of writing implying a translation from inner speech). But the grammar of thought is not the same in the two cases. One might even say that the syntax of inner speech is the exact opposite of the syntax of written speech, with oral speech standing in the middle.

Written speech lags behind oral speech, Vygotsky explains, because the child lacks "skill in abstract, deliberate activity. As our studies showed, the psychological functions on which written speech is based have not even begun to develop in the proper sense when instruction in writing starts. It must build on barely emerging, rudimentary processes."[7]

SUMMARY

In this chapter we have seen that written language is not simply speech written down. There is both a relationship and a disrelationship between oral and written language, more subtle than it is often assumed to be. Chomsky points out that conventional orthography adequately represents spoken language and thus the semantic component for the mature reader. It conveys the necessary information required for reading. It seems to be based on the expectation that the reader has mastered the spoken language. There are potential spoken language reference errors that a child never makes because he knows his language—unless by misguided instruction he is led into them. For example, he will not pronounce the *s* in *was* as / s/, but will pronounce it as /z/ because that is the way he speaks his language. It is the same with the word *walked*. The child will read the word as "walkt," and not "walk-ed," because that is the way he naturally talks. This should caution us against attempting to teach many commonly taught phonic generalizations which children may not need to learn.

On the other hand, written language, in some respects, is more difficult to process and to discover the meaning of than oral language. Because written language lacks some of the features of oral language, processing requires a more conscious effort. Usually more words are required in written language to convey meaning. This helps to explain why the child's skill in spelling and writing lags behind his skill in reading. Thus we should be cautioned about the emphasis we give to oral language in the language-experience approach to reading. Too, we should be warned against placing too much stress on the importance of writing activities in workbooks accompanying reading programs.

SUMMARY OF CHAPTERS 1—7

Let us, at this time, recapitulate what we have said so far. We started out by saying that children learn to read from a variety of different methods of instruction—phonics, whole-word, language-experience, and the like. Children apparently possess inherent characteristics that they actively use in assisting the teacher and themsleves in learning to read. This would explain why improvements in children's learning to read seem to result from the application of the results of basic, theoretical research rather than from superficial changes in methods. Because reading is a language-related activity and because learning language (like learning to read) involves innate characteristics of the child, the study of language and how it is acquired is a legitimate area of study for reading instructors. Therefore, chapters 3 through 7 of this book have been devoted to preparing the way for a greater understanding of language and its relation to reading. In chapter 3 we introduced the concept that the child does not learn language through passive imitation, but is actively involved in using his language-producing capacities to induce his own language development. Chapters 4, 5, and 6, further elaborate this basic concept. In chapter 4 we learned that the child already has an elaborate language before he enters school and is confronted with the task of learning to read. The child does not learn language by combining small units of language together, but by differentiating and elaborating whole language patterns. He learns a general structure of rules that gradually becomes more and more differentiated. This system of rules is what makes it possible for him to understand language he has never heard or seen before. Oral and written language have features that are common to both, and features that are unique to each. Evidence that oral and written language have common features is that written language provides just enough information for the native speaker to read it. However, because written language does not contain all the features of oral language, written language must be more complex in certain respects than oral language.

In the next five chapters, we turn our attention to the mental development of the learner. We will again see that the child is not a passive, but an active, learner, and that the thinking of the child is not simply less in amount than that of the adult, but has distinctive characteristics that make it qualitatively different from mature thought.

In addition, we will be exploring the relation between language and thought, and will review pertinent literature on concept learning.

NOTES FOR CHAPTER 7

1. The following section is a summary of pages 5–14 of *The Sound Pattern of English,* by Noam Chomsky and Morris Halle (New York: Harper & Row, 1968).
2. Drawn from Chomsky and Halle, p. 221.
3. Noam Chomsky, "Comments for Project Literacy Meeting," *Project Literacy Reports* 2 (September 1964), pp. 1–8 (Cornell Univ.).
4. Lev S. Vygotsky, *Thought and Language* (Cambridge: MIT Press, 1962), p. 142.
5. Ibid., p. 144
6. Ibid., pp. 98–99.
7. Ibid., p. 100.

8

the nature of mental development and learning to read
Chomsky noted in the preceding chapter what the nonliterate speaker must learn if he is to learn to read, but he did not describe the nature of the mental development of such a nonliterate person. To begin this exploration of the nature of the learner, let us explore the developmental theories of Jean Piaget. They seem to parallel at many points Chomsky's description of a grammar and its acquisition. Because there are many exhaustive studies of Piaget's work, including his own, the following account presents only highlights, and attempts to avoid interpretative distortion.

From birth till death, the human being's encounters with his environment result in adaptation to that environment. Several months after birth, this process of adaptation involves the exercise of intelligence, which begins to develop the moment the baby is born and originates in reflexes, which are hereditary structures. Intelligence governs the interaction between the organism and its environment. However, it presupposes intention: the conscious desire to act.

This adaptation of an organism motivated to explore the environment has two components. One is assimilation, the process of internalizing data of whatever sort; the other is accommodation, the process of internal change in the organism brought about by assimilation. In development, assimilation leads to accommodation, which in turn leads to further assimilation, and so on.

One can imagine a chemical compound: it is capable of combining with certain substances; one of these is added, bringing about a change in the molecular structure of the resulting compound, and this change, in turn, allows the new compound to combine with substances that would have resulted in only a mixture with either of the previous substances. Though the molecular structure of the new compound is different from that of its separate constituents, the atoms remain the same. Something similar to this apparently goes on in the assimilation-accommodation model. In adaptation, intelligence organizes the assimilated input; and as intelligence develops, an increasing number of organizations—structures—are formed, new organizations assimilate older ones, organizations coordinate with one another, and organizations combine with one another.

At birth, Piaget states, "the physiology of the organism furnishes a hereditary mechanism which is already completely organized and virtually adapted but has never functioned. Psychology begins with the use of this mechanism."[1] The mechanism includes reflexes. It incorporates new objects to it—the newborn child does not suck just objects that give milk; he sucks everything—and this leads to what Piaget calls "motor recognition," the origin of meaning. The touch of something on the lips means "Milk! Suck it." Subsequently, as the organism utilizes experience, this global schema—a structure that would include an internal-external behavior pattern—is differentiated. As we have seen, the global schema of cooing and babbling, intercoordinated with hearing, is differentiated; the baby gains the ability to make an increasingly wide array of sounds. At first he makes the same sounds he has always made, ones discovered by chance as crying and sounds of eating occur; he babbles to make interesting things last—that is, to provide himself with pleasure in hearing the sounds. But then he begins to play with these sounds, to vary them. These two processes are what Piaget calls "circular reactions," and they occur throughout life as we develop new schemata.

The child acts on his environment, perceives new data, and gradually assimilates it to his cognitive structures. However, some of it doesn't gibe. The child cannot make it fit exactly into an existing structure; he cannot quite assimilate it without distorting it or without changing the structure. He tries at first to fit it into an existing schema—what Piaget calls an "anticipatory schema." But this won't work. The child tries to suck a new toy, discovers it won't give milk, but also discovers that it has other properties, such as an interesting appearance.

Briefly, assimilation and accommodation are not in equilibrium. The child is sucking everything but senses that though some things give milk, others do not. This brings about a change in the cognitive organization: accommodation. In the example of the mixture, it is as though we added a catalyst, causing a chemical reaction to take place. A new schema evolves, with an organization of data about properties of things that give milk and things that do not; in other words, adaptation occurs. Gradually the child comes to be able to predict that a set of certain properties signify that the object possessing them gives milk, even if he cannot do so in words. He achieves this end, however, by inventing new means to test out his hypotheses dealing with combinations of properties of devices that might give milk. He will be unable to undertake systematic exploration and manipulation of these properties, however, until he reaches the age of eleven or twelve.

One might term the awareness that some objects do not give milk a "discrepant event." One way a teacher can motivate students is by offering such events—ones that do not quite fit a structure—for example, a youngster's explanation of a particular cause-and-effect relationship. A discrepant event throws assimilation and accommodation out of equilibrium; the data won't fit the cognitive organization; and to bring about adaptation, a new and higher level organization develops. This is because, as Piaget maintains, "there is an intrinsic need for cognitive organs or structures, once generated by functioning, to perpetuate themselves by more functioning. Schemata are structures, and one of their important, built-in properties is that of repeated assimilation of anything assimilable in the environment."[2]

In this sense, motivation is intrinsic in the child. What does it mean, then, to motivate a child? And how does cognitive growth and development occur? Flavell poses the questions this way:[3]

First, how does the action of assimilation and accommodation permit the organism to make cognitive progress as opposed to remaining fixated at the level of familiar and habitual cognitions? That is, how is the organism able to do something other than repeat past accommodations and assimilate the results of these accommodations to the same old system of meanings? Secondly, assuming that cognitive progress, or development, can somehow result from assimilatory and accommodatory operations, what prevents it from occurring all at once and of a piece? That is, why is intellectual development the slow and gradual process we know it to be? To indulge in metaphor, we need to know both what makes the cognitive engine progress at all and what limits its velocity and acceleration, assuming the possibility of movement.

Cognitive progress, in Piaget's system, is possible for several reasons. First of all, accommodatory acts are continually being extended to new and different features of the surroundings. To the extent that a newly accommodated-to feature can fit somewhere in the existing meaning structure, it will be assimilated to that structure. Once assimilated, however, it tends to change the structure in some degree and, through this change, make possible further accommodatory extensions. Also, assimilatory structures are not static and unchanging, even in the absence of environmental stimulation. Systems of meanings are constantly becoming reorganized internally and integrated with other systems. This continuous process of internal renovation is itself, in Piaget's system, a very potent source of cognitive progress. Thus both kinds of changes—reorganizations of purely endogenous origin and reorganizations induced more or less directly by new accommodatory attempts—make possible a progressive intellectual penetration into the nature of things. Once again, [assimilation and accommodation] innervate each other in reciprocal fashion: changes in assimilatory structure direct new accommodations, and new accommodatory attempts stimulate structural reorganizations.

If cognitive progress is insured under this interpretation of [assimilation and accommodation], it is certainly well established empirically that this progress is typically slow and gradual. It is not immediately clear why this should be so. What prevents the organism from mastering, in one fell swoop, all that is cognizable in a given terrain? The answer is that the organism can assimilate only those things which past assimilations have prepared it to assimilate. There must already be a system of meanings, an existing organization, sufficiently advanced that it can be modified to admit the candidates for assimilation which accommodation places before it. There can never be a radical rupture between the new and the old; events whose interpretation requires a complete extension or reorganization of the existing structure simply cannot be accommodated to and thence assimilated. As Piaget states, ... assimilation is by its very nature conservative, in the sense that its primary function is to make the unfamiliar familiar, to reduce the new to the old. A new assimilatory structure must always be some variate of the last one acquired, and it is this which insures both the gradualness and continuity of intellectual development.

In summary, the functional characteristics of the assimilatory and accommodatory mechanisms are such that the possibility of cognitive change is insured, but the magnitude of any given change is always limited. The organism adapts repeatedly, and each adaptation necessarily paves the way for its successor. Structures are not infinitely modifiable, however, and not everything which is potentially assimilable can in fact be assimilated by organism A at point X in his development. On the contrary, the subject can incorporate only those components of reality which its ongoing structure can assimilate without drastic change.

Here are some tentative questions spawned by the preceding few paragraphs. For one thing, what is readiness? What is the nature of the intellectual task that the child will be asked to perform? In reading, how do we define the task? How do we sample the child's behavior to determine whether or not he is ready? To what extent do readiness tests sample relevant behaviors? Is each child's intelligence when he enters school such that he is ready to be taught to read?

Teachers have for generations adhered to the maxim "You go from the known to the unknown," but what does this mean in terms of the child's cognitive development? What does it mean, say, for the child who does not know how to read and in whom we want to develop reading skills?

STAGES OF DEVELOPMENT

There is another important property of cognitive development, again one that is important to both language development and reading instruction: cognition stems from the organism's actions, and as the child develops, these become increasingly internalized, abstract, schematic, and organized according to their inner rules of consistency. In this regard, Piaget terms verbal behavior "a rough draft of action."[4]

Piaget asserts that language appears about the time a child is one and a half or two, with the appearance of the "semiotic function." This is the ability to represent something internally by means of a differentiated signifier.

Until this time, the child possesses only perceptual signifiers, which are not yet differentiated from that which they signify. Whiteness, a property of milk, is not differentiated from milk itself. Differentiated signifiers, however, are those that refer to elements that are not physically present. (The concept of signifiers could include Chomsky's views of formatives.)

The achievement of differentiated signifiers is implied by the almost simultaneous appearance of certain behavior patterns about the time the child is two. These behavior patterns include *deferred imitation*—that is, imitation that starts after the disappearance of the model; *symbolic play,* the game of pretending; *drawing*, or graphic image; *mental image*, internalized imitation; and finally *verbal evocation*, as when a child says *meow* after a cat has disappeared.[5]

Piaget makes a distinction between symbols and signs. When a child pretends that a pebble is a piece of candy, he has arbitrarily chosen the pebble to signify the candy. A child, however, may regard the name of something—its sign—as an inherent property of the thing named. He regards the name "as a label attached in substance to the designated object."[6]

Vygotsky also notes this. He asserts:[7]

The word, to the child, is an integral part of the object it denotes. Such a conception seems to be characteristic of primitive linguistic consciousness. We all know the old story about the rustic who said he wasn't surprised that savants with all their instruments could figure out the size of stars and their course—what baffled him was how they found out their names. Simple experiments show that preschool children "explain" the names of objects by their attributes. According to them, an animal is called "cow" because it has horns, "calf" because its horns are still small, "dog" because it is small and has no horns; an object is called "car" because it is not an animal. When asked whether one could interchange the names of objects, for instance call a cow "ink," and ink "cow," children will answer no, "because ink is used for writing, and the cow gives milk." An exchange of names would mean an exchange of characteristic features, so inseparable is the connection between them in the child's mind. In one experiment, the children were told that in a game a dog would be called "cow." Here is a typical sample of questions and answers:

"Does a cow have horns?"

"Yes."

"But don't you remember that the cow is really a dog? Come now, does a dog have horns?"

"Sure, if it's a cow, if it's called cow, it has horns. That kind of dog has got to have little horns."

We can see how difficult it is for children to separate the name of an object from its attributes, which cling to the name when it is transferred, like possessions following their owner.

According to Piaget, language serves to represent concepts or concrete objects seen as classes having only one member (for example, "my father"). The mental image of an object bears a schematized resemblance to the object it symbolizes. Concepts develop as summarized schemata. There are two types of images: *reproductive*, which enable you to visualize sights you have never seen before, and *anticipatory*, which allow you to imagine movements or transformations of objects as well as their results. Not until the child is seven or eight, however, is he capable of reproducing movements and transformations, "and by this stage the child can also anticipate in his imagery movements and transformations";[8] that is, change or turn an object around in his mind and imagine how it would be after the change without actually performing the action. The child must first have been able to perform operations; that is, he must first have been able to internalize actions.

Likewise, memory appears at the time of mental images and the beginning of language. Piaget notes *recognition* memory, which occurs in the presence of an object already encountered, and *evocation* memory, consisting of evoking the image of an absent object. Interestingly, Piaget has shown that the child's memory of an event improves as his schemata develop, independent of his perceptual schemata.

Possible actions become increasingly internalized and organized into systems. Piaget uses the term *operations* for these systems. He has organized his thinking about the development of children into five stages. Following the first, or sensorimotor, stage of development, the direct-action stage, there are four principal periods that are contiguous and merge into one another:[9]

After the appearance of language or, more precisely, the symbolic function that makes its acquisition possible (1 1/2–2 years), there begins a period which lasts until nearly 4 years and sees the development of a symbolic and preconceptual thought. [See chapter 7.]

From 4 to about 7 or 8 years, there is developed, as a closely linked continuation of the previous stage, a stage of intuitive thought whose progressive articulations lead to the threshhold of the stage of operations.

From 7–8 to 11–12 years "concrete operations" are organized, i.e. operational groupings of thought concerning objects that can be manipulated or known through the senses.

Finally, from 11–12 years and during adolescence, formal [logical] thought is perfected and its groupings characterize the completion of reflective intelligence.

Two kinds of shifts go on in reference to these stages; one is a shift within a stage—a horizontal shift. For example, suppose a child can read a mathematical sentence but cannot read a word sentence. Later he is able to read the word sentence, and the structure used to read the word sentence may be essentially the same as that used to read the mathematical sentence. This concept is similar to the one often used in learning theory.

The second shift is a vertical one. For example, during the concrete operational stage a child may indicate that he "knows" his grammar by his use and understanding of language, but he may be unable to represent this symbolically until after he reaches the stage of formal thought. In effect, the child in one stage has to solve again, but in a different way, problems that he earlier solved in a preceding stage.

On the one hand, the advent of a new stage signals itself by a kind of abrupt restructuring. For instance, the child may be able to perform a task by rote; suddenly he does an identical task, shouts "I get it!" and performs the task subsequently almost without consciously thinking about it. There is, says Piaget, a "sudden mobility . . . the satisfaction of arriving at a system."[10]

The movement from one stage to the next represents what Piaget calls "equilibration." The concept is necessary for this reason:[11]

[As] structures continually move toward a state of equilibrium, and when a state of relative equilibrium has been attained, the structure is sharper, more clearly delineated, than it had been previously. But that very sharpness points up inconsistencies and gaps in the structure that had never been salient before. Each equilibrium state therefore carries with it the seeds of its own destruction, for the child's activities are thenceforth directed toward reducing those inconsistencies and closing the gaps.

Perhaps "cracking the code" in reading is a behavioral example of this "restructuring." Previously the child was struggling to decode one word at a time. Suddenly he "gets" the system and moves quite rapidly thereafter. And since equilibration occurs at all developmental levels, another example might be the common experience of the teenager struggling with geometry who suddenly gets the system.

GROUPINGS

Earlier it was noted that operations are internalized actions. At the stage of logical thought, these operations form well-defined complex structures in equilibrium, called "groupings," and the properties of the groupings describe the actual work of the mind. Piaget's description of these properties, therefore, describes operations, say, for doing math problems, reading, spelling, and so forth; that is, operations for solving problems. According to Piaget:[12]

Every problem, whether it concerns the anticipatory hypothesis regarding the solution or its detailed checking, is thus no more than a particular system of operations to be put into effect within the corresponding complex grouping. In order to find our way, we do not have to reconstruct the whole of space, but simply to complete its filling out in a given sector. In order to foresee an event, repair a bicycle, make out a budget or decide on a program of action, there is no need to build up the whole of causality and time, to review all accepted values, etc.; the solution to be found is attained simply by extending and completing the relationships already grouped, except for correcting the grouping when there are errors of detail, and above all, subdividing and differentiating it, but not by rebuilding it in its entirety. As for verification, this is possible only in accordance with the rules of the grouping itself, by the fitting of the new relations into the previously existent system.

Since predicting outcomes, following directions, and applying what one has read are usually considered comprehension skills in reading, one can see the importance of the groupings. To perform the tasks successfully, the child must possess groupings. There are essentially two systems of these. The first system is formed by logical operations. These operations start with individual elements that are constants and simply classify and serialize them and so forth. Says Piaget:[13]

The simplest logical grouping is that of classification or the formation of hierarchies of more or less inclusive classes. It is based on a primary, fundamental operation: the combining of individuals in classes, and of classes with other classes. The ideal example is found in zoological or botanical classification, but all qualitative classification follows the same dichotomous pattern. [For example, the alphabet is a class of letters.]

A second grouping brings into play "the operation which consists ... in assembling asymmetrical relations which express" the differences between elements.[14] Again considering the alphabet: A comes before B; B comes before C; therefore A comes before C. Then there are the differences between capital and lowercase letters. Also, the letter A plus the letters that are not A equals the alphabet; and the alphabet minus the letters that are not A equals A.

"Another operation is substitution which," as Piaget states, "joins together the various individuals in a class or different simple classes included in a composite class." [15] According to Piaget, there must be qualitative equivalence for substitution to be successful. In reading, for instance, consider the child who has been taught initial consonant substitution. Given *man,* the child is taught to read new words by substituting an initial consonant for the *m* and he reads *fan, can, pan,* and *ran.* However, he might be asked to read *bead* and make a *nonequivalent* substitution. He reads the word as though it were "bed," substituting the checked, or short, *e* for the free, or long, one because he has seen words such as *bread* and *breakfast*, and because he does not know the code for transcribing sounds.

The next grouping pertains to operations of reciprocity between symmetrical relationships. If I am a brother of John, John is a brother of mine. If the letter *a* codes a certain sound, the sound can be coded by the letter *a*. And if *dog* is another word for *canine, canine* is another word for *dog.* Synonymy would involve substitution; reciprocity would involve a statement of equivalence. The point is, however, that the groupings must exist if the operations are to be performed consistently.

The next grouping deals with what Piaget calls "multiplication of classes." For example, a word might be to a pattern of words (in terms of their class of sound-spelling relationships) what a sentence is to a pattern of sentences with the same surface-to-deep structural relationships. *Fan* is to *man, ran, pan, can* what "The yellow-eyed dog was chewing a bone" is to "The red-haired man dashed after his hat," "The white-hatted man was preparing breakfast," "The red-feathered birds were circling the park."

The converse of this grouping, adds Piaget, is abstraction. For instance, *f* is the first letter of *fan* and the sixth letter of the alphabet. We may disregard the fact that it is the sixth letter of the alphabet and consider it only as the first letter of *fan.* Or, the word *what* is a pronoun, an adverb, or an adjective, depending on its syntactic and semantic relationships. (What's the problem? or, What you said troubles me. What with the weather the way it is, we can't go sailing. What fun it is to ride....) Perhaps a child will make a mistake in reading when he is unable to differentiate between the various functions of *what.*

The sixth grouping deals with the multiplication of two series of relations; that is, we may find all the relationships between ordered objects according to two sorts of relations at once. Suppose Billy is the son of Tom, the father in a married couple, Tom and Mary. Then Billy is also the son of Mary. If Tom and Mary have another son, Jim, then Jim is a brother of Tom. Or, if *dawn* is a synonym for *sunrise*, and *sunup* is a synonym for *sunrise*, then *dawn* is a synonym for *sunup*. This is a case of one-to-one correspondence.

Suppose now that we consider the fusing of groupings one and two: the letters of the alphabet and the relationships between them. We have arrived at the "group," an ordered series of elements—in this case, the letters in alphabetical order. Piaget asserts that a similar example of fusing is "the best proof of the natural character of the totalities constituted by these groupings of operations."[16]

The work of Flavell has important implications for our discussion. He believes that a group—that is, a structure in equilibrium—consists of an arbitrary, specified set of elements *and* an arbitrary operation performed on those elements. The structure in equilibrium has four properties.

First, any two sets of elements—for example, any two classes—may combine to form a third set of elements. This, says Piaget, makes possible the coordination of operations.

Second, every change is reversible. That is, what is combined can be disconnected; what is done can be undone.

Third, a combination of operations is associative; thought can make detours.

And fourth, an operation combined with its converse is annulled. If you proceed somewhere, then go back to where you started, the starting point is still the same place.

In addition there is a system of groupings, termed "infralogical." These groupings analyze and synthesize objects that are variable; for instance, they lead to the notions of space and time. Flavell observes that these groupings[17]

(1) ... bear on sets of discrete, discontinuous objects. (2) Their operation is independent of the spatio-temporal proximity, or lack of it, of the objects they deal with. (3) They do not require any actual modification of their objects, neither alteration of their structure nor modification in the sense of changing their spatial or temporal location.

These groupings also seem to be important to reading.

The first grouping permits the joining together of parts into progressively more inclusive wholes. For example, we can join the letters *m, a, n* in order and get *man;* we can join *h, a, n, d* in order and get *hand;* we can join *l, e,* in order and get a bound morpheme. Then we can join *man, hand, le* in order and get *manhandle*. We can also join *s* and get *manhandles,* and so on.

The second infralogical grouping permits locating something in space and time. Consider the ambiguous sentence "He follows Fred." This sentence could refer to a person who was born after Fred or to someone who trails behind Fred. This grouping could also refer to a simple change of order without measurement. Consider the ordered letters *s, a, w* in *saw;* the infralogical grouping might well result in the common reading error of reversal, because it would specify that if *a* is next to *s,* then *s* is next to *a*. The child transposes the *s* and the *w*—the spelling relationship—without realizing the impact on the sound relationship, in much the same way that he might believe a rectangular container would be preserved if he rotated it 180 degrees.

The next infralogical grouping permits spatio-temporal substitutes and symmetrical relations. Again, considering the ordered *s, a, w,* this grouping specifies that *s* is to the left of *a* and that *a* is to the left of *w*. This grouping would be necessary, then, to avoid optical reversal.

The last such grouping permits the combining of the preceding operations according to several systems or dimensions simultaneously. Not only is the letter *s* to the left of *a*, but also the sound that it stands for occurs in time before the sound that *a* stands for when we say the word *saw*.

It seems that the point of these infralogical groupings so far as reading is concerned is this: the groupings are necessary to account for the resynthesizing of spoken words when one looks at printed words and for resynthesizing spoken sentences when one reads written sentences.

PERCEPTUAL STRUCTURES

For Piaget, perceptual structures also develop. At first the organism centers on an arbitrary property—for example, the dot over the *i* in the word *pig* or the fact that *astronaut* is a long word. He also notes the problem of comparing objects that are too distant from one another for direct comparison.[18] For example, consider the sentences "John is the one to send candy to" and "John is the one to send home." At the beginning stage of reading instruction, it is possible that the distance between *John* and the last word in each sentence will interfere with the child's ability to use syntactical rules to help him decode. That is, even if he uses both patterns in speech, he may still not be able to understand the sentence after he decodes it.

However, Piaget adds that as the child matures, his perception *decenters:* it is no longer occupied by a syncretic or arbitrary property—one that has been erroneously fused with another. Piaget defines syncretism[19] as

the spontaneous tendency on the part of children to take things in by means of a comprehensive act of perception instead of by the detection of details, to find immediately and without analysis analogies between words or objects that have nothing to do with each other, to bring heterogeneous phenomena into relation with each other, to find a reason for every chance event; in a word, it is the tendency to connect everything with everything else.

Discovering that the dot over the *i* in *pig* does not count or that there are many long words besides *astronaut* brings about decentering.

Once operations are established, they react on perceptions, integrating them. Perceptions pave the way to operations, which then lead to the development of perceptual strategies—that is, intelligence acting on perception. And just as earlier there are centerings and decenterings on physical properties, this later occurs with thought.

Perception and intelligence evolve in thought which at first, says Piaget,[20] allows

the knowledge of the successive phases of an action to be molded into one simultaneous whole. Next, an awareness, not simply of the desired results of action, but its actual mechanism, thus enabling the search for the solution to be combined with a consciousness of its nature. Finally, an increase in distances, enabling actions affecting real entities to be extended by symbolic actions affecting symbolic representations and thus going beyond the limits of near space and time.

The child's affective and social development parallels his cognitive development. In fact, says Piaget, the three systems are inseparable. At first the child is egocentric; he sees the world in terms of himself. But during the period of concrete operations—from seven to twelve—he moves from egocentrism to the externalization of thought; that is, he is able to put himself in another person's shoes. The ability to do this, however, depends on the development of reciprocity, which is related to reversible thought: what I do affects someone else, and what someone else does affects me.

SUMMARY

In this chapter we have learned some facts about the mental development of children. Central to our understanding are the concepts of assimilation and accommodation. Central to these concepts is the understanding that the individual attempts to keep his mental organization abreast of his information, achieved through interaction, as to the organization of the outside world. We can say that he is constantly reorganizing to be in a state of equilibrium or adaptation. However, he is a seeker through the use of his senses. He gathers in, or assimilates, information from the environment that does not easily fit into what he knows, and he must therefore reconstruct his conceptual framework. This process of reconstruction is called accommodation. How he accommodates depends on the kind of equilibrium or adaptation he has so far achieved. At first the infant can assimilate only through the senses. Later his mental and physical development enables him to manipulate objects physically. When he is seven or eight, the child is able to manipulate objects mentally, but they are nevertheless conceptualized with reference to his imagined direct action on them. By the age of eleven or twelve, he can perform these mental operations abstractly and consciously. He knows a formula for problems; he does not need to conceive of a problem as actual behavior. At this stage these operations become well-defined structures, called groupings. These logical groups include such operations as the classification of elements, the assembling of relationships between elements, the substitution of one element for another, and the ordering of a number of relationships simultaneously.

We have examined the properties of groupings, groups, and operations that mark a stage between the age of seven or eight and the age of eleven or twelve. Piaget terms this stage "concrete," because its operations can occur only when the child is in contact with and active in relation to objects. He is not able to make purely verbal hypotheses. Being constantly tied to action—that is, external action—concrete operations give actions "a logical structure, embracing also the speech accompanying it, but they by no means imply the possibility of constructing a logical discourse independently of action."[21]

Throughout this chapter we have attempted to suggest implications of the various concepts regarding the mental development of children. There is, however, one general implication that requires emphasis: educators are probably expecting too much from young children. Children in the primary grades require many opportunities to act out problems and to arrive at solutions by manipulating actual objects. The teacher of reading, recognizing the nature of children and of their learning, will prepare the reading environment so as to support the child's maximum use of his functional capacities for learning to read. The reading situation must be one of active, manipulating children, building in relation to their background of direct, relevant experience. Their relatively highly developed language skills and their graphic activities and capacity to discover and order regularities when they are available show them to be well adapted for learning to read where the environment is prepared and ready for them. Written symbols can be tied to behavior. Children learn by action. They do not learn by listening to other children except by interaction which, if geared by them, is responsive to their manipulation needs. The teacher prepares the focus of action and interaction within the reading instruction by ensuring opportunity for action specific to learning to read. She does not need to instruct in meaning and in language expression per se at this time, but prepares for action and manipulation of written symbols relative to other written symbols and to spoken sounds. In materials where the teacher can be sure the child does know the meaning, she will take advantage of the meaning to heighten discrimination of written word forms. She will plan to juxtapose the functional capacity to assimilate (even to overgeneralize) against the need to accommodate, which requires a focus on discrimination and on revision of concepts toward differentiation and integration. Reading instruction will proceed on many fronts, each tied to its particular manipulative correlate—letter-letter, letter-sound, written word–spoken word, and so on. The teacher should bear in mind that children before they are eleven or twelve are incapable of logical thought; requiring them to verbalize complex mental operations (such as stating phonic generalizations) will result either in frustration or in verbalization without understanding.

NOTES FOR CHAPTER 8

1. Jean Piaget, *Origins of Intelligence in Children* (New York: Norton, 1963), p. 39.
2. John H. Flavell, *The Developmental Psychology of Jean Piaget* (New York: Van Nostrand, 1963), p. 78.
3. Ibid., pp. 49–50.
4. Jean Piaget, *The Psychology of Intelligence* (Totowa, N.J.: Littlefield, Adams, 1966), p. 32.
5. Jean Piaget and Bärbel Inhelder, *The Psychology of the Child* (New York: Basic Books, 1969), pp. 54–55.
6. *The Psychology of Intelligence,* p. 124.
7. Lev S. Vygotsky, *Thought and Language* (Cambridge: MIT Press, 1962), pp. 128–29.
8. *The Psychology of the Child,* pp. 70–72.
9. *The Psychology of Intelligence,* p. 123.
10. Ibid., p. 139.
11. John L. Phillips, Jr., *The Origins of Intellect: Piaget's Theory* (San Francisco: W. H. Freeman, 1969), p. 10.
12. *The Psychology of Intelligence,* p. 39.
13. Ibid., p. 43.
14. Ibid., p. 44.
15. Ibid.
16. Ibid., p. 46.
17. *The Developmental Psychology of Jean Piaget,* p. 196.
18. *The Psychology of Intelligence,* p. 81.
19. Ibid., p. 121.
20. Ibid.
21. Ibid., p. 146.

9

the development of formal thinking

Some years ago a Denver fifth-grade teacher was about to quit her job. She couldn't understand the children, she explained. Their thinking was not logical and she wanted to know, "How can you teach them logic?" The question should have been stated this way: *Can* you teach a child logic? Would the intensive study of syllogisms, for instance, accomplish the task? A reading of *Judgment and Reasoning in the Child,* by Piaget,[1] suggests possible answers.

Before the age of seven or eight, the child justifies things psychologically rather than logically—for example, when he uses the word *because.* The child says that four is not half of nine "because someone can't count," rather than "because four and four makes eight."

Piaget states that "the child, unconscious as he is of his own thought-process, can only reason about isolated or about more or less special cases," and that his judgments reflect co-occurrence of events rather than necessary causes.[2]

He continues: "The consequence of this fact that the child's formulated thought only takes place in connection with particular or specific cases is that we cannot speak about deductive thought as such before a very advanced stage of development."[3]

As Piaget has noted, the child is unaware of his own thought processes; his thinking lacks general propositions, and he is unable to think deductively. Certainly this would have considerable impact on his progress in reading programs, especially in those in which he is drilled on rules, generalizations, and exceptions for decoding words and in which he is asked, in discussing selections, to perform cognitive tasks that, in fact, he is incapable of performing. What, then, are the bases for formal thinking? Piaget replies:[4]

Two factors were particularly necessary for the right functioning of any formal reasoning: (1) a sort of detachment from one's own point of view or from the point of view of the moment, enabling one to place oneself at that of others and to reason first from premises admitted by them, then more generally from every kind of purely hypothetical proposition; (2) owing to the mere fact of having placed oneself inside the beliefs of others, or more generally inside a hypothesis, one must, in order to reason formally, be able to remain on the plane of mere assumption without surreptitiously returning to one's private point of view or to that of the reality of the moment. To be formal, deduction must detach itself from reality and take up its stand upon the plane of the purely possible, which is by definition the domain of hypothesis. In a word, formal thought presupposes two factors, one social (the possibility of placing oneself at every point of view and of abandoning one's own), the other, which is connected with the psychology of belief (the possibility of assuming alongside of empirical reality a purely possible world which shall be the province of logical deduction).

In moving toward formal thought, adds Piaget,[5]

there would seem ... to be two critical periods in the social and intellectual life of the child: the one at the age of 7–8 which is accompanied by the decline of egocentrism, the beginning of earliest motivated ... arguments and the first appearance of the desire for verification or for logical justification; and the second at the age of 11–12 which is the age of societies governed by rules, and that in which formal thought first comes into being.

THE RELATIVITY OF IDEAS

In moving toward formal thought, children universally face the difficulty of grasping the relativity of ideas. They manifest this difficulty in the use of the word *than*. Given a question such as "Bill is heavier than Fred, and Bill is lighter than Oscar; who is the heaviest?" the child answers on the basis of membership in the group of "heavy people" rather than on the relation between people in terms of their actual weight. He seems to reason that Bill and Fred are heavy, and that Bill and Oscar are light. That means that Fred is the heaviest, Oscar the lightest, and Bill is somewhere in-between. Piaget explains:[6]

In so far as the field of consciousness is restricted, relations pass unnoticed, and only individuals are taken in with their particular characteristics independently of comparison. Hence the possibility of judgments of membership, since these call only for perception of individuals taken singly, or taken as a whole but without comparison. But in so far as the field of consciousness expands, individuals are no longer given singly or "en bloc"; they are compared in groups of two or more. At this point judgments of relation or comparison become possible.

Why should "the child's field of consciousness ... be so narrow," and why should "individuals be perceived singly without any relation to each other or to the child himself"?[7] Piaget suggests that children have difficulty in formal thought because they always take their own point of view as being absolute. He adds[8] that

it is once more to the egocentrism of thought that we must appeal in order to explain the incapacity for even the most elementary relativism of thought. To understand a relation ... means thinking of at least two points of view at the same time.

Piaget further notes[9] that

the difficulties we have been describing in making judgments of relationships

are independent of language, and even take place in ordinary life. They may therefore be said to disappear sooner than verbal difficulties. . . .
The difficulty is one of conscious realization. . . . The subject must have quite definitely and consciously become aware of a distinction which, though it may play a part in his actions, can do so without necessarily obtruding itself upon his notice. This is why language is so important. It is the index of what has become conscious, and too much care cannot be taken in the study of verbal forms used by the child. . . . Verbal forms point to logical difficulties; they show that the child has not yet consciously realized the difference existing between operations which on the practical plane he perhaps finds it quite easy to keep separate.

In other words, the child has to struggle to use language to solve problems that he can already solve in action.

Piaget hopes that his studies will shed light on the child's verbal thought:[10]

By verbal thought we mean the child's faculty for adapting himself, not to actual reality, but to words and expressions . . . of adults and other children and through which he tries to imagine reality. And just because verbal thought is partly divorced from reality, the pedagogue must refrain from cultivating it in the child, except with certain necessary precautions. [He warns that] whatever the child has heard, since it is not bound up with any concrete perception, is distorted and selected from according to laws of thought peculiar to each stage in the child's development.

In the following discussion, Piaget again cites egocentrism as the villain.[11]

Even when he is reasoning about single objects, the child cannot generalize relative notions sufficiently to apply them to all possible cases. Here again we have a spurious generality in place of true generalization. The child unconsciously extends his own immediate point of view to all points of view (realism), instead of consciously generalizing a relation which he has conceived clearly as relative and reciprocal (relativism).
Realism is therefore a kind of immediate, illegitimate generalization, while relativism is a generalization that is mediate and legitimate. . . . The realistic or immediate character of the reasoning process prevents the establishment of relations and stands in the way of generalization. . . .
Until the age of 11–12 children were incapable of reasoning from pure assumptions, of reasoning correctly from premises which they did not believe in. Now at this age of 11–12 at which reasoning becomes possible, [they possess] desubjectivation of thought and the power to see relations as such and handle them in an objective manner. . . .
The thought of the child passes from a state of egocentric immediacy, in which single objects only are known and thought of absolutely, and made to bear no relation to one another, to a state of objective realism in which the mind extracts from these objects innumerable relations capable of bringing about the generalization of propositions and reciprocity of different points of view. . . . It is because he fails to grasp the *reciprocity* existing between different points of view that the child is unable to handle relations properly. . . . Necessity and reciprocity constitute an essential character of logical thought—its *reversibility*.

How, then, does one eradicate egocentrism and develop formal thought? The answer is through argument and opposition:[12]

The fact that the child's thought is less conscious of itself than ours has already been hinted at. . . . For egocentrism of thought necessarily entails a certain degree of unconsciousness. Anyone who thinks for himself exclusively and is consequently in a perpetual state of belief, i.e. of confidence in his own ideas, will naturally not trouble himself about the reasons and motives which have guided his reasoning process. Only under the pressure of argument and opposition will he seek to justify himself in the eyes of others and thus acquire the habit of watching himself think, i.e. of constantly detecting the motives which are guiding him in the direction he is pursuing.

This seems to be an especially strong argument against lecturing to children—against the teacher doing too much of the talking—in the primary and intermediate classrooms. It also seems to be a strong argument against any form of instruction in which there cannot be a give and take actively involving the children. Passive listening is not likely to spur the development of reasoning.

The function of argument and objection is clarified:[13]

The difference between objects strikes us sooner than their resemblance. . . . Because their resemblance is subjective, it is the product of our own thought, or rather the identity of our reaction to these objects. Difference, on the other hand, is objective, i.e. is given by the things themselves. . . . Never without the shock of contrast with the thought of others and the effort of reflection which this shock entails would thought as such come to be conscious of itself.

Just as the child may acquire certain skills, learning by contrast, now he acquires reasoning by using language and having his own reasoning come into conflict with the reasoning of others. The conflicts, the contrasts, are necessary.

Piaget also considers children's definitions, which offer insight into children's ability to make generalizations:[14]

[They] are always interesting, but they are not easy to interpret, for all definition is conscious realization. . . . The more automatically an idea is handled, the harder is the process of its conscious realization. Ask even an educated adult what is the difference between "because" and "since"! Even though he is perfectly capable of assigning different though slightly overlapping uses to these terms, this does not mean that he can realize the difference straight away.

In this light, he sees definition, psychologically, as the conscious "realization of the use which one makes of a word or a concept in the course of a process of reasoning."[15]

At first, the child resorts to the well-known "definition by usage": a chair is to sit on, a grandmother is to hug. Says Piaget:[16]

The real nature of an object lies neither in its physical cause, nor in the concept one has of it, but in a reason or in a motive for its existence which implies both a directing intelligence and a physical realization. [Definitions of this sort are] permeated with intention and finalism. Or, to put it another way, the child will fail to distinguish between logical justification (since all definition, whether logical or conceptual, consists in a justification of the use made of a concept in reasoning) and explanation.

[However, after the age of 7–8] we meet with the first logical definitions, i.e. definitions according to the formula by genus and specific difference (e.g. A mother is a lady who has children). When these definitions are perfect and exhaustive they presuppose conscious knowledge (1) of a general proposition (All mothers are ladies) and (2) of an interference or "multiplication" of two general propositions (All ladies are not mothers, nor are all people with children mothers: mothers therefore entail interference of these two conditions). But these logical definitions do not appear in perfected form from the beginning. At first and up till the age of about 11–12 the child is incapable of giving exhaustive definitions: he simply defines by the genus (A mother is a lady), or by a feature that is particular but not specific (A cousin is the son of an aunt or an uncle) without generalization of the notion.

SYNTHESIS BETWEEN DIFFERENT ELEMENTS

These considerations led Piaget to conclude:[17]

When the child has to deal with complex conceptions (such as those in which the notion in question is determined by several heterogeneous factors) he is, as is only natural, even less conscious of the definition of the concepts than when he makes use of simpler notions. . . . This inability to become conscious of the guiding factors of one's own thought entails a second phenomenon which is of the utmost importance for the psychology of childish reasoning, and in particular for the analysis of contradiction in the child. We mean the absence of logical hierarchy or of synthesis between the different elements of the same conception. . . . [Adults] always have the component parts of the concept *simultaneously* in mind. . . . The child, on the contrary, thinks not simultaneously, but *alternately* of the two determining factors.

This is what Piaget calls "concepts by conglomeration." They are not true concepts.

The child has never become conscious of the factors in a concept,[18] which

act upon his reason in alternation with one another, penetrating the field of attention at different moments in time. The concept therefore resembles a metal ball that is attracted successively and in no fixed order by six electromagnets, and jumps without rhyme or reason from one to the other. . . . The complexity of an adult concept on the other hand does not exclude equilibrium. The mind has become conscious of each factor, not in isolation from, but in relation to, the others, so all these factors act on the concept at once; there is synthesis and hierarchy.

We can see, now, why children so often contradict themselves: they are incapable of consciously considering two propositions simultaneously. Noncontradiction, though, is equilibrium, and that is reversibility. A childish train of thought is not reversible, whereas directed thought is;[19]

for it is obvious that nondirected thought, i.e. that in which the individual has set himself no real problem, but seeks only to satisfy some desire which is not conscious, or not wholly so—it is obvious that such thought is by its nature irreversible.... A train of associations is irreversible, because association of ideas is nearly always directed by an affective tendency which nothing obliges to remain the same.... But in thought that is really directed, that obeys conscious direction ... assimilation and imitation will have to collaborate instead of pulling in different directions as they do in the early stages of mental growth.

Imitation arises from divorcing accommodation from assimilation. Thus by performing Daddy's action I am Daddy; I can ignore the fact that I am not Daddy. Thus rote learning is imitation. Imitation of reality is the fundamental tendency of childish activity to reproduce, first by gesture and then by imagination, the external movements to which the organism is compelled to adapt itself, and later and more generally the succession or partial successions of events and phenomena which call for the same adaptation.[20] In undirected thought, "assimilation is always deforming to begin with."[21] For example, the child condenses images and deforms them in attempting to fit them into an existing schema. When he guesses wildly at a sentence as he is reading aloud during a reading lesson, he often reads the sentence as though it were one that could occur, one that might fit in with the story he has been hearing others read. He makes it what he wants it to be.

Again, egocentrism is the villain, for it brings about antagonism between assimilation and imitation, according to Piaget:[22]

But as soon as thought becomes socialized, a momentous factor comes into play; imitation and assimilation are transformed, solidarity is established between them, and thought becomes increasingly capable of reversibility. For the capacity for leaving one's own point of view and entering into that of other people robs assimilation of its deforming character, and forces it to respect the objectivity of its data. The child will henceforth attempt to weave a network of reciprocal relations between his own point of view and that of others. This *reciprocity* of viewpoints will enable him both to incorporate new phenomena and events into his ego, and to respect their objectivity, i.e. the specific characters which they present. Gradually, this same reciprocity of viewpoints will accustom the child to the reciprocity of relations in general. Henceforth, imitation of reality will find its completion in assimilation of reality by the mind.

Social life, by developing the reciprocity of relations side by side with the consciousness of necessary implications, will therefore remove the antagonistic characters of assimilation and imitation, and render the two processes mutually dependent. Social life therefore helps to make our mental processes reversible, and in this way prepares the path for logical reasoning.

The challenge of the teacher, then, is to harness the children's social life and use it in the classroom to help them develop logical thought.

TRANSDUCTION

Piaget also notes that childish reasoning has a characteristic that he calls *transduction,* a kind of reasoning much like that of the medicine man who explains that it did not rain because he did not burn incense. In this kind of reasoning, the child is unable to generalize, because the reciprocity of relations has escaped him. Between the ages of 7–8 and 11–12, this kind of reasoning begins to diminish.[23]

The child is no longer content to explain one phenomenon by another simply by recalling their common history; he wants to connect the two phenomena by a necessary relation. Transductive reasoning yields before the increasing need for combined induction and deduction. Generalization has become possible.

Piaget concludes:[24]

We may say that during the first stage the reasoning mind doesno more than to "imitate" reality as it is, without reaching any necessary implications; during the second stage the mind "operates upon" reality, creating partly reversible experiments and thus reaching the consciousness of implications between certain affirmations and certain results; finally, in the third stage, these operations necessitate each other in the sense that the child realizes that by asserting such and such a thing he is committing himself to asserting such and such another thing. . . . The correct use of relations is what appears last, but what is last in chronological order is often first in the order of values. Indeed one may say that the possibility of reasoning logically is subordinate to that of handling relations correctly.

VERIFICATION OF THOUGHT

Piaget states:[25]

Logical activity is not the whole of intelligence. One can be intelligent without being particularly logical. The main functions of intelligence, that of inventing solutions, and that of verifying them, do not necessarily involve one another; the first partakes of imagination, the second alone is properly logical. Demonstration, research for truth is therefore the true function of logic.

But on what occasions do we experience the need to verify our thought? This need does not arise spontaneously in us. On the contrary, it appears very late, and for two reasons. The first is that thought puts itself at the service of the immediate satisfaction of desire long before forcing itself to seek for truth. Thought's most spontaneous manifestation is play, or at any rate that quasi-hallucinatory form of imagination which allows us to regard desires as realized as soon as they are born. All the writers who have concerned themselves with the play, the testimony, and the lies of children have realized this. . . .

But this is not all. Even when thought turns away from immediate satisfaction and play, and gives itself up to disinterested curiosity in things for their own sakes (and this curiosity appears very soon, certainly from the age of 3), the individual still has the peculiar capacity for immediate belief in his own ideas.

It is, therefore, not for ourselves that we try to verify our statements ... but up to the age of 7–8, a large number of the questions asked are rhetorical....

It must be remembered, moreover, that experience itself does not undeceive minds oriented in this fashion. Things are in the wrong, not they. The savage who calls down the rain by a magic rite explains his failure as the work of an evil spirit. He is, according to a famous saying, "impervious to experience."...

What then gives rise to the need for verification? Surely it must be the shock of our thought coming into contact with that of others, which produces doubt and the desire to prove. If there were not other people, the disappointments of experience would lead to overcompensation and dementia. We are constantly hatching an enormous number of false ideas, conceits, Utopias, mystical explanations, suspicions, and megalomaniacal fantasies, which disappear when brought into contact with other people. The social need to share the thought of others and to communicate our own with success is at the root of our need for verification. Proof is the outcome of argument.... Reflection is the act by which we unify our various tendencies and beliefs.... Argument is, therefore, the backbone of verification. Logical reasoning is an argument which we have with ourselves, and which reproduces internally the features of a real argument.

But isn't Piaget's last statement a valid description of "critical reading"? If it is, all the more reason for fostering debates and social interaction in the classroom.

In respect to communication between adult and child, Piaget asserts:[26]

The child feels he is inferior to the adult in every way, and is also for a long time under the delusion that the adult understands everything he says. Consequently, he never tries to express his thoughts clearly when he speaks to his parents, and conversely, he remembers only as much as he chooses of what is said by adults, because of his inability to enter into the world of "grownups."

Piaget recognized the relation between perceived status differences and communication, the situation that influences the comments of an upward-aspiring manager when he talks to the boss. His communication may be guarded and nervous. This apparently is one of the reasons why Piaget warned "pedagogues" to be careful in attempting to develop the child's ability to verbalize thought. Another is the child's inability to learn from certain experiences. Perhaps it also explains why Piaget seems to stress the importance of social interaction for children.

CONSCIOUS REALIZATION OF THOUGHT

Piaget states: "We only become conscious [of differences] in proportion to our disadaptation."[27] But he asks:[28]

How does this conscious realization take place?... What are the means and the obstacles to this conscious realization?... For to become conscious of an operation is to make it pass over from the plane of action to that of language: it is therefore to re-invent it in imagination in order to express it in words. As regards reasoning in particular, to become conscious of its operations means ... to remake "mentally" experiments that one has already made in action. In other words, the process of learning an operation on the verbal plane will reproduce the same incidents as had arisen when this operation was being learned on the plane of action; a process of shifting will take place from one apprenticeship to the other. The dates will differ, but the rhythms will probably be analogous. This shifting from action to thought can be observed at every turn. It is of fundamental importance to the understanding of child logic and explains all the phenomena which have been the object of our enquiry. For example, the child has difficulty in realizing that a part or a fraction is relative to a whole. He has difficulty, when told that a given color is both darker than one and lighter than a third, in discovering which of the three is the lightest. Now these difficulties still show very clearly on the verbal plane between the years of 7 to 11, whereas on the plane of action they have ceased to exist. But the way the child has to grope and feel in order to overcome these difficulties reproduces what a few years ago he had known on the plane of action. For on this plane too he was unable to divide a whole into two or four parts without forgetting the whole, and of comparing the features of three objects without committing the fallacies which reappear at a later date in his thinking. Thus, the mere fact of thinking an operation instead of actually carrying it out causes circumstances to reappear that had been forgotten long ago on the plane of action.

Now consider reading in the primary grades. One may ask, in relation to what Piaget has stated, to what extent a child can perform the reasoning tasks asked of him. Suppose, for example, that the child is not particularly adept at decoding; that is, he cannot read the words well enough to get the message from the story. To what extent, if any, is he equipped to discuss it? To what extent will the teacher's questions develop the child's comprehension, if at all? To what extent is the child ready to answer the "thought" questions the teacher asks? If there is improvement in the child's comprehension, perhaps it stems more from the improvement in his decoding ability and his social interaction on the playground than it does from his experiences in the classroom. In any event, Vygotsky will have something to say about this in a later chapter. For the time being, he and Piaget would agree that deeds take precedence over words. Psychologically, just as physically, actions speak louder than words.

Until the age of eight or nine, the child's attention is the prisoner of the first thing to catch his eye, and his thought also is caught in the web of immediate perception. Says Piaget:[29]

Such habits of thought, acquired as they are over a period of many years, will naturally have some effect upon the schematism of attention. In the first place this realism prevents the child from looking at things as they are in themselves. He sees them always in terms of the momentary perception which is taken as absolute and, in a manner of speaking, hypostasized. He therefore makes no attempt to find the intrinsic relations existing between things. Again, by the mere fact of not being considered in their internal relations, but only as presented by immediate perception, things are either conglomerated into a confused whole (syncretism), or else considered one by one in a fragmentary manner devoid of synthesis. Herein lies the narrowness of the child's field of attention. The child sees a great many things, often more than we do; he observes, in particular, a whole mass of detail which escapes our notice, but he does not organize his observations; he is incapable of thinking of more than one thing at a time. Thus he squanders his data instead of synthesizing them.

Summarizing, Piaget states:[30]

This evolution in the structure of childish reasoning has very important consequences. We have already put forward the view, which has since been confirmed by a more recent study, that formal thought does not appear till the age of 11–12, at the period, therefore, when the child comes to reason about pure possibility. For to reason formally is to take one's premises as simply given, without enquiring whether they are well-founded or not; belief in the conclusion will be motivated solely by the form of the deduction. Previous to this, and even in the minds of children from 7–8 to 11–12, deduction is never pure, by which we mean that belief in the validity of the conclusion is still bound up with belief in the validity of the premises. For before the age of 7–8, there is no awareness of logical implications. Thought is still realistic, and in reasoning, the child looks always to an "inner model" which is considered as true reality, even when his reasoning bears upon it all the marks of deduction. This is mental experiment pure. The pseudo-assumptions of children of 6–7 are of this type. ("If I was an angel and had wings and if I flew up into the fir trees, would the squirrels run away or would they stay . . .") Between the years of 7–8 and 11–12, there is certainly awareness of implications when reasoning rests upon beliefs and not upon assumptions, in other words, when it is founded on actual observation. But such deduction is still realistic, which means that the child cannot reason from premises without believing in them. Or even if he reasons implicitly from assumptions which he makes on his own, he cannot do so from those which are proposed to him. Not till the age of 11–12 is he capable of this difficult operation, which is pure deduction, and proceeds from any assumption whatsoever. . . .

11–12 is therefore the age at which we must situate the appearance of what a little earlier we called "logical experiment." Logical experiment, in conclusion, presupposes and may be defined by the two following conditions: (1) a "mental experiment" carried out on the plane of pure hypothesis or of pure possibility, and not as before on the plane of reality reproduced in thought; and (2) an ordering and awareness of the operations of thought as such, as for example of definitions or assumptions that one has made and has decided to retain identical with themselves.

It is not without interest to note that this new awareness is once again under the dependence of social factors, and that conversely, incapacity for formal thought is very directly the result of childish egocentrism. For what prevents the child from reasoning from data that he does not agree to but is asked simply to "assume," is that he is untutored in the art of entering into other people's points of view. For him, there is only one comprehensible point of view—his own. Hence the fact that up till the age of 11–12, physical reality is not accompanied by subjective reality (the child being unaware of the personal character of his opinions, his definitions, and even his words), nor, consequently, even by a logical reality in which everything conceivable would be possible. Previous to this, there is only the real and the unreal. There is undoubtedly a plane of physical possibility, but there is no plane of logical possibility. The real alone is logical. At about the age of 11–12, on the contrary, social life starts on a new plane, and this obviously has the effect of leading children to a greater mutual understanding, and consequently of giving them the habit of constantly placing themselves at points of view which they did not previously hold. This progress in the use of assumptions is probably what lends greater suppleness to the child's conception of modality, and teaches him the use of formal reasoning.

SUMMARY

Before the age of seven or eight the child does not justify things logically but according to his personal preferences or biases. The child can only reason about isolated cases or what happens to be immediately present. His judgments reflect a concurrence of events rather than of necessary causes.

Piaget lists two factors that are required in formal reasoning: (1) being able to detach oneself from one's own point of view, and then reasoning from the premises of the other person's point of view; (2) being able to remain completely detached from one's own point of view and then reasoning on the plane of mere assumption. Deductive reasoning detaches itself from the personal viewpoint and from the reality of the moment. Piaget further states that the two critical periods in the social and intellectual life of a child occur around the age of seven–eight, when there is a decline of egocentrism, and around the age of eleven–twelve, when the rules of society are discovered. Formal thought comes into being at this time.

All children face the difficulty of grasping the relativity of ideas, such as in the word *than*. Children have difficulty in formal thought because they have always taken their own point of view as absolute. The child must be able to use language rather than participation to adapt himself to words and expressions so that he will in turn be able to imagine reality. He must be able to use language to solve problems that he could previously solve only in action. Conscious realization takes place when an operation passes from the plane of action to that of language, when the child can reinvent a problem in imagination and then express it in words.

The eradication of egocentric thought comes through argument and opposition. Conflict and contrast are necessary to the functioning of argument and objection. Under pressure of argument and opposition, the child must be able to justify his own reasoning.

An adult is able to formulate the component parts of a concept simultaneously, but a child is unable to do so. He thinks of the determining factors one at a time. Remaining incapable of consciously considering two propositions simultaneously, he often contradicts himself. It is not until the age of eleven or twelve that he begins to take account of necessary relationships between two phenomena instead of explaining them with reference to concurrence or common history. Generalization now becomes possible.

The main functions of intelligence are inventing solutions and verifying them. Thus, as Piaget contends, while inventing solutions relates to imagination, demonstration or the search for truth or verifying solutions is the true function of logic. The need for verification arises when one's own thought comes into contact with that of others. One then possesses doubt and the need to prove. The underlying basis of this need for verification lies in the social need for sharing the thoughts of others and communicating our own. The need for proof results from argument; the act of reflection is a unification of our various inclinations and beliefs.

The human organism is biologically adapted to learn in certain ways at different stages in development. Recognition of the requirements of these stages will help us provide an environment that fosters learning. Between the ages of six and twelve, children must be active participants in classroom activities and in oral discussions of all learning tasks. As we saw in the preceding chapter, teachers often seem to be expecting children to reason objectively and explain verbal problems logically before they have reached the age when formal thought is possible. Purely verbal instruction and demands for intelligent solutions based on thought alone leave the young child without the necessary learning resources and promote feelings of inadequacy. Besides, time is being wasted that could be used to expand and enhance the child's preparation for the formal reasoning he will be capable of when he is eleven or twelve years old.

We shall see in the next chapter that intelligence tends toward reversible mobility; this is a characteristic of the equilibrium necessary for adapted thought (in which reality is appropriately reconstructed in the mind) and can be suitably represented in logical operations. Even after twelve years of age, encounters with spoken or written language episodes that we cannot understand are best tackled by a return to direct manipulation of objects or events. This builds the concepts needed for the use of the logical operations to introduce them into logical thought.

Discussion in the classroom is most suitable among peers of similar developmental status and of fairly similar background, and should be based on some common experience in which the class members are actors, so that, especially before the age of twelve, logical discussion can be backed up by direct and interactive experience.

NOTES FOR CHAPTER 9

1. Jean Piaget, *Judgment and Reasoning in the Child* (Totowa, N.J.: Littlefield, Adams, 1966).
2. Ibid., pp. 55–56.
3. Ibid., p. 57.
4. Ibid., p. 71.
5. Ibid., p. 74.
6. Ibid., p. 89.
7. Ibid.
8. Ibid., p. 91.
9. Ibid., pp. 92–93.
10. Ibid., p. 115.
11. Ibid., pp. 132–34.
12. Ibid., p. 137.
13. Ibid., p. 144.
14. Ibid., p. 114.
15. Ibid., p. 147.
16. Ibid., pp. 148–49.
17. Ibid., pp. 156–57.
18. Ibid., p. 159.
19. Ibid., pp. 172–73, 177.
20. Ibid., p. 173.
21. Ibid., p. 175.
22. Ibid., p. 180.
23. Ibid., p. 191.
24. Ibid., pp. 194–95.
25. Ibid., pp. 201–4.
26. Ibid., pp. 204–5.
27. Ibid., p. 213.
28. Ibid., pp. 213–14.
29. Ibid., p. 220.
30. Ibid., pp. 251–53.

the relation between language and thought

What is the relation between language and thought? According to Piaget, language provides an entire system of notation to serve thought, much like mathematics. Though language may serve to develop logic, it is not the source of all logic, he maintains. Action learning is still necessary. The roots of logic are to be found in the coordination of actions, including verbal behavior. Thus language is structured by logic:[1]

LANGUAGE

In the normal child, language appears at about the same time as the other forms of semiotic thought. In the deaf-mute, on the other hand, articulate language does not appear until well after deferred imitation, symbolic play, and the mental image. This seems to indicate that language is derived genetically, since its social or educational transmission presupposes the preliminary development of these individual forms of *semiosis*. However, this development, as is proved by the case of deaf-mutes, can occur independent of language.[2] Furthermore, deaf-mutes, in their collective life, manage to elaborate a gestural language which is of keen interest. It is both social and based on imitative signifiers that occur in an individual form in deferred imitation, in symbolic play, and the image, which is relatively close to symbolic play. Because of its adaptive properties rather than its playful purpose, this gestural language, if it were universal, would constitute an independent and original form of semiotic function. In normal individuals it is rendered unnecessary by the transmission of the collective system of verbal signs associated with articulate language.

1. EVOLUTION

Articulate language makes its appearance, after a phase of spontaneous vocalization (common to children of all cultures between six and ten or eleven months) and a phase of differentiation of phonemes by imitation (from eleven or twelve months), at the end of the sensori-motor period, with what have been called "one-word sentences" (C. Stern). These single words may express in turn desires, emotions, or observations (the verbal scheme becoming an instrument of assimilation and generalization based on the sensori-motor schemes).

From the end of the second year, two-word sentences appear, then short complete sentences without conjugation or declension, and next a gradual acquisition of grammatical structures. The syntax of children from two to four has been observed in some extremely interesting studies by R. Brown, J. Berko, and others at Harvard and S. Ervin and W. Miller at Berkeley.[3] These studies, which were inspired by Noam Chomsky's hypothesis of the structure of grammatical rules, have shown that the acquisition of syntactical rules cannot be reduced to passive imitation. It involves not only an important element of generalizing assimilation, which was more or less known, but also certain original constructions. R. Brown isolated models of these. Moreover, he has shown that reductions of adult sentences to original infantile models obey certain functional requirements, such as the conservation of a *minimum* of necessary information and the tendency to add to this *minimum*.

2. LANGUAGE AND THOUGHT

In addition to this problem of the relationship of infantile language to linguistic theory, and to information theory, the great genetic problem raised by the development of infantile language concerns its relationship to thought, and in particular to the logical operations. Language may increase the powers of thought in range and rapidity, but it is controversial whether logico-mathematical structures are themselves essentially linguistic or non-linguistic in nature.

As to the increasing range and rapidity of thought, thanks to language we observe in fact three differences between verbal and sensori-motor behavior. (1) Whereas sensori-motor patterns are obliged to follow events without being able to exceed the speed of the action, verbal patterns, by means of narration and evocation, can represent a long chain of actions very rapidly. (2) Sensori-motor adaptations are limited to immediate space and time, whereas language enables thought to range over vast stretches of time and space, liberating it from the immediate. (3) The third difference is a consequence of the other two. Whereas the sensori-motor intelligence proceeds by means of successive acts, step by step, thought, particularly through language, can represent simultaneously all the elements of an organized structure.

These advantages of representative thought over the sensori-motor scheme are in reality due to the semiotic function as a whole. The semiotic function detaches thought from action and is the source of representation. Language plays a particularly important role in this formative process. Unlike images and other semiotic instruments, which are created by the individual as the need arises, language has already been elaborated socially and contains a notation for an entire system of cognitive instruments (relationships, classifications, etc.) for use in the service of thought. The individual learns this system and then proceeds to enrich it.

3. LANGUAGE AND LOGIC

Must we then conclude, as has been suggested, that since language possesses its own logic, this logic of language constitutes not only an essential or even a unique factor in the learning of logic (inasmuch as the child is subject to the restrictions of the linguistic group and of society in general), but is in fact the source of all logic for the whole of humanity? These views derive from the pedagogical commonsense characteristic of the sociological school of Durkheim and also the logical positivism still adhered to in many scientific circles. According to logical positivism, in fact, the logic of the logicians is itself nothing but generalized syntax and semantics (Carnap, Tarski, etc.).

We have available two sources of important information on this subject: (1) The comparison of normal children with deaf-mutes, who have not had the benefit of articulate language but are in possession of complete sensori-motor schemes, and with blind persons, whose situation is the opposite. (2) The systematic comparison of linguistic progress in the normal child with the development of intellectual operations.

The logic of deaf-mutes has been studied by M. Vincent[4] and P. Oléron,[5] in Paris, who have applied the operatory tests of the Genevan school, and by F. Affolter in Geneva. The results indicate a systematic delay in the emergence of logic in the deaf-mute. One cannot speak of deficiency as such, however, since the same stages of development are encountered, although with a delay of one to two years. Seriation and spatial operations are normal (perhaps a slight delay in the case of the former). The classifications have their customary structures and are only slightly less mobile in response to suggested changes of criteria than in hearing children. The learning of arithmetic is relatively easy. Problems of conservation (an index of reversibility) are solved with a delay of only one or two years compared with normal children. The exception is the conservation of liquids, which gives rise to special technical difficulties in the presentation of the assignment, since the subjects must be made to understand that the questions have to do with the contents of the containers and not with the containers themselves.

These results are even more significant when compared with the results obtained in studies of blind children. In studies made by Y. Hatwell, the same tests reveal a delay of up to four years or more compared with normal children, even in elementary questions dealing with relationships of order (succession, position "between," etc.). And yet in the blind children verbal seriations are normal (A is smaller than B, B smaller than C, therefore . . .). But the sensory disturbance peculiar to those born blind has from the outset hampered the development of the sensori-motor schemes and slowed down general coordination. Verbal coordinations are not sufficient to compensate for this delay, and action learning is still necessary before these children develop the capacity for operations on a level with that of the normal child or the deaf-mute.

4. LANGUAGE AND OPERATIONS

The comparison of progress in language with progress in the intellectual operations requires both linguistic and psychological competence. Our collaborator, H. Sinclair, who fulfills both conditions, undertook a group of studies of which we offer one or two samples.

Two groups of children were chosen. The first was clearly pre-operatory; that is, these children did not possess the least notion of conservation. The children in the second group accepted one of these notions and justified it by arguments of reversibility and compensation. Both groups were shown several pairs of objects (a large object and a small one; a group of four or five marbles and a group of two; an object that is both shorter and wider than another, etc.) and were asked to describe the pairs when one element of the pair is offered to one person and the other to a second person. This description is thus not related to a problem of conservation. The language of the two groups differs systematically. The first group uses "scalars" almost exclusively (in the linguistic sense): "this man has a big one, that man a small one; this one has a lot, that one little." The second group uses "vectors": "this man has a bigger one than the other man"; "he has more," etc. Whereas the first group describes only one dimension at a time, the second group says: "This pencil is longer and thinner," etc. In short, there is a surprising degree of correlation between the language employed and the mode of reasoning. Similarly, a second study shows a close connection between the stages of development of seriation and the structure of the terms used.

How should this relationship be interpreted? A child at the pre-operatory level understands the expressions of the higher level when they are integrated into orders or assignments ("Give that man a longer pencil," etc.), but he does not use them spontaneously. If you train him to use these expressions, he learns them but with difficulty, and the training seldom influences his notions of conservation (it does in approximately one case in ten). Seriation, on the other hand, is somewhat improved by verbal training, because then the linguistic process also relates to the act of comparison and therefore to the concept itself.

These data, combined with those described [earlier], indicate that language does not constitute the source of logic but is, on the contrary, structured by it. The roots of logic are to be sought in the general coordination of actions (including verbal behavior), beginning with the sensori-motor level, whose schemes are of fundamental importance. This schematism continues thereafter to develop and to structure thought, even verbal thought, in terms of the progress of actions until the formation of the logico-mathematical operations. This is the culmination of the logic implied in the coordinations of actions, when these actions are ready to be internalized and organized into unified structures.

Vygotsky agrees with Piaget on the precedence of deeds over words:[6]

The relation between thought and word is a living process; thought is born through words. A word devoid of thought is a dead thing, and a thought unembodied in words remains a shadow. The connection between them, however, is not a pre-formed and constant one. It emerges in the course of development, and itself evolves. To the Biblical "In the beginning was the Word," Goethe makes Faust reply, "In the beginning was the deed." The intent here is to detract from the value of the word, but we can accept this version if we emphasize it differently: In the *beginning* was the deed. The word was not the beginning—action was there; it is the end of development, crowning the deed.

Piaget comments further about language and its relation to thought. Consider excerpts from his article "Linguistic Structuralism."[7]

Language is a group institution. Its rules are imposed on individuals. One generation coercively transmits it to the next, and this has been true for as long as there have been men. Any given form of it, any particular spoken language, derives from some earlier form, which in turn flows from some still more primitivee form, and so on, indefinitely, without a break, all the way back to the one or more ancestral languages.

Every word in a language designates a concept, which constitutes its signification. The most resolute antimentalists, Bloomfield, for example, go so far as to maintain that the idea of concepts is completely reducible to that of a word's signification.

More exactly, Bloomfield says that there are no concepts, that what is mistakenly so called is simply the signification of words. But surely this is one way of defining and granting existence to concepts.

The syntax and semantics of a language yield a set of rules to which any individual speaking that language must submit, not only when he expresses his thoughts to others, but even when he expresses it "internally."

Language, in short, is independent of the decisions of individuals; it is the bearer of multi-millennial traditions; and it is every man's indispensable instrument of thought. As such, it appears to be a privileged domain of human reality, so it is only natural that it should sometimes be regarded as the source of structures which, on account of their age, generality, and power, are of special significance (that language and its structures far antedate science goes without saying)....

Linguistic structures lose none of their interest by being looked at in this way, but their relations to the structures of the signified become different. In whatever way the problem as to the relation between linguistic and logical structure be solved eventually, it is a fundamental problem for any general theory of structure....

The verbal sign, ... since it is merely conventional, has no intrinsic nor, consequently, fixed relation to its meaning; there is nothing in the phonic character of the signifier to call forth the value or content of the signified.... There can be no disputing the fact that, on the whole, the word designating a concept has fewer connections with it than does the concept with its definition and its contents. Granted that verbal signs are sometimes "motivated" ... and that there is occasionally a resemblance between the symbol and what it symbolizes; granted too that ... to the speaker the word does not seem arbitrary at all (young children think of the names of things as physically a part of them—a mountain has always had its name, even before men, by looking at it, find out what that name is!), still, the conventional character of the verbal sign is incontestable, as the multiplicity of languages proves. Note that "conventional" does not mean simply "arbitrary"—verbal signs depend upon implicit or explicit agreements based on custom, in contrast to symbols, which may be of individual origin, as in symbolic games or dreams.[8] ...

In other domains [than linguistics], ... structure belongs, not to the means of expression, but to the expressed, to the signified rather than to the signifier, in short, to realities which have intrinsic value and normative power. The defining character of norms is that they are obligatory, that they conserve their own value by binding men to such conservation. *Their* equilibrium at any given time depends upon their antecedent history, for the distinctive character of development here is that it is always directed toward such equilibrium.[9] The history or rather chronicle of a word, however, may simply consist of a series of changes of meaning without any mutual relations except such as result from the necessity of answering to the expressive requirements of the successive synchronic systems to which the word belongs....

Piaget notes that logical positivists insist that logic and mathematics supply both syntactic and semantic structures of the intellect. He counters that, instead, these derive from the activity of coordinating one's own acts. Reacting to Chomsky's idea that language is innate to man, he states:[10]

We meet with facts which, though presenting certain connections with Chomsky's

assumption, differ as to the importance or range of the hereditary points of de-
parture. . . . And the reason for this is, undoubtedly, that where Chomsky sees
only two alternatives—either an innate schema that governs with necessity, or
acquisition from outside (cultural and therefore variable determination such as
cannot account for the limited and necessary character of the schema in question)—there are in fact three possibilities. There is heredity versus acquisition
from outside, true; but there is also the process of internal equilibration. . . .

The relatively late appearance of language in the course of the second year
of life seems to confirm the constructivist thesis. For why should speech begin
at this level of development and not earlier? Contrary to the too facile explanations
by conditioning, which imply that language acquisition starts as early as the second
month, the acquisition of language presupposes the prior formation of sensori-motor
intelligence, which goes to justify Chomsky's ideas concerning the necessity of
a prelinguistic substrate akin to rationality. But this intelligence which antedates
speech is very far from preformed from the beginning; we can see it grow step
by step out of the gradual coordination of assimilation schemes.

Piaget then summarizes his views regarding the relation between
language and thought. He reviews some of the same studies he cited previously in this chapter. We have included them because they are pertinent
to his argument.[11]

Let us return to the problem with which we started, which remains one of the
most controversial issues of structuralism and, indeed, of epistemology in general.
Any serious answer to the question of how linguistic and logical structures are
related must, of course, be provisional. Even a Soviet linguist like Saumjan, working
in a culture center where only a few years ago the Pavlovian theory of language
as a "secondary signal system" seemed to have taken care of all problems, admits
that the question of the relation between language and thought is "one of the
hardest and most profound of contemporary philosophical problems." We can
obviously not even begin to solve the problem here; all we mean to do is to indicate
what, from the structuralist perspective and taking recent developments in linguistics into account, the state of the question is.

But we must backtrack and recall two important facts: The first is that, since
Saussure and many others, we know that verbal signs exhibit only one aspect
of the semiotic function and that linguistics is really only a limited though especially
important segment of that more inclusive discipline which Saussure wanted to
establish under the name of "general semiology." The symbolic or semiotic function
comprises, besides language, all forms of imitation:[12] mimicking, symbolic play,
mental imaging, and so on. Too often it is forgotten that the development of representation and thought (we are not as yet speaking of properly logical structures)
is tied to this *general* semiotic function and not just to language. How otherwise
could we explain that deaf-mute children (those, that is, whose brain has not
been damaged) play at make believe, invent symbolic games and a language of
gestures? By studying their concrete logical operations—seriation, classification,
conservation, and so forth—as investigators like P. Oléron, H. Furth, M. Vincent, and F. Affolter[13] have done, one can watch the development of these logical
structures; this development is occasionally slowed down, but much less so than
in the case of children blind from birth (studied by Y. Hatwell). In the case of
blind children, language, which is quite normal, only slowly makes up for gaps

in their sensori-motor schemata, whereas the deaf-mute child's deprivation of language does not interfere with the development of operational structures (the one-to-two-year average retardation as compared to normal children being attributable to lack of social stimulation).

The second fact to be recalled is that intelligence precedes language not only ontogenetically ... but also phylogenetically—the numerous studies of the intelligence of the great apes amply prove this. Even sensori-motor intelligence already involves certain definite structures (order, subordination schemes, correspondences, and so on), which derive from the activity of coordinating acts and are prior to rather than derivative from language.

This much said, it is obvious that, if speech depends upon an at least partially structured intelligence, the reverse is also true; speech structures this intelligence, and here begin the real problems. They have certainly not been solved. But the two methods now at our disposal—*transformational analysis* (see, for example, M. D. S. Braine's psycholinguistic studies of the acquisition of syntax) and *operational analysis* (see Inhelder's, Sinclair's, and Bovet's experimental studies of the acquisition of logical structures)—enable us to analyze the correlations between syntactic and operational structures, at least at certain particular points; we are even in a position to guess just where there is interaction between the two and which of the linguistic or logical structures are prior, which posterior, in the process of construction.

Let us, for example, briefly consider H. Sinclair de Zwaart's novel and precise experiments.[14] She formed two groups of children, choosing as criterion for their "operational level" their ability or inability to deduce the conservation of a certain volume of liquid upon seeing it poured into containers of different shapes. The first, clearly "pre-operational," group was made up of children who denied conservation, while those of the second group admitted it at once and explained it in terms of principles of reversibility and compensation. She also analyzed the speech of these children by asking them questions that did not refer to the conservation experiments but rather to couples or collections of things which they were to compare with one another—a long and a short pencil, a long thin one and a short thicker one, a collection of four or five blocks and a collection of just two, and so on. Next she asked the children to carry out certain orders: "Give me a smaller pencil" or "Give me one that is smaller and thinner," and so forth.

She found that there is a systematic difference in the language of the two groups. The children in the "pre-operational" group rarely use any except scalar adjectives: "That one is big"; "This one is little"; or "Over there there's a lot"; "Here there aren't a lot"; and so on. The children in the second group, on the other hand, employ vector vocabulary: "That one is bigger than the other"; "There are more here"; and so on. Besides, where the things they are asked to compare differ in more than one respect, the children in the first group tend to ignore one or else juxtapose "kernel" sentences: "That one is big, this one is little; that one (the first) is thin, this one is thick," and so forth. Those in the second group, on the other hand, note binary connections like "That one is longer and thinner, the other shorter and thicker." Obviously, there is a correlation between the operational and the linguistic level, and we see immediately how the verbal structuration of the children in the second group can help their reasoning. The children in the first group do understand the expressions which they do not as yet themselves employ, as is shown by their ability to execute orders given in terms of that higher echelon vocabulary. Mrs. Sinclair therefore subjected them to linguistic training, difficult, but possible. After this training, she re-examined them and found their progress quite small; about one in six now recognized that the quantity of liquid remained the same.

There must, of course, be additional experiments of this sort. It seems that on the level of "concrete operations" ... operational structure precedes linguistic structure, the latter somehow growing out of the former to rely upon it subsequently. It remains to be investigated by some analogous procedure what exactly happens at the level of "propositional operations," where the language of children is modified so strikingly while their reasoning becomes hypothetico-deductive. If we can say today that it is as much as demonstrated that language is not the source of logic, that Chomsky is right in grounding language in reason, it must nevertheless also be said that the detailed study of their interaction has only begun. What is wanted is further experimentation and correlative formalization.[15]

SUMMARY

We have learned that basic to both language and thought is action. Although there may be some type of thinking (for example, visualizing the face of a pretty girl) in which language is not involved, much thought involves language. However, language is not the source of all thought. The contrary seems to be true; language is structured by thought. Syntactic rules involve generalizing assimilations. Language apparently is an instrument of thought which provides a system of notation. Thus language is a facilitator of thought. It increases the power of thought by increasing its rate and by liberating thought from time and space. Language detaches thought from action and is the source of representation in much thought.

On the other hand, verbal signs—for example, words—are conventions based on custom and have no fixed relation to meaning. As a whole, language differs from other forms of representational thought in that it is learned in a social setting. Although syntactic rules are acquired through generalizing assimilation—that is, mental activity—syntax is made up of structures specifically related to language. Syntactic rules are needed to make communication possible; thus, while language facilitates thought, it is also a constraining force. Actions are the source of thought and there is a correlation between language and thought. Language is used in thought but it restricts thought, although some aspects of thought may be independent of language. Language provides thought with summarization, abstraction, and mobilization. Thought without language carries concepts and relationships in imagined actions. It waits upon the necessary process of generalization and labeling to be introduced into the realm of logical operations. Suitably imagined, it must still be verified to achieve the status of reality. Without language, thinking would surely be too cumbersome to ever become logical or realistic. We may speculate that language and syntax do not freeze out the emergence of new concepts and relationships from time to time, but require their suitable evaluation and appropriate status in thought. We may begin to respect and appreciate the long period of time a child spends at the level of the sensorimotor behavior and concrete operations building up the vast bed of concepts and meanings that are summarized in language. Without sufficient grounding in meaning and concepts an unmeaningful, even though syntactically appropriate, rearrangement of vocabulary items does not direct us to an understanding of the nature of objects and relationships. In much the same way reading materials that lead us into abstractions beyond our competence are useless for developing thought.

It is also possible that the roots for the achievement of deeper understanding of the nature of man in his world and of new relationships of familiar concepts lie in the sensorimotor and concrete operational level of thought. We have every reason to expect that this period of development and those modes of thought are to be valued and fostered for their own sake. Suitably selected reading materials can make an important contribution to the enhancement of these modes, as well as contribute to the necessary foundation for the later achievement of intelligent and adapted behavior.

NOTES FOR CHAPTER 10

1. Jean Piaget and Bärbel Inhelder, *The Psychology of the Child* (New York: Basic Books, 1969), pp. 84–90.
2. One finds in the chimpanzee a beginning of symbolic function which enables him, for example, to save tokens with which to obtain fruits from an automatic dispenser (experiment by J. B. Wolfe) and even to offer them as gifts to less fortunate companions (H. W. Nissen and M. P. Crawford).
3. U. Bellugi and R. Brown, eds., *The Acquisition of Language,* Monographs of the Society for Research in Child Development, no. 92 (1964).
4. M. Vincent and M. Borelli, "La naissance des opérations logiques chez des sourds-muets," *Enfance* (1951), pp. 222–38, and *Enfance* (1956), pp. 1–20.
5. P. Oléron, "L'acquisition des conservations et le langage," *Enfance* (1961), pp. 201–19.
6. Lev S. Vygotsky, *Thought and Language* (Cambridge: MIT Press, 1962), p. 153.
7. In Jean Piaget, *Structuralism* (New York: Basic Books, 1970), pp. 74–79.
8. Compare *Origins of Intelligence in Children,* pp. 189ff., where Piaget speaks of the symbol and the sign as "the two poles, individual and social, of the same elaboration of meanings." [Trans.]
9. In the case of norms this equilibrium depends on the possibility of ever more dramatic reversals, while in linguistics it is rather a question of mere oppositions, without ruling out a mechanism (as yet, however, very little understood) of collective self-regulation.
10. *Structuralism,* pp. 89–91.
11. Ibid., pp. 92–96.
12. See Piaget's *Play, Dreams, and Imitation in Childhood* (New York: Norton, 1951). [Trans.]
13. On account of the ingenuity of its techniques and the copiousness of its illustrations, Furth's *Thought without Language* is particularly interesting.
14. H. Sinclair de Zwaart, *Acquisition du langage et développement de la pensée* (Paris: Dunod, 1967).
15. Selected bibliography from *Structuralism:*
    • Chomsky, Noam, *Syntactic Structures* (The Hague: Mouton, 1957).
    • Foucault, Michel, *Les mots et les choses* (Paris: Gallimard, 1966).
    • Lacan, J., *Ecrits* (Paris: Editions du Seuil, 1966).
    • Piaget, Jean, *Traité de logique* (Paris: Colin, 1949).
    • ——, *Biologie et connaissance* (Paris: Gallimard, 1967).
    • —— et al., *Logique et connaissance scientifique* (Encyclopédie de la Pléiade, vol. 22).
    • Saussure, Ferdinand de, *Course in General Linguistics,* edited by C. Bally and A. Séchehaye; translated by Wade Baskin (New York: Philosophical Library, 1959).
    • De Zwaart, H. Sinclair, *Acquisition du langage et développement de la pensée* (Paris: Dunod, 1967).

Piaget's theory of development and other theories

Piaget has compared aspects of his own theory of development with those of other theories, paying special attention to different points of view concerning the nature and development of intelligence. For example, he says[1] that intelligence can be defined

by the direction towards which its development is turned, without insisting on the question of boundaries, which become a matter of stages or of successive forms of equilibrium. We can therefore regard the matter from the point of view both of the functional situation and of the structural mechanism. From the first of these points of view, we can say that behaviour becomes more "intelligent" as the pathways between the subject and the objects on which it acts cease to be simple and become progressively more complex. Thus perception only requires simple paths, even if the object perceived is very remote. A habit might seem more complex, but its spatio-temporal articulations are welded into a unique whole with no independent or separable parts. An act of intelligence, on the other hand, such as finding a hidden object or recognizing the meaning of a picture, involves a certain number of paths (in space and time) which can be both isolated and synthesized. Thus, from the point of view of the structural mechanism, elementary sensori-motor adaptations are both rigid and uni-directional, while intelligence tends towards reversible mobility. That, as we shall see, is the essential property of the operations which characterize living logic in action. But we can see straight away that reversibility is the very criterion of equilibrium (as physicists have taught us). To define intelligence in terms of the progressive reversibility of the mobile structures which it forms is therefore to repeat, in different words, that intelligence constitutes the state of equilibrium towards which tend all the successive adaptations of a sensori-motor and cognitive nature, as well as all assimilatory and accommodatory interactions between the organism and the environment.

From the biological point of view, intelligence thus appears as one of the activities of the organism, while the objects to which it adapts itself constitute a particular sector of the surrounding environment. But as the knowledge that intelligence builds up achieves a privileged equilibrium, because this is the necessary limit of sensori-motor and symbolic interaction, while distances in space and time become indefinitely extended, intelligence engenders scientific thought itself, including biological knowledge. It is therefore natural that the psychological theories of intelligence should come to be placed among biological theories of adaptation and theories of knowledge in general. It is not surprising that there should be some relationship between psychological theories and epistemological doctrines since, even if psychology has been freed from philosophical tutelage, there happily remains some bond between the study of mental functions and that of the processes of scientific knowledge. But what is more interesting is that there exists a parallelism, and a fairly close one, between the great biological doctrines of evolutionary variation (and therefore of adaptation) and the particular theories of intelligence as a psychological fact; psychologists have, in fact, often been unaware of the currents of biological inspiration behind their interpretations, just as biologists have sometimes unwittingly adopted one particular psychological position among other possible ones (cf. the role of habit in Lamarck or of competition and strife in Darwin); moreover, in view of the affinity between the problems, there may be a simple convergence of solutions and so the latter may confirm the former.

From the biological point of view, the relations between the organism and the environment admit of six possible interpretations according to the following combinations (each of which has led to its own solution, classical or contemporary): either (I) we reject the idea of a genuine evolution, or else (II) we admit its existence; then, in both cases (I and II) we attribute adaptations (1) to factors external to the organism, or (2) to internal factors, or (3) to an interaction between the two. So (I) from the non-evolutionist point of view, we may attribute adaptation (I1) to a pre-established harmony between the organism and the properties of the environment, (I2) to a preformism allowing the organism to respond to every situation by actualizing its potential structures, or else (I3) to the "emergence" of complete structures, irreducible to elements and determined simultaneously from within and from without.[2]

As for the evolutionist points of view (II), they likewise explain adaptive variations, by environmental pressure (Lamarckism II1), or by endogenous mutations with subsequent selection (mutationism II2),[3] or (II3) by a progressive interaction between internal and external factors.

Now it is striking to note how we find the same broad currents of thought in the interpretation of knowledge itself, regarded as a relationship between the thinking subject and objects. Corresponding to the pre-established harmony of creationist vitalism, there is (I1) the realism of those doctrines which see in reason an innate adaptation to eternal forms or essences; corresponding to preformism, there is (I2) apriorism which explains consciousness by internal structures which precede experience; and corresponding to the "emergence" of new structures there is (I3) contemporary phenomenology, which simply analyses the various forms of thought, refusing either to derive them genetically from each other or to distinguish in them the roles of subject and object. Evolutionist interpretations, on the other hand, reappear in those epistemological schools which allow for the progressive development of reason; corresponding to Lamarckism there is (II1) empiricism, which explains knowledge by the pressure of objects; corresponding to mutationism there are (II2) conventionalism and pragmatism, which attribute the fittingness of mind to reality to the untrammelled creation of subjective ideas, subsequently selected according to a principle of simple expediency. Finally, interactionism (II3) involves a relativism, which would describe knowledge as the product of an indissociable collaboration between experience and deduction.

Without insisting on this parallelism in its most general form, we may now note how contemporary strictly psychological theories of intelligence are inspired by the same currents of thought, whether biological emphasis is dominant or whether philosophical influences related to the study of knowledge are felt.

There is no doubt, to begin with, that a fundamental incompatibility divides two kinds of interpretations: those which, while recognizing the existence of the facts of development, cannot help considering intelligence as a primary datum, and thus reduce mental evolution to a sort of gradual awakening of consciousness without any real construction of anything, and those which seek to explain intelligence by its own development. It should be noted moreover that the two schools collaborate in the discovery and analysis of actual experimental facts. That is why it is fitting to classify objectively all contemporary all-embracing interpretations, inasmuch as they have helped to throw light on one particular aspect or another of the facts to be explained; the demarcation line between psychological theories and philosophical doctrines is in fact to be found in this appeal to experience, and not in the initial hypotheses.

Among the non-evolutionist theories, there are first of all (I1) those which remain constantly faithful to the idea of an intelligence-faculty, a sort of direct knowledge of physical entities and of logical or mathematical ideas by a pre-established harmony between intellect and reality. We must confess that few experimental psychologists still adhere to this hypothesis. But the problems arising from the common frontiers of psychology and the analysis of mathematical thought have caused certain symbolic logicians, e.g. Bertrand Russell, to formulate such a conception of intelligence and even wish to impose it on psychology itself (cf. his *Analysis of Mind*).[4]

A more prevalent hypothesis (I2) is that according to which intelligence is determined by internal structures, which are likewise not formed but gradually become explicit in the course of development, owing to a reflection of thought on itself. This apriorist current has in fact inspired a good deal of the work of the German *Denkpsychologie* and is consequently found at the root of numerous experimental researches on thought, using the familiar methods of introspection, which have been developing from 1900–1905 to the present day. Naturally this does not mean that every use of these methods of investigation leads to this explanation of intelligence: Binet's work testifies to the contrary. But for K. Bühler, Selz and many others, intelligence eventually became, as it were, "a mirror of logic," which imposes itself from within with no possible causal explanation.

In the third place (I3), corresponding to emergence and phenomenology (with the actual historical influence of the latter), there is a recent theory of intelligence which has raised the problem anew in a very suggestive way: the Configuration (*Gestalt*) theory. The notion of a "complex configuration," resulting from experimental researches in perception, involves the assertion that a whole is irreducible to the elements which compose it, being governed by special laws of organization or equilibrium. Now, having analysed these laws of structuring in the realm of perception and having come across them again in motor functions, memory, etc., the Configuration theory has been applied to intelligence itself, both in its reflective (logical thought) and its sensori-motor form (intelligence in animals and in children at the pre-linguistic stage). Thus Köhler, in connection with chimpanzees, and Wertheimer, in connection with the syllogism, etc., have spoken of "immediate restructurings" seeking to explain the act of insight by the "goodness" (*Prägnanz*) of well organized structures, which are neither endogenous nor exogenous but embrace subject and object in a total field. Furthermore, these *Gestalten*, which are common to perception, movement, and intelligence, do not evolve, but represent permanent forms of equilibrium, independent of mental development (we may in this respect find all intermediate stages between apriorism and the Configuration theory, although the latter is normally found linked with a physical or physiological realism of "structures").

Such are the three principal non-genetic theories of intelligence. It may be noted that the first reduces cognitive adaptation to pure accommodation, since it sees thought only as the mirror of ready–made "ideas," that the second reduces it to pure assimilation, since it regards intellectual structures as exclusively endogenous, and that the third unites assimilation and accommodation in a single whole, since, from the *Gestalt* point of view, there exists only the field linking objects and the subject, with neither activity on his part nor the isolated existence of the object.

As for genetic interpretations, we find once more those which explain intelligence in terms of the external environment only (associationist empiricism corresponding to Lamarckism), the activity of the subject (the trial-and-error theory at the level of individual adaptation, corresponding to mutationism at the level of hereditary variations), and the relationship between subject and object (operational theory).

Empiricism (II1) is scarcely upheld any longer in its pure associationist form, except for some authors, of predominantly physiological interests, who think they can reduce intelligence to a system of "conditioned" responses. But we find less rigid forms of empiricism in Rignano's interpretations, which reduce reasoning to mental experience, and especially in Spearman's interesting theory, which is both statistical (factor analysis of intelligence) and descriptive; from this second point of view, Spearman reduces the operations of intelligence to the "apprehension of experience" and to the "eduction" of relations and "correlates," that is to say, to a more or less complex reading of immediately given relations. These relations, then, are not constructed but discovered by simple accommodation to external reality.

The notion of trial-and-error (II2) has given rise to several interpretations of learning and of intelligence itself. The trial-and-error theory elaborated by Claparède constitutes in this respect the most far-reaching exposition: intelligent adaptation consists of trials or hypotheses, due to the activity of the subject, and of their selection, effected afterwards under the pressure of experience (successes or failures). This empirical control, which from the outset selects the subject's trials, is subsequently internalized in the form of anticipations due to awareness of relations, just as motor trial-and-error is extended into symbolic trial-and-error or imagination of hypotheses.

Finally, emphasizing the interaction of the organism and the environment leads to the operational theory of intelligence (II3). According to this point of view, intellectual operations, whose highest form is found in logic and mathematics, constitute genuine actions, being at the same time something produced by the subject and a possible experiment on reality. The problem is therefore to understand how operations arise out of material action, and what laws of equilibrium govern their evolution; operations are thus concerned as grouping themselves of necessity into complex systems, comparable to the "configurations" of the Gestalt theory, but these, far from being static and given from the start, are mobile and reversible, and round themselves off only when the limit of the individual and social genetic process that characterizes them is reached.

This sixth point of view is the one we shall develop.

Piaget criticizes both Russell's theory of intelligence and the thought psychology of Bühler and Selz for their failure to account for the genetic development of intelligence in children. He cites "concepts successively constructed by the child at different stages of his development" to refute Russell,[5] and as for thought psychology, he asserts that its "very method ... prevents it from going beyond pure description,"[6] adding that it fails to explain the actual constructive mechanisms of intelligence, because introspection, even when controlled, surely deals only with the products of thought and not with its formation. Furthermore, it is restricted to subjects capable of reflection; whereas we should perhaps look for the secret intelligence in children under the age of seven or eight!

Note the similarities between Piaget's and Chomsky's views of "descriptive adequacy" and "explanatory adequacy" of theory. Note, too, that Piaget is hinting that theories pertaining to children who are still undergoing development, when based on experiments employing adults as subjects, may suffer from a fatal methodological defect.

He criticizes thought psychology because it analyzes "only the final stages of intellectual development." Thus the researcher "discovers the wholes which characterize systems of thought as well as the role of anticipatory schemata in the solution of problems. . . . He does not trace their genetic formation."[7]

These comments seem especially applicable to research involving concept formation and attainment as well as stimulus–response theory. Psychological journals are crammed with articles in which the subjects in an experiment are college students. The emerging principles, hypotheses, or replications suffer because they may be applicable only to adults. It is possible that the gap between psychological theory, on the one hand, and successful methods of teaching reading, on the other, exists because the theory is based on the behavior of adults while the methods deal with the behavior of children.

Piaget insists that "the essential characteristic of logical thought is that it is operational, i.e., it extends the scope of action by internalizing it."[8] Actions or operations, not definitions, are necessary for the child to construct concepts. "A concept is in fact only a plan of action or of operation, and only carrying out the operations producing A and B will decide whether they are compatible or not."[9]

These same points are brought to bear by Piaget in his critique of Gestalt psychology:[10]

We are bound to admit how well founded are the descriptions given by Gestalt psychology. The essential "wholeness" of mental structures (perceptual as well as intelligent), the existence of the "good *Gestalt*" and its laws, the reduction of variations of structure to forms of equilibrium, etc., are justified by so many experimental studies that these concepts have acquired the right to be quoted throughout contemporary psychology. In particular, the method of analysis that consists in always interpreting facts in terms of a total field is alone justifiable, since reduction to atomistic elements always impairs the unity of reality.

But it is as well to recognise that, if the "laws of organisation" are not derived, beyond psychology and biology, from absolutely general "physical *Gestalten*" (Köhler), then the language of wholes is merely a mode of description, and the existence of total structures requires an explanation which is not at all included in the fact of wholeness. We have admitted this in connection with our own groupings and we must also admit it in connection with "configurations" or elementary structures.

The general and even "physical" existence of "laws of organisation" implies at the very least—and Gestalt theorists are the first to vouch for it—their constancy in the course of mental development. The essential question for the orthodox Gestalt doctrine (we shall adhere to this orthodoxy for the moment, but we must point out that certain of the more cautious partisans of the Gestalt school, such as Gelb and Goldstein, have rejected the hypothesis of "physical *Gestalten*") is thus that of the permanence of certain essential forms of organisation throughout mental development, e.g. that of perceptual constancy.

However, as far as the main point is concerned, we think it is possible to maintain that, in the present state of knowledge, the facts are opposed to such an assertion. . . .

The existence of a development with age of the mechanisms underlying perceptual constancy (and later we shall see many other developmental changes in perception) undoubtedly leads to a revision of the Gestalt School's explanation. To begin with, if there is an actual development of perceptual structures, we can no longer dismiss either the problem of their formation or the possible role of past experience in the process of their coming into being. Concerning this last point, Brunswik has demonstrated the frequency of empirical *Gestalten* side by side with "geometrical *Gestalten*." In this way, a figure that is intermediate between the image of an open hand and a geometrical pattern with five exactly symmetrical extensions, when seen tachistoscopically, yielded in adults 50 per cent in favour of the hand (learned shape) and 50 per cent in favour of the geometrical "good *Gestalt*."

Concerning the genesis of *Gestalten*, which raises an essential problem as soon as we reject the hypothesis of permanent "physical *Gestalten*," we may first of all point out the illicit nature of the dilemma: either wholes or the atomism of isolated sensations. In point of fact there are three possible terms. A perception may be a synthesis of elements, or else it may constitute a single whole, or it may be a system of relations (each relation being itself a whole, but the complete whole becoming unanalysable and not relying at all on atomism). This being the case, there is no reason why complex structures should not be regarded as the product of a progressive construction which arises, not from "syntheses," but from adaptive differentiations and combined assimilations, nor is there any reason why this construction should not be related to an intelligence capable of genuine activity as opposed to an interplay of pre-established structures.

With regard to perception, the crucial point is that of "transposition." Should we follow Gestalt theory and interpret transpositions (of a melody from one key to another or of a visual form by enlargement) as the simple reappearance of the same form of equilibrium between new elements whose relations have been retained (cf. the horizontal levels of systems of sluice-gates), or should we regard them as the product of an assimilatory activity which integrates comparable elements into the same schema? The fact of improvement with age in ability to transpose . . . seems to us to demand this second solution. Moreover, transposition as ordinarily understood, which is external to the figures, should undoubtedly be connected with the internal transpositions between elements of the same figure, which explain the role of the factors of regularity, equality, symmetry, etc., inherent in "good *Gestalten*."

These two possible interpretations of transposition mean quite different things with respect to the relations between perception and intelligence and especially the nature of the latter.

In attempting to reduce the mechanisms of intelligence to those characterising perceptual structures, which are in turn reducible to "physical *Gestalten*," the Gestalt theory reverts essentially to classical empiricism, although by far more refined methods. The only difference (and considerable though it is, it has little weight in the face of such a reduction) is that the new doctrine replaces "associations" by structured "wholes." But in both cases operational activity in sensory processes fades into pure receptivity, and abdicates in favour of the passivity of automatic mechanisms.

We cannot insist too strongly on the fact that, although operational structures are bound to perceptual structures by a continuous series of intermediate structures (and we grant this without any difficulty), there is, nevertheless, a fundamental contradiction in meaning between the rigidity of a perceived "configuration" and the reversible mobility of operations. Thus Wertheimer's attempted comparison between the syllogism and the static "configurations" of perception runs the risk of remaining inadequate. What is essential in the mechanism of a grouping (by which syllogisms are formed) is not the structure assumed by premises, not that which characterises conclusions, but rather the process of combination which makes it possible to pass from the one to the other. No doubt this process is an extension of perceptual restructurings and recentrings (such as those enabling us to see an "ambiguous" design alternately as convex and concave). But it is even more than this, since it is constituted by the whole system of mobile and reversible operations of conjunction and disjunction ($A + A' = B$; $A = B - B'$; $A' = B - A$; $B - A - A' = 0$, etc.). So it is no longer static forms that are important in intelligence, nor the simple uni-directional transition from one state to another (or even oscillation between the two); the general mobility and reversibility of operations are what give rise to structures. It follows that the structures involved themselves differ in the two cases. A perceptual structure is characterised, as the Gestalt theory itself has insisted, by its irreducibility to additive combination—it is thus irreversible and non-associative. So there is considerably more in a system of reasoning than a "recentring" (*Umzentrierung*); there is a general decentralisation, which means a dissolution or melting down of static perceptual forms in favour of operational mobility, and consequently there is the possibility of constructing an infinite number of new structures which may be perceptible or may exceed the limits of all true perception.

As for the sensori-motor intelligence described by Köhler, it is clear that here perceptual structures play a much bigger part. But by the very fact that Gestalt theory is bound to consider them as arising directly from situations as such, without historical development, Köhler found himself constrained to exclude from the realm of intelligence, on the one hand, the trial-and-error which precedes the discovery of solutions and, on the other hand, the corrections and checks which follow it. Study of the child's first two years of life has led us, in this context, to a different viewpoint. There are indeed complex structures or "configurations" in the infant's sensori-motor intelligence, but far from being static and non-historical, they constitute "schemata" which grow out of one another by means of successive differentiations and integrations, and which must therefore be ceaselessly accommodated to situations by trial-and-error and corrections at the same time as they are assimilating the situations to themselves. The response with the stick is thus prepared by a series of anticipatory schemata, such as that of pulling the objective to oneself by means of its extensions (string or struts) or that of striking one object against another.

The following reservations must therefore be made.... An act of intelligence is doubtless determined by past experience only in so far as it resorts to it. But this relationship involves assimilatory schemata which in turn are the product of previous schemata, from which they are derived through differentiation and co-ordination. Schemata thus have a history; there is interaction between past experience and the present act of intelligence, not uni-directional action of past on present as empiricism demands nor uni-directional appeal to the past by the present. . . . It is even possible to formulate these relations between present and past by saying that equilibrium is reached when all previous schemata are embedded in present ones and intelligence can equally well reconstruct past schemata by means of present ones and vice versa.

On the whole, then, we see that the Gestalt theory, although correct in its description of forms of equilibrium or well-structured wholes, nevertheless neglects the reality, in perception as in intelligence, of genetic development and the process of construction that characterises it.

Piaget minces no words in his criticism of theories dealing with sensory stimuli and motor responses:[11]

The distinction between motor functions and perceptual functions is legitimate only for purposes of analysis. As von Weizsäcker[12] has convincingly shown, the classical division of phenomena into sensory stimuli and motor responses, which is introduced by the reflex-arc schema, is just as fallacious, and refers to laboratory products, which are just as artificial, as the idea of the reflex arc itself, conceived in isolation. Perception is influenced by motor activity from the outset, just as the latter is by the former. This is what we, for our part, have asserted when speaking of sensori-motor schemata in order to describe the simultaneously perceptual and motor assimilation which characterises the behaviour of the infant.[13]

Beyond initial reflex behavior, he adds, "the infant acquires habits as a result of experience. Do these habits provide the basis for intelligence or have they nothing to do with it?"[14] He continues:[15]

Nothing is better fitted to illustrate the continuity which links the problem of the birth of intelligence to that of the formation of habits than a comparison of the various answers to these two questions. The same hypotheses appear in both cases, as though intelligence were an extension of those mechanisms which in their automatic form appear as habit.

In connection with habit, we once again find the genetic schemata of association, of trial-and-error or of assimilatory structuring. In its treatment of the relations between habit and intelligence, associationism goes so far as to make habit into a primary fact which explains intelligence; the theory of trial-and-error reduces habit to a matter of responses selected in the course of random behaviour and becoming automatic, this being characteristic of intelligence itself; the theory of assimilation sees intelligence as a form of equilibrium of that assimilatory activity which, in its original form, constitutes habit. As for non-genetic interpretations, we shall again meet the three combinations corresponding to vitalism, apriorism and Gestalt: habit deriving from intelligence, habit unrelated to intelligence and habit explained, like intelligence and perception, by structurings whose laws remain independent of development.

Piaget suggests[16] that there is

a certain continuity between the limited and comparatively rigid co-ordinations that we usually call habits, and co-ordinations characterising intelligence, which have greater mobility and extreme limits which are further removed.

This was fully realised by Buytendijk, who has brilliantly analysed the formation of elementary animal habits, especially in invertebrates. However, the greater the complexity this writer finds in the factors affecting habit, the more he tends, on account of his vitalist system of interpretation, to subordinate the co-ordination peculiar to habits to intelligence itself, a faculty inherent in the organism as such. The formation of a habit always involves a fundamental means-end relation; an action is never a succession of mechanically associated movements but is directed towards a satisfaction such as contact with food or release, e.g., Limnaea, when placed upside down, return more and more rapidly to their normal position. But the means-end relation characterises intelligent actions; habit would then be the expression of an intelligent organisation which, moreover, must be co-extensive with all living structure. Just as Helmholtz explained perception by the intervention of unconscious inference, so vitalism ends by describing habit as the result of an unconscious organic intelligence.

But although we must fully acknowledge the justice of Buytendijk's observations regarding the complexity of the simplest acquisitions and the irreducibility of the relation of need to satisfaction, which is the origin and not the effect of associations, there is no justification for hastily explaining everything by intelligence, considered as a primary fact. Such a thesis involves a series of difficulties which are exactly the same as those of the parallel interpretation with respect to perception. In the first place, habit, like perception, is irreversible because it is always orientated in one direction towards the same result, while intelligence is reversible. Reversing a bit (e.g. writing backwards or from right to left, etc.) means acquiring a new habit, while a "reverse operation" of intelligence is psychologically implied by the original operation (and logically constitutes the same change, but in the opposite direction). In the second place, just as intelligent insight only slightly modifies a perception (knowledge has little influence on an illusion, as Hering pointed out in reply to Helmholtz) and, reciprocally, elementary perception does not automatically turn itself into an act of intelligence, so intelligence only slightly modifies an acquired habit and, above all, the formation of a habit is not immediately followed by the development of intelligence. There is actually an appreciable break in the genetic series between the appearance of the two types of structures. Piéron's sea-anemones, which close up at low tide and thus store the water they need, are not evidence for a really mobile intelligence and, in particular, they retain their habit in the aquarium for several days before it is extinguished. Goldsmith's Gobii learn to pass through a hole in a sheet of glass to reach food and keep to the same route after the glass is removed: we may name this behaviour sub-cortical intelligence, but it is still considerably inferior to what is ordinarily called intelligence without qualification.

Hence the hypothesis which for a long time seemed the simplest: that habit constitutes a primary fact, explicable in terms of passively experienced associations, and intelligence grows out of it gradually, by virtue of the growing complexity of the acquired associations. We are not going to call associationism to trial here, since the objections to this mode of interpretation are as well known as its resurrection in different and often disguised forms. However, it is essential, in order to arrive at the true development of the structures of intelligence, to remember that the most elementary habits are still irreducible to the pattern of passive association.

But the idea of the conditioned reflex, or of conditioning in general, has afforded a recrudescence of vitality to associationism by providing it with both a precise physiological model and a revised terminology. Hence the series of applications attempted by psychologists in the interpretation of intellectual functions (language, etc.) and occasionally of the act of intelligence itself.

But if the existence of conditioned behaviour is a fact, and even a very important one, its interpretation does not imply the reflexological associationism with which it is too often identified. When a response is associated with a perception there is more in this connection than a passive association (i.e. becoming stamped in as a result of repetition alone); meanings also enter into it, since association occurs only in the presence of a need and its satisfaction. Everyone knows in practice, although we too often forget it in theory, that a conditioned reflex is stabilised only as long as it is confirmed or reinforced; a signal associated with food does not give rise to an enduring reaction if real food is not periodically presented together with the signal. Association thus comes to be part of a complex piece of behaviour, which starts from a need and finishes with its satisfaction (actual, anticipated or even make-believe, etc.). This amounts to saying that this is not a case of association in the classical sense of the term, but rather of the constitution of a complex schema bound up with a meaning. Moreover, if a system of conditioned responses is studied with reference to their historical sequence (and those concerning psychology always present such a sequence, as opposed to over-simplified physiological conditioning), the role of complex structuring is seen to even better advantage. Thus André Rey placed a guinea-pig in compartment A of a box with three adjacent compartments, A, B, and C, and administered an electric shock preceded by a signal. On the repetition of the signal, the guinea-pig jumped into B, then returned to A, but only a few more trials were required for it to jump from A into B, from B into C and to return from C into B, and so into A. Thus, in this case, the conditioned response is not the simple substitution of responses originally due to a simple reflex, but new behaviour which arrives at stability only by a structuring of the whole environment.

Now if this is the case with the most elementary types of habit, the same must hold *a fortiori* in the case of the increasingly complex "associative transfers" which carry behaviour to the threshold of intelligence. Wherever there is an association between response and perception, the so-called association really consists in integrating the new element with a previous schema of activity. Whether this previous schema is in the nature of a reflex, as in the conditioned reflex, or belongs to much higher levels, association is always, in point of fact, assimilation of such a kind that the associative link is never simply the reproduction of a relation which is given, already formed, in external reality.

This is why the study of the formation of habits, like that of the structure of perceptions, concerns the problem of intelligence in the highest degree. If early intelligence consisted merely in exerting its action (which is a later acquisition belonging to a higher plane) on a completed world of associations and relations, corresponding term for term with relations written, once and for all, in the external environment, then this action would, in point of fact, be illusory. On the other hand, in so far as the organising assimilatory process, which eventually arrives at the operations peculiar to intelligence, appears from the outset in perceptual activity and in the formation of habits, the empiricist models of intelligence that some writers try to build up are inadequate at all levels, since they disregard assimilatory construction.

Suppose a person is confronted by a novel or unique situation: what means does he use to adapt to it (if it's a problem, to solve it; if it's an obstacle, to overcome it)? Piaget asserts that either by sensorimotor or by internalized trial and error the person seeks to "contrive solutions from which experience will select afterwards."[17] Citing the work of Tolman, he suggests that these trials really result from hypotheses about how the situation might be managed, the problem solved, or the obstacle overcome. Piaget continues:[18]

As for Tolman, he brings out the role of generalisation in the formation of habits themselves. Thus, when an animal is placed in a new maze different from the one known to it, it perceives general analogies and applies to the new case behaviour that met with success in the previous case (particular routes). So there is always complex structuring, but, for Tolman, the structures concerned are not simple "configurations" in the sense of Köhler's theory; they are *sign-gestalts*, i.e. schemata provided with meanings. This double property of general validity and meaning belonging to the structures considered by Tolman is a fairly good indication that he is concerned with what we call assimilatory schemata. Thus, from elementary learning to intelligence, there seems to be involved an assimilatory activity, which is as necessary to the structuring of the most passive forms of habits (conditioned responses and associative transfers) as it is to the unfolding of visible manifestations of activity (directed trial-and-error). In this respect, the problem of the relations between habit and intelligence is a fair parallel to that of the relations between intelligence and perception. Just as perceptual acitivity is not identical with intelligence, but links up with it as soon as it is freed from centring on the immediate and present object, so the assimilatory activity that engenders habits is not the same as intelligence but leads to the latter as soon as irreversible and isolated sensori-motor systems are differentiated and coordinated in mobile articulations. Besides this, the affinity between these two kinds of activity is obvious, since perceptions and habitual responses are constantly united in complex schemata, and since the "transfer" or generalisation characteristic of habit is the exact equivalent, on the motor side, or "transposition" in the domain of spatial figures, both involving the same generalised assimilation.

By the time a child is two, according to Piaget,[19]

instead of new means being exclusively discovered by active experimentation, as at the previous level, there may henceforth be inventions by rapid internal co-ordination of processes now unknown to the subject. To this last category belong the phenomena of sudden restructuring described by Köhler in chimpanzees and Bühler's *Aha-Erlebnis* or experience of sudden insight. Thus, in children who have no occasion to experiment with sticks before the age of one year six months, the first contact with a stick affords insight into its possible relations with the objective to be reached, and this without actual trial-and-error. Similarly, it seems obvious that certain of Köhler's subjects discovered the use of the stick, so to speak, by looking and without previous practice.

The main problem, then, is to understand the mechanism of these internal co-ordinations, which imply both invention without trial-and-error and a mental anticipation closely related to representation. We have already seen how the Gestalt theory explains things by a simple perceptual restructuring without reference to past experience. But it is impossible not to see in the behaviour of an infant at this sixth stage the end-result of all the development characterizing the previous five levels. In fact, it is clear that once he becomes used to tertiary circular reactions and to the intelligent trial-and-error that constitutes true active experimentation the child sooner or later becomes capable of internalizing this behaviour. When the subject no longer acts when confronted with the data of a problem, and appears to be thinking instead (one of our children, after having tried without success to widen the opening of a box of matches by random behaviour, interrupted his activity, looked carefully at the chink then visible, then opened and closed his own mouth), everything seems to indicate that he continues his attempts, but with implicit trials or internalised actions (the imitative movements of the mouth in the foregoing example are a very clear indication of this sort of motor thinking). What happens then, and how do we explain the discovery that yields the sudden solution? Sensori-motor schemata that have become sufficiently mobile and amenable to co-ordination among themselves give rise to mutual assimilations, spontaneous enough for there to be no further need for actual trial-and-error and rapid enough to give an impression of immediate restructuring. Internal co-ordination of schemata will, then, bear the same relation to the external co-ordination of the earlier levels, as inner speech, a simple, rapid, internalised rough draft of overt language, bears to outer speech.

But does the greater spontaneity and speech of assimilatory co-ordination between schemata fully explain the internalisation of behaviour, or does representation begin at the present level, thus indicating the transition from sensori-motor intelligence to genuine thought? Independently of the advent of language, which the child begins to acquire at this age (but which is absent in chimpanzees who are, nevertheless, capable of remarkably intelligent inventions), two types of behaviour at this sixth stage testify to the beginnings of representation, but beginnings which scarcely go beyond the rather rudimentary representation of chimpanzees. On the one hand, the child becomes capable of delayed imitation, i.e. of producing a copy which occurs for the first time after the perception of the model has disappeared; now whether delayed imitation is derived from imaginal representation or whether it causes it, it is certainly closely linked with it. . . . On the other hand, the child simultaneously arrives at the simplest form of symbolic play, consisting in using the body to produce an action foreign to the present context (e.g. pretending to sleep for fun, while he is actually wide awake). Here again there appears a sort of image which is enacted, and therefore motor, but it is already almost representative. Do not these enacted images, characteristic of delayed imitation and of the early make-believe symbol, act as significants in the internalised co-ordination of schemata? This is what seems to be illustrated in the example we mentioned a short while ago of the child who used his mouth to imitate the widening of the visible gap in a box he was trying to open.[20]

SUMMARY

Piaget highlights groups of issues relevant to a discussion on the nature of intelligence. One group of issues deals with whether intelligence develops or whether it is preformed as an endowment of the genes and awakened within the individual. Another set of issues is concerned with the source of intelligence. Is its source to be found in the external environment, or in the activity of the subject, or as some combination of both?

Piaget subscribes to the idea that there is an actual development of intelligence rather than a stimulus-induced awakening of intelligence. In this regard his views differ from those of the Gestaltists.

Thus, although Piaget agrees with the Gestalt principles of organization, he believes that organization comes from an interaction with the environment rather than from a stable internal schema.

The Gestaltic concept of stable internal schema preorganized to process incoming information is more static than Piaget's concept that internal structures or schemata are developed by active efforts to discover the nature of the order of the external world. Piaget's concept helps to explain how new structures are developed and shows the learner as highly active in building his intelligence. But, if Piaget is right in believing that structures are developed, there must be an exploration of this development to understand the thought processes of children. Furthermore, it means that children's thought is somewhat different from that of adults. Contrary to what many Gestaltists have done, children's thought must be studied independently, and research findings from adult thinking cannot be generalized to children, and environments for children must be carefully planned.

Furthermore, Piaget's more dynamic concept (that there are structures to organize thought, developed through accommodation and assimilation, which provide functional modes for relating man to his environment) indicates not only that present experiences are built upon past experiences, but also that past experiences can be reorganized from present experiences in mature thought. This interplay between past and present experiences has important implications for reading activities. Not only is reading comprehension dependent on past experiences, but also new insights can be given to old experiences through reading.

In summary, whereas Piaget disagrees with the Gestaltists about the source of internal schemata, he agrees with them that such structures exist and that intelligence comes from an interaction of the individual and the environment. The main difference between Piaget and the Gestaltists is that Piaget believes that the schemata are developed, whereas the Gestaltists believe that preexisting schemata are awakened by environmental events.

Piaget's ideas can also be compared and contrasted with those of behavior theorists. One particular contrast between his theory and that of the behaviorists lies in the area of motivation in learning. Whereas behavior theorists believe that behavior is modified through extrinsic rewards, Piaget sees the human organism as actively seeking stimulation. Rewards result internally when equilibrium is restored to the organism after the mental correlates of encounters with unanticipated circumstances have been suitably analyzed and categorized by mental structures.

To sensory stimuli, to which the behaviorists give much weight in learning, Piaget adds motor responses. He believes that the child learns by interacting with the environment through directed motor activities.

What would be the pertinent sensory data and objects to be manipulated when the task is learning to read? There is considerable motor activity displayed in language learning as the child explores sounds, converses with family and acts according to the messages given and received, and verbally tests hypotheses regarding syntax. Oral reading and writing are obvious motor activities.

In addition, actual manipulation of written forms, copying letters and words, manipulating parts of words, and matching shapes of words and letters might support the initial phase of learning to read. Discovering and mastering letter-sound relationships is a major learning-to-read task. Just as mothers provide a specialized language environment for beginning language learning, so teachers must prepare the kind of environment that supports learning to read and changes appropriately with respect to the nature of the reading materials provided as the child develops. Early reading materials must provide immediate feedback to ensure that the child knows when his hypotheses are correct, thus assuring that the activity will be intrinsically rewarding.

Piaget has discussed habits that are automatic mechanisms. Unlike behaviorists, Piaget believes that there cannot be a stimulus followed by an automatic response. Meaning must also be present. This meaning, derived from the association between stimulus and response, is supplied by the individual in an attempt to structure the whole environment. The association consists of integrating the new element with a previous schema of activity. This idea may have an application to reading. It seems to explain how the child is able to apply associations of sound-symbol relationships to words he has not seen before.

For similar reasons Piaget rejects the concept that learning is accomplished through a simple trial-and-error procedure in which the right responses are selected for later use and the wrong responses rejected. He believes that learning is possible without trial and error, because central correlates of earlier behavior have been internalized through generalized assimilation and because trials are not random behaviors but each is a directed effort reflecting a guess or hypothesis on the part of the child. This would explain how individuals can function in seemingly new circumstances.

So far our discussion of mental development has centered mainly on the ideas of Piaget. Let us, in the next chapter, explore the work of other investigators.

NOTES FOR CHAPTER 11

1. Jean Piaget, *The Psychology of Intelligence* (Totowa, N.J.: Littlefield, Adams, 1966), pp. 10–17.
2. Pre-established harmony (I1) is the solution inherent in classical creationism and it constitutes the only explanation of adaptation which is in fact at the disposal of vitalism in its pure form. Preformism (I2) has sometimes been associated with vitalist solutions, but it can become independent of them and often persists in mutationist guises among authors who deny all constructive character to evolution and consider every new characteristic as the actualization of potentialities which hitherto were merely latent. Conversely, the view based on emergence (I3) reverts to explaining the innovations which arise in the hierarchy of beings by complex structures which are irreducible to the elements of the previous level. From these elements there "emerges" a new totality, which is adaptive because it unites in an indissociable whole both the internal mechanisms and their relations with the external environment. While admitting the fact of evolution, the hypothesis of emergence thus reduces it to a series of syntheses, each irreducible to the others, so that it is broken up into a series of distinct creations.
3. In mutationist explanations of evolution subsequent selection is due to the environment itself. In Darwin it was attributed to competition.
4. The author desires to indicate that his discussion of Russell's views on this and subsequent pages refers only to that writer's first period. Russell has since rejected this position in favour of an extreme empiricism. (*Translator's note.*)
5. *The Psychology of Intelligence*, p. 21.
6. Ibid., p. 25.
7. Ibid., pp. 25–26.
8. Ibid., p. 34.
9. Ibid., p. 28.
10. Ibid., pp. 60–61, 63–66.
11. Ibid., p. 87.
12. *Der Gestaltkreis*, 1941.
13. *La naissance de l'intelligence chez l'enfant*, 1936.
14. *The Psychology of Intelligence*, p. 87.
15. Ibid., pp. 87–88.
16. Ibid., pp. 89–92.
17. Ibid., p. 94.
18. Ibid., p. 98–99.
19. Ibid., pp. 105–7.
20. A short bibliography from *The Psychology of Intelligence*:
    - Binet, A., *Etude expérimentale de l'intelligence* (Paris: Schleicher, 1903).
    - Bühler, K., *Die Krise der Psychologie*, 2d ed. (Jena: Fischer, 1929).
    - Burloud, A., *La Pensée d'après les recherches expérimentales de Watt, de Messer et de Bühler* (Paris: Alcan, 1927). Includes references for these three writers.
    - Claparède, Ed., "La Genèse de l'hypothèse," *Archives de Psychologie* (Geneva), 1934.
    - Claparède, Ed., "La Psychologie de l'intelligence," *Scientia* 22 (1917), 253–68.
    - Delacroix, H., "La Psychologie de la raison," in *Traité de Psychologie*, by Dumas, vol. 1, 2d ed. (Paris: Alcan, 1936), pp. 198–305.
    - Duncker, K., *Zur Psychologie des produktiven Denkens* (Berlin, 1935).
    - Guillaume, P., *La Formation des habitudes* (Paris: Alcan, 1936).
    - Guillaume, P., *La Psychologie de la forme* (Paris: Flammarion, 1936).
    - Hull, C. L., *Principles of Behavior* (New York, 1943).
    - Köhler, W., *Gestalt Psychology* (London, 1929).
    - Köhler, W., *The Mentality of Apes* (London, 1924).
    - Krechevsky, I., "The Docile Nature of Hypotheses," *J. Comp. Psychol.* 15 (1933), 425–43.
    - Lewin, K., *Principles of Topological Psychology* (London: McGraw-Hill, 1935).
    - Lindworsky, I., *Das Schlussfolgernde Denken* (Freiburg-im-Breisgau, 1916).
    - Montpellier, G. de, *Conduites intelligentes et psychisme chez l'animal et chez l'homme*
    - (Louvain and Paris: Vrin, 1946).
    - Piaget, J., *Classes, relations et nombres: Essai sur les "Groupements" de la logistique et la réversibilité de la pensée* (Paris: Vrin, 1942).

- Piaget, J., *La Construction du réel chez l'enfant* (Neuchâtel: Delachaux et Niestlé, 1937).
- Piaget, J., *La naissance de l'intelligence chez l'enfant* (Neuchâtel: Delachaux et Niestlé, 1936).
- Piaget, J., and Lambercier, M., "Recherches sur le développement des perceptions," I to VIII, *Archives de Psychologie* (Geneva), 1943–46.
- Selz, O., *Zur Psychologie des produktiven Denkens und des Irrtums* (Bonn, 1924).
- Spearman, C., *The Nature of Intelligence* (London, 1923).
- Thorndike, E. L., *The Fundamentals of Learning* (New York: Teachers College, Columbia Univ., 1932).
- Tolman, E. C., "A Behavioristic Theory of Ideas," *Psychol. Rev.* 33 (1926), 352–69.
- Wertheimer, M., *Über Schlussprozesse im produktiven Denken* (Berlin, 1920).

12

concept learning and verbal learning

So far we have examined the developmental psychological theories of Piaget. There are, however, other insights about the nature of the learner that can help in our consideration of the teaching of reading; for example, the studies of concept learning and verbal learning. Consider a statement by Robert M. Gagné:[1]

Most of us have, in fact, fallen into the habit of using the word *conceptual* in a pretty broad sense to refer to the kind of behavioral change that is often verbal in its expression, but actually is a change in the symbolic or representational capabilities of the human learner. Thus, we tend not to think of acquiring capability to tie a shoelace or print a letter as conceptual. However, we do think of the performance of answering the following question as conceptual: "What must I do if my shoelace comes untied?" Bartlett (1958),[2] however, reminds us that these two categories may not be so entirely different as we sometimes like to think. . . .

Despite differences in the language used to describe a concept, there is considerable agreement among research psychologists as to what the word means. Let me give some examples.

Berlyne (1965)[3] believed that a concept is formed when overt behavior comes to depend on certain properties of a stimulus pattern while disregarding other properties. "It means forming what logicians and mathematicians call an *equivalence class* of stimulus situations, which share some characteristics but are distinct in other respects, and performing the same response to all members of the class."

Kendler (1964)[4] defined concept learning as the acquisition of a common response to dissimilar stimuli. But he also went on to say that concepts are associations, and that they function as cues or mediators of learned behavior. This conception of the concept is basically similar to that of Osgood (1953),[5] who emphasized the acquisition of a mediating process that can be "detached" or "abstracted" from the stimulus objects with which it may initially have been associated. From a somewhat different point of view, Carroll (1964)[6] defined a concept as an abstraction from a series of experiences which defines a class of objects or events.

Although these examples of the definition of a concept are not exhaustive, they nevertheless derive from a sample of research people who are prominent in this field, and therefore cannot with wisdom be ignored. All these definitions have some general properties in common, and I judge these to be as follows.

1. A concept is an inferred mental process.
2. The learning of a concept requires discrimination of stimulus objects (distinguishing "positive" and "negative" instances).
3. The performance which shows that a concept has been learned consists in the learner being able to place an object in a class.

The common examples of concept learning which would presumably be acceptable to each of these investigators might include the following: learning *chair* as a class of objects; learning *red* as a property of objects detachable from particular objects; learning classes of direction or position, such as *up, down, middle, right*, and *left*, as classes of position or movement not invariably associated with particular positions or movements.

James J. Jenkins contends that concepts belong to three general classes.[7]

The first class is that of concepts that depend on the isolation of some aspect (or set of aspects) of the stimuli which are instances of that concept. The second class is that of concepts that depend on community or agreement of particular responses to the stimuli. The third class is that of concepts that are constructs in general systems of relationships. Instances may be recognized by submitting them to some test procedure or set of procedures. Neither the test procedures nor the rules of the concept system may be clear to the subject who possesses the concept.

Concepts appear to entail the development of groupings, which Piaget has postulated, since concept formation requires the ability to form classes and hierarchies of classes, and the ability to perceive and organize positive and negative instances. These ideas of Piaget lead to inferences about the nature of the knower. Piaget's ideas provide insight as to how the knower comes to develop concepts and principles. At the same time, studies by other researchers on concept and verbal learning identify various means for developing concepts. These studies, therefore, provide a natural link between the knower and the known: between a theory of learning and a theory of instruction. They also help solve the problem of how to enable the nonliterate person to come to recognize in written form language that he already understands and uses in speech.

Studies of concept learning are important for another reason. This stems in part from a simple definition of a concept by E. James Archer. A concept, he states, is "the label of a set of things that have something in common."[8] This definition suggests a relation between a word and a concept. It can be expected, then, that studies of concept formation will shed light on problems of developing a child's vocabulary. And since concept-formation studies also explore the nature of meaning, we can expect that such studies will in addition provide the classroom teacher with strategies for developing the child's comprehension.

First, consider the relation between words, meanings, and concepts described by John B. Carroll:[9]

THE NATURE OF CONCEPTS

In a totally inorganic world there could be no concepts, but with the existence of organisms capable of complex perceptual responses, concepts become possible. In brief, concepts are properties of organismic experience—more particularly, they are the abstracted and often cognitively structured class of "mental" experience learned by organisms in the course of their life histories. There is evidence that animals other than human beings behave with regard to concepts in this sense, but we shall confine our attention to human organisms. Because of the continuity of the physical, biological, and social environment in which human beings live, their concepts will show a high degree of similarity; and through language learning, many concepts (classes of experience) will acquire names, that is, words or phrases in a particular language, partly because some classes of experience are so salient and obvious that nearly every person acquires them for himself, and partly because language makes possible the diffusion and sharing of concepts as classes of experience. We use the term "experience" in an extremely broad sense—defining it as any internal or perceptual response to stimulation. We can "have experience of" some aspect of the physical, biological, or social environment by either direct or indirect means; we can experience heat, or light, or odor directly, while our experiences of giraffes or atoms, say, may be characterized as being indirect, coming only through verbal descriptions or other patterns of stimuli (pointer readings, etc.) that evoke these concepts.

One necessary condition for the formation of a concept is that the individual must have a series of experiences that are in one or more respects similar; the constellation of "respects" in which they are similar constitutes the "concept" that underlies them. Experiences that embody it may be called "negative instances." A further necessary condition for the formation of a concept is that the series of experiences embodying the concept must be preceded, interspersed, or followed by other experiences that constitute negative instances of the concept. As the complexity of the concepts increases (i.e., as there is an increase in the number of interrelations of the respects in which experiences must be similar in order to be positive instances), there is a greater necessity for an appropriate sequencing of positive and negative instances in order to insure adequate learning of the concept.[10] At least this is true when the concept has to be formed from non-verbal experiences only, i.e., from actual exemplars or referents of the concept as contrasted with non-exemplars. But concept learning from verbal explanation, as will be noted below, must, as it were, put the learner through a series of vicarious experiences of positive and negative instances. For example, in telling a child what a lion is, one must indicate the range of positive and negative instances—the range of variations that could be found in real lions and the critical respects in which other animals—tigers, leopards, etc.—differ from lions.

We have been describing what is often called the process of abstraction. We have given a number of necessary conditions for the formation of a concept; exactly what conditions are sufficient cannot yet be stated, but in all likelihood this will turn out to be a matter of (a) the number, sequencing, or timing of the instances presented to the individual, (b) the reinforcements given to the individual's responses, and (c) the individual's orientation to the task. The evidence suggests that the learner must be oriented to, and attending to, the relevant stimuli in order to form a concept. The public test of the formation of a concept is the ability to respond correctly and reliably to new positive and negative instances of it; we do not wish to imply, however, that a concept has not been formed until it is put to such a test.

The infant acquires "concepts" of many kinds even before he attains anything like language. One kind of concept that is acquired by an infant quite early is the concept embodied in the experience of a particular object—a favorite toy, for example. As the toy is introduced to the infant, it is experienced in different ways—it is seen at different angles, at different distances, and in different illuminations.

It is felt in different positions and with different parts of the body, and experienced with still other sense-modalities—taste, smell. But underlying all these experiences are common elements sufficient for the infant to make an identifying response to the particular toy in question—perhaps to the point that he will accept only the particular specimen that he is familiar with and reject another specimen that is in the least bit different. The acceptance or rejection of a specimen is the outward sign of the attainment of a concept—as constituted by the class of experiences associated with that particular specimen. The experiences themselves are sufficiently similar to be their own evidence that they constitute a class—a perceptual invariant, therefore, together with whatever affective elements that may be present to help reinforce the attainment of the concept (pleasure in the sight, taste, smell, and feel of the toy, for example).

Even the concept contained in a particular object represents a certain degree of generality—generality over the separate presentations of the object. But preverbal infants also attain concepts which from the standpoint of adult logic have even higher degrees of generality. A further stage of generality is reached when the infant comes to recognize successive samples of something—e.g., a particular kind of food—as equivalent, even though varying slightly in taste, color, temperature, etc. Because the different samples of food are about equally reinforcing, the infant gradually learns to overcome the initial tendency to reject a sample that is experienced as not quite the same as one previously experienced. That is, what seems to be initially a negative instance turns out to be a positive instance because it provides the same reinforcement as the earlier instance—the reinforcement being in this case a "sign" that the new experience is to be taken in the same class as former ones. An even higher stage of generality is achieved when the child will accept and make a common response to any one of a number of rather different stimuli—for example, any one of a number of different foods. In adult terms, he has attained the concept of "food" in some elementary sense. The explanation of this phenomenon may indeed draw upon the usual primary reinforcement theory (the equivalence of different foods in satisfying a hunger drive) but it also depends upon various secondary reinforcements, as when the parent punishes the child for eating something not considered "food," like ants or mud. This is an elementary case in which culture, as represented by parents, provides signs as to what the positive and negative instances of a concept are.

Direct experience, i.e., the recognition of experiences as identical or similar, allows the infant to attain concepts that in adult language have names such as redness, warmth, softness, heaviness, swiftness, sweetness, loudness, pain, etc. In some cases, the infant's concepts of sensory qualities may be rather undifferentiated. For example, because big things are generally experienced as heavy and strong, and small things are generally experienced as lightweight and weak, the infant's concept of size may not be adequately differentiated from his concepts of weight and strength. Without any social reinforcement to guide him, his concept of "redness" may range over a rather wide range of the color spectrum, and if he happens to have been born into a culture which pays little attention to the difference, say, between what we would call "red" and "orange," his concept of "redness" may remain relatively undifferentiated even after he has learned a language—just as it has been demonstrated that different varieties of blue are not well coded in everyday English.[11]

Furthermore, we can infer from various investigations of Piaget[12] that the child's concepts of size, weight, and other physical attributes of objects do not contain the notion of "conservation" that his later experiences will teach him. For all the infant or young child knows of the physical universe, objects can change in size, weight, etc., in quite arbitrary ways. It is only at a later stage, when the child has had an opportunity to form certain concepts about the nature of the physical universe that his concepts of size, weight, and number can incorporate the notion of constancy or conservation that mature thinking requires. Experience with objects that can expand or contract through stretching or shrinking gives the child a concept of size that can properly explain the fact that a balloon can be blown up to various sizes. Indeed, this explanation may involve the concepts of "expansion" and "contraction." At a still later stage, the child may learn enough about the relation of heat to expansion to explain why it is necessary to have seams in concrete roads, or why one allows for expansion in the building of large bridges. And it will be relatively unlikely that even as an adult he will learn enough about the concept of size to understand the concept of relativity—that the size of a body is relative to the speed at which it is traveling and the system in which it is measured.

Thus, concepts can in the course of a person's life become more complex, more loaded with significant aspects. Concepts are, after all, essentially idiosyncratic in the sense that they reside in particular individuals with particular histories of experiences that lead them to classify those experiences in particular ways. My concept of "stone" may not be precisely your concept of "stone" because my experiences with stones may have included work with pieces of a peculiar kind of vitreous rock that you have seldom seen. To a large extent, how I sort out my experiences is my own business and may not lead to the same sortings as yours.

Nevertheless, I can specify the way I sort out my experiences by noting the *critical attributes* that differentiate them. I can specify what sensory qualities and attributes are necessary before I will classify an experience as being an experience of what I call a stone. But it is not even necessary for a person to be able to specify such attributes. A child who has learned a certain concept—who has learned to recognize certain experiences as being similar—may not necessarily be able to verbalize what attributes make them similar; he may not even be aware of the fact that he has attained a certain concept, since it may be the case that only his behavior—the fact that he consistently makes a certain response to a certain class of stimuli—indicates that he has formed a concept. Such would be the case, for example, for the classic instance where the child is afraid of the barber because he wields instruments (scissors) that look like those of the doctor whom he has already learned to fear, and because he wears a similar white smock.

Indeed, this last instance exemplifies the fact that concepts may include affective components. Because concepts are embodied in classes of experiences they include all the elements of experiences that may occur in common—perceptual and cognitive elements as well as motivational and emotional elements. My concept of "stone" may reflect, let us say, my positive delight in collecting new varieties of minerals, whereas your concept may reflect the fact that you had unpleasant experiences with stones—having them thrown at you in a riot, or finding lots of them in your garden. Osgood's "semantic differential,"[13] in which one is asked to rate one's concepts on scales such as good-bad, strong-weak, fast-slow, active-passive, light-heavy, pungent-bland, etc., is a way of indexing certain relatively universal cognitive and affective components of individual experiences as classed in concepts; it would perhaps more properly be called an "experiential differential" than a "semantic differential." The fact that fairly consistent results are obtained when concept ratings from different people are compared or averaged implies that people tend to have generally similar kinds of experiences, at least within a given culture.

It has already been suggested earlier that since man lives in an essentially homogeneous physical and biological environment and a partially homogeneous social environment, it is inevitable that a large number of concepts arrived at by individual people should be the same or at least so nearly identical in their essential attributes as to be called the same; these concepts we may call *conceptual invariants*. We can be sure that throughout the world people have much the same concepts of *sun, man, day, animal, flower, walking, falling, softness,* etc., by whatever names they may be called. The fact that they have names is incidental; there are even certain concepts that for one reason or another (a taboo, for example) may remain nameless.

It is probably when we enter into the realms of science and technology and of social phenomena that the concepts attained by different people will differ most. In science and technology concepts vary chiefly because of differences, over the world, in the levels of scientific and technological knowledge reached; and in the social sphere they will differ chiefly because of the truly qualitative differences in the ways cultures are organized. Nevertheless, within a given community there will be a high degree of commonality in the concepts recognized and attained, in the sense that there will be relatively high agreement among people as to the attributes that are criterial for a given concept. For example, even though types of families vary widely over the world, the concept of *family* within a given culture is reasonably homogeneous. At the same time, differences in intellectual and educational levels will account for differences in the sheer number of concepts attained by individuals within a given culture.

WORDS AND THEIR MEANINGS

In the learning of language, words (and other elements in a linguistic system, including phonemes, morphemes, and syntactical patterns) come to be perceived as distinct entities, and in this sense they form one class of perceptual invariants along with the perceptual invariants that represent common objects, feelings, and events. The child must learn to perceive the various instances of a given sound or word as similar, and eventually to differentiate the several contexts in which a given sound or sound pattern is used. (We know of an instance of a very young child who somehow learned to react violently to the word "no," but she would react just as violently to the word "know," even when it was embedded in a sentence. The process of differentiation took a considerable time.)

Many words or higher units of the linguistic system come to stand for, or name, the concepts that have been learned pre-verbally. Certainly this is true for a long list of words that stand for particular things or classes of things, qualities, and events. For the English language, these categories correspond roughly to proper and common nouns; adjectives; and verbs of action, perception, and feeling. It is perhaps less clear that "function words" like prepositions and conjunctions, or grammatical markers like the past tense sign can represent concepts, but a case can be made for this. For example, prepositions like *in, to, above, below, beside, near* correspond to concepts of relative spatial position in a surprisingly complex and subtle way; and conjunctions like *and, but, however, or* correspond to concepts of logical inclusion and exclusion, similarity and difference of propositions, etc.

The processes by which words come to "stand for" or correspond to concepts can best be described in psychological terms. Without going into the details here, we can only say that in every case there is some sort of reinforcing condition that brands a word as being associated with a given concept. This is true whether the word is learned as what Skinner[14] calls a *mand* (as when a child learns the meaning of *water* as a consequence of having water brought whenever he says "water") or as a *tact* (as where the child is praised or otherwise reinforced for saying "water" when he sees or experiences water), because in either case the word is paired contiguously with the concept *as an experience*. The connection between a word and the concept or experience with which it stands in relation must work in either direction: the word must evoke the concept and the concept must evoke the word.

As a physical symbol, a word is a cultural artifact that takes the same, or nearly the same, form throughout a speech community. It is a standardized product on which the speech community exercises a considerable degree of quality control. Not so with concepts, which as we have seen may vary to some extent with the individual, depending on his experiences of the referents of the words. Society does, however, maintain a degree of "quality control" on the referential meaning of words. The conditions under which the use of words is rewarded or not rewarded—either by successful or unsuccessful communication or by direct social approval or disapproval—can be looked upon as constituting the "rules of usage" of a word, and these rules of usage define the *denotative meaning* of a term. Thus, there is a rule of usage such that the noun *mother* can be used only for a certain kind of kinship relation. One thinks of denotative meaning as something that is socially prescribed. Connotative meaning, however, banks heavily on those aspects of concepts that are widely shared yet non-criterial and perhaps affective (emotional) in content. "Mother" as a noun might evoke various emotional feelings depending upon one's experience with mothers.

Perhaps it is useful to think of words, meanings, and concepts as forming *three* somewhat independent series. The words in a language can be thought of as a series of physical entities—either spoken or written. Next, there exists a set of "meanings" which stand in complex relationships to the set of words. These relationships may be described by the rules of usage that have developed by the processes of socialization and communication. A "meaning" can be thought of as a standard of communicative behavior that is shared by those who speak a language. Finally, there exist "concepts"; the classes of experience formed in individuals either independently of language processes or in close dependence on language processes.

The interrelations found among these three series are complex: almost anyone can give instances where a word may have many "meanings," or in which a given "meaning" corresponds to several different words. The relationships between societally-standardized "meanings" and individually-formed "concepts" are likewise complex, but of a somewhat different nature. It is a question of how well each individual has learned these relationships, and at least in the sphere of language and concepts, education is largely a process whereby the individual learns either to attach societally-standardized words and meanings to the concepts he has already formed, or to form new concepts that properly correspond to societally-standardized words and meanings. A "meaning" of a word is, therefore, a societally-standardized concept, and when we say that a word stands for or names a concept it is understood that we are speaking of concepts that are shared among the members of a speech community.

To the extent that individual concepts differ even though they possess shared elements, misunderstandings can arise. My concept of "several" may correspond to the range "approximately three to five," where yours may correspond to "approximately five to fifteen." Speech communities may differ, too, in the exact ranges in which they standardize meanings. The word *infant* seems to include a higher age range in Great Britain (in the phrase "infants' schools") than it does in the United States, and in legal contexts the word may even refer to anyone who has not attained some legal age like twenty-one years.

The fact that words vary in meaning according to context has given rise to one form of a "context theory of meaning" which seems to allege that the meaning of a word is to be found in its context; this is only true, however, in the sense that the context may provide a *clue* as to the particular meaning (or standardized concept) with which a word is intended to be associated. In fact, the clue usually takes the form of an indication of one or more elements of a concept. For example, in the phrase *A light load* the context suggests (though it does not determine absolutely) that *light* is to be taken as the opposite of heavy because loads vary more importantly in weight than in their color, whereas the context in *A light complexion* suggests the element of color because complexions can vary in color but only very improbably in weight. It is not surprising that normal language texts have been found to have redundancy, for the elements of concepts suggested by the words in a sentence are often overlapping.

Frequently context is the key to the fact that a word is being used in an archaic or unusual sense. A student who cannot square the usual meaning of *smug* with its use in the following lines from Shakespeare's *Henry IV* (Part I):

> And here the smug and silver Trent shall run
> In a new channel, fair and evenly

had better resort to a dictionary, where he will find that an earlier meaning of *smug* is *trim, neat*. We cannot dwell here on the interesting ways in which words change in meaning historically, often in response to changes in emphasis given to the various criterial attributes embodied in the concepts corresponding to words. Just as one example, though, consider the historical change of meaning of "meat" from (originally) "any kind of food" to "edible part of animal body, flesh," where the criterial attribute "part of animal body" gradually came to be reinforced alongside the attribute "edible thing."

DEFINITIONS

What, by the way, is the function of a dictionary definition in the light of the system of ideas being presented here? Aside from the few instances where dictionary definitions present pictures or drawings of the items being defined, two main techniques are used in dictionary entries: (1) the use of verbal equivalents, and (2) the use of formal definition by stating *genus et differentia*. The use of verbal equivalents, as where we are told that *smug* can mean "trim, smooth, sleek," has the function of evoking either a (hopefully) previously known concept to which both the defined word and the defining word stand in the same relation, or a series of (hopefully) previously known concepts from whose common elements the reader can derive the concept to which the defined word properly stands in relation. The use of a formal definition, on the other hand, literally "marks off the boundaries of" the concept by first indicating what it has in common with other experiences (*genus*) and then indicating in what respects or attributes (*differentia*) it differs from other experiences. For example, if we are told that *tarn* is a small mountain lake or pool, we know that in many respects it is similar to other lakes or pools—that it is an enclosed, contained body of water, but that it is a special kind of lake of a given size and location. One could, therefore, presumably acquire the concept named *tarn* by learning to make this response only in connection with the criterial attributes defining it. What could be simpler, particularly if one is verbally told what the criterial attributes are? The only kind of intellectual mishap would occur, one would think, when one of the attributes is misunderstood or overlooked. Calling Lake George (in the Adirondacks) a *tarn* would be grossly to neglect or misunderstand the element of small size.

CONCEPT FORMATION RESEARCH

We are now in a position to inquire into the possible relevance of concept formation research to the learning of the meanings and concepts associated with words in a language.

Practically all concept formation research since the days of Hull[15] has been concerned with essentially the following task: the subject is presented with a series of instances which are differentiated in some way; either the task is finding out in what way the several instances match up with one of a small number of names, or (in the simpler case) it is one of discovering why some instances are "positive" (i.e., instances of the "concept" the experimenter has in mind) or "negative" (not instances of the "concept"). Typically the stimulus material consists of simple visual material characterized by a number of clearly salient dimensions—e.g., the color of the figures, the geometrical shape of the figures, the number of figures, the number of borders, the color of the background, etc. Occasionally the critical characteristics of the concept are not clearly in view—as in Hull's experiment where the critical stroke elements of Chinese characters tended to be masked by the rest of the figures, or as in Bouthilet's[16] experiment where the critical feature was the inclusion of letters found in the stimulus word. Sometimes the critical elements are semantic elements of words, as in Freedman and Mednick's experiment[17] in which the task was to find the common semantic element in a series of words such as *gnat, needle, stone,* and *canary.*

Thus, there are two elements to be studied in any concept-formation task: (1) the attributes which are criterial to the concept—their nature and number, the number of values each attribute has and the discriminability of these values, and the salience of the attributes themselves—that is, whether the attributes command attention and are readily perceivable, and (2) the information-handling task required of the subject in view of the order in which positive and negative instances are presented and the amount of information concerning the concept that is furnished by each presentation. Most of what we know about this kind of concept attainment task can be summarized in the following statements:

1. Concept attainment becomes more difficult as the number of relevant attributes increases, the number of values of attributes increases, and the salience of the attributes decreases.
2. Concept attainment becomes more difficult as the information load that must be handled by the subject in order to solve the concept increases, and as the information is increasingly carried by negative rather than positive instances.

3. Various strategies for handling the information load are possible, and some are in the long run more successful than others.

Lenneberg seems to agree with much that Carroll stated. He stresses the flexibility of criteria for categorization. In this regard, he asserts that categorization "is a creative process of cognitive organization rather than an arbitrary convention." He considers concept formation a primary cognitive process—considering Piaget, we can certainly see how this would be true—but he considers naming a secondary process. Thus he concludes that a word labels a process (a concept-formation process) or a family of such processes, rather than a concept or a category of concepts:[18]

TOWARD A BIOLOGICAL CONCEPTION OF SEMANTICS

The activity of *naming* or, in general, of using words may be seen as the human peculiarity to make explicit a process that is quite universal among higher animals, namely, the organization of sensory data. All vertebrates are equipped to superimpose categories of functional equivalence upon stimulus configurations, to classify objects in such a way that a single type of response is given to any one member of a particular stimulus category. The criteria or nature of categorization have to be determined empirically for each species. Frogs may jump to a great variety of flies and also to a specific range of dummy-stimuli, provided the stimuli preserve specifiable characteristics of the "real thing."

Furthermore, most higher animals have a certain capacity for discrimination. They may learn or spontaneously begin to differentiate certain aspects within the first global category, perhaps by having their attention directed to certain details or by sharpening their power of observation. In this differentiation process initial categories may become subdivided and become mutually exclusive, or a number of coexisting general and specific categories or partially overlapping categories may result. Again, the extent of a species' *differentiation capacity* is biologically given and must be ascertained empirically for each species. Rats cannot make the same range of distinctions that dogs can make, and the latter are different in this respect from monkeys. The interspecific differences cannot merely be explained by differences in peripheral sensory thresholds. Apparently, a function of higher, central processes is involved that has to do with cognitive organization.

Most primates and probably many species in other mammalian orders have the capacity to relate various categories to one another and thus to respond to *relations* between things rather than to things themselves; an example is "to respond to the largest of any collection of things." Once more, it is a matter of empirical research to discover the limits of relations that a species is capable of responding to.

In summary, most animals organize the sensory world by a process of *categorization*, and from this basic mode of organization two further processes derive: *differentiation* or discrimination, and interrelating of categories or the perception of and tolerance for *transformations*.... In man these organizational activities are usually called concept-formation; but it is clear that there is no formal difference between man's concept-formation and animal's propensity for responding to categories of stimuli. There is, however, a substantive difference. The total possibilities for categorization are clearly not identical across species.

1. *Words as Labels for Categorization Process* The words that constitute the dictionary of a natural language are a sample of labels of categories natural to

our species; they are not tags of specific objects. When names have unique referents, such as Michelangelo, Matterhorn, Waterloo, they may be incorporated into discourse but are not considered part of the lexicon. Thus most words may be said to label realms of concepts rather than physical things. This must be true for otherwise we should have great difficulty in explaining why words refer to *open* classes. We cannot define the category labeled *house* by enumerating all objects that are given that name. Any new object that satisfies certain criteria (and there is an infinity of such objects) may be assigned that label. It is easier to say what such criteria are *not* than to say what they are. They are not a finite set of objectively measurable variables such as physical dimensions, texture, color, acidity, etc. (except for a few words, which constitute a special case . . .). We cannot predict accurately which object might be named *house* and which not by looking only at the physical measurements of those objects. Therefore, categorization and the possibility of word-assignment must usually be founded on something more abstract.

The infant who is given a word and has the task of finding the category labeled by this word does not seem to start with a working hypothesis that a specific, concrete object (his father) uniquely bears the name *daddy*; instead, initially the word appears to be used as the label of a general and open category, roughly corresponding to the adult category *people* or *men*. Thus categorization by a principle, or the formation of an (abstract) concept is apparently prior to and more primitive than the association of a sound pattern with a specific sensory experience. The same thing may be expressed in different words; stimulus generalization is prior to stimulus discrimination.

Let us consider more closely the process of categorization that underlies semantics. Is it possible to characterize this cognitive activity any further? For instance, if the classification criteria are not usually physical dimensions, what are they? The most outstanding feature of the "criteriality" is its great flexibility. Sometimes the criterion is primarily one of "use that man makes of the objects"; sometimes it is a given aspect; sometimes a certain emotional state that all objects in that class may elicit in the viewer. Any one category is not definable by only one, consistently applied criterion. For instance, the word *house* is usually applicable to structures that serve as shelter for men, animals, or objects. But the criterion for categorizing is frequently changed by metaphorical or quasi-metaphorical extensions, as in House of Lords, house of cards, house of God, the house of David, etc. The ease with which the criterion for categorization may be changed and the naturalness with which we understand such extensions point to the fact that categorization is a creative process of cognitive organization rather than an arbitrary convention. It is precisely due to the absence of rigidly adhered to classification criteria that not only the physical world can be grouped and the groups named, but the classification criteria may be bent, stretched, and altered to include virtual figments, that is, physically nonexisting entities, resulting in words without reference (or obvious referents), but which label a concept (for example, the word *ghost*). The procedure also makes possible the development of the meaning of the word *times* in the phrase four *times* five.

The abstractness underlying meanings in general, which has been the focus of so much philosophizing since antiquity, may best be understood by considering concept-formation the primary cognitive process, and naming (as well as acquiring a name) the secondary cognitive process. Concepts are superimpositions upon the physically given; they are modes of ordering or dealing with sensory data. They are not so much the *product* of man's cognition, but conceptualization is the *cognitive process itself*. Although this process is not peculiar to man (because it essentially results from the mode of operation of a mechanism that can only respond in limited ways to a wide variety of inputs), man has developed the behavioral peculiarity of attaching words to certain types of concept formation. The words (which persist through time because they may be repeated) make the underlying conceptualization process look much more static than it actually is, as we shall demonstrate presently. Cognition must be the psychological manifestation of a physiological process. It does not appear to be a mosaic of static concepts, or a storehouse of thoughts, or an archive of memorized sense-impressions. The task of cognitive organization never comes to an end and is never completed "in order to be used later." Words are not the labels of concepts completed earlier and stored away; they are the labels of a *categorization process or family of such processes*. Because of the dynamic nature of the underlying process, the referents of words can so easily change, meanings can be extended, and categories are always open. *Words tag the processes by which the species deals cognitively with its environment.*

This theoretical position also elucidates the problem of translation or the equation of meanings across natural languages. If words label modes of cognizing, we would expect that all semantic systems have certain formal commonalities. For instance, if we hear a given word used in connection with a given object or phenomenon, we are able to intuit the general usage of that word—it does not have to be paired with 200 similar objects or phenomena before we can make predictions whether the name applies to a new object. Man's cognition functions within biologically given limits. On the other hand, there is also freedom within these limits. Thus every individual may have highly idiosyncratic thoughts or conceptualize in a peculiar way or, in fact, may choose somewhat different modes of cognitive organization at different times faced with identical sensory stimuli. His vocabulary, which is much more limited and unchangeable than his capacity for conceptualizing, can be made to cover the novel conceptual processes, and other men, by virtue of having essentially the same cognitive capacities, can understand the semantics of his utterances, even though the words cover new or slightly different conceptualizations. Given this degree of freedom, it becomes reasonable to assume that natural languages always have universally understandable types of semantics, but may easily have different extensions of meanings, and that, therefore, specific semantic categories are not coterminous across languages.

It does not follow from this that differences in semantics are signs of obligatory differences in thought processes, as assumed by Whorf (1956)[19] and many others. The modes of conceptualization that happen to be tagged by a given natural language need not, and apparently do not, exert restrictions upon an individual's freedom of conceptualizing. This will be discussed subsequently.

2. *Differentiation of Categories*   Since there is freedom, within limits, to categorize, there must also be freedom to substructure a category. Not only can the infant adjust his initial broad category *doggy* from all quadrupeds to the species *Canis familiaris*, but child and man alike are free to superimpose further classifications upon inclusive categories, and the criteria for the formation of these narrower categories or for the process of substructuring in general are as variegated as those for the initial categories. Thus differentiation may result from labeling the direction of attention to one aspect of the object (high, wet, bulging) or from differentiating some relationship that exists between the speaker and the object (*this* noun, *that* noun). Instances of this type of differentiation process make it obvious that words cannot be attachment to things, but only acoustic markers

of cognitive processes—signals of how the individual deals with the task of organizing input. Since languages may differ in the peculiar cognitive process that is being tagged lexically, the semantics of a language reflect merely one of many possible ways of dealing with the cognitive organization task.

Differentiation may result in peculiar hierarchies of inclusiveness-exclusiveness of categories or in contrasting categories as in antonyms, partially overlapping categories as synonyms, etc. The manifold structures produced by the basic freedom of differentiation points, once more, points to the underlying dynamics of the semantic process. A lexicon is like a photograph that freezes motion. Differentiation is part of the organization processes, and it goes on continuously and in many ways. A natural language captures some of those ways, but it is not as fixed or as rigid a system as it may appear; in fact, it does reflect the ongoing creative or productive process if analyzed with care. Naming is a method and a process more than it is a rigidly established relationship. The speaker who must communicate a peculiar form of substructuring a category will immediately take recourse to novel ways of naming, as we shall see from the empirical experiments described below.

3. *Interrelating of Categories (Transformations)* The transformational process of syntax . . . has its counterpart in semantics also. Just as certain structural principles underlying given sentence-types bear relations to one another, so do the similarity-principles that are the basis for the formation of categories. For instance, there are objects called knife, fork, and spoon. We may extract some common denominator from these and choose to give the abstraction a label, say *flatware*. Other objects, such as cork-screw, ladle, and rolling pin may be subsumed under the categorical label *utensils*. There are certain relationships between the two categories that are completely constant. For instance, certain similarity-relationships hold for any object that is part of *flatware* and any object that is part of *utensils*. The cognitive calculus with categories is easily reflected in naming habits. This goes so far as to enable us to write semantic rules that have the same formal structure as syntactic rules and that predict what kinds of words may be interchanged in sentence frames without changing the grammaticality of the sentence. . . .

Categories may also be related to one another such that the relationship itself is labeled by morphemes or words (for example, *by*, *-ing*, *for*, $-s_{pl}$, *is*, etc.). The semantics of these relational elements perhaps illustrates best how words do not refer to real things but to cognitive processes. It is in connection with the cognitive process of relating abstract concepts (name categories or structural sentence-types) that the intimate relationship between semantics and syntax is most clearly revealed.

4. *Preliminary Conclusions* The basic cognitive mechanisms underlying semantics appear to be similar to those of syntax, namely processes of categorization, differentiation, and interrelation (transformation). Indeed, the latter two are merely aspects of the categorization process itself. This argument may also be extended to include the cognitive processes underlying phonology. Although categorization is a universal phenomenon in the animal kingdom, the categorizations peculiar to language operate through the application of highly species-specific principles.

Naming is a process, not a catalogue of rigid conventions. There are two types of constraints that determine naming-behavior: the biological constraint upon the physiological processes that determine the species' cognitive capacities, particularly the conditions under which similarities are recognized; and the constraint necessitated by the communicative function subserved by naming. Notice, however, that the naming process may go on in the absence of communication. Neologisms are created and assigned meanings by the schizophrenic patient or the genius creating words for his highly idiosyncratic concepts, regardless of whether they will actually transfer information from one individual to another.

It is a matter of social dynamics, roles, values, or group-mechanisms whether anybody will take the trouble to discover what conceptualization process was being tagged by such neologisms. Communication is a social phenomenon, whereas naming is an intrapersonal one; the intrapersonal process may become a social one by virtue of enormous similarities between the cognitive functioning of all individuals and an apparent specific motivation in humans to interact socially. Again, group cohesiveness is a widespread phenomenon in the animal kingdom, but the mechanisms vary greatly from species to species. In man, the prime vehicle of this interaction is the mutual adjustment of concept formation, tagged by words.

CONCEPTS VARY WITH DEVELOPMENT

If concept formation is viewed as a process, it should not be surprising to discover that human being's concept-formation ability varies with development. A relationship would be anticipated between developmental psychology and the discipline of psychology that has traditionally examined concept formation. Indeed, there is such a bridge.

Kagan makes the point "that an individual's conceptual structure passes through different stages over the course of development. These stages are characterized by qualitatively different structures, not by mere accretion of more or richer concepts."

Here are the highlights of Kagan's comments concerning a developmental approach to a conceptual growth. He postulates *"cognitive units, cognitive processes,* and *determinants of attention"*:[20]

Cognitive units are the hardware of mental work; the things that get manipulated in mentation. Three basic classes of cognitive units include *perceptual schemata, language units,* and *rules of transformation* or principles. Cognitive processes refer to the more dynamic events that act on the cognitive units, much like catalysts act on basic compounds in chemical solution. The processes of *labeling, evaluation, hypothesis production,* and *transformation* are fundamental. Consider a typical problem-solving situation in which the child is confronted with a set of initial thoughts that are problematical or external information which he has to resolve. The first task is to label the information presented, a phase that Guilford calls "cognition." The child then generates hypotheses in accord with these labels. At this point the process of evaluation becomes relevant. The child should pause to evaluate the validity of his hypotheses and initial labels. Finally, the child implements the hypothesis he decided on with appropriate transformation rules. Labeling, hypothesis generation, evaluation, and implementation of transformations are basic cognitive processes. Perceptual schemata, language symbols, and rules are the units that are acted on by these cognitive processes.

The final category in our vocabulary list includes determinants of attentional involvement. Problems of learning, relearning, recall, and problem solving require attention to the task at hand. Attentional involvement is the basic medium in which cognitive activity occurs, and degree of attention governs the accuracy and efficiency of the final cognitive product. Without attentional involvement, these processes are not effectively activated and new information is not assimilated. The basic determinants of attention fall into two categories: violations of expected events and personological variables which we usually call motivation and conflict.

One of the motivational factors is to differentiate self from peers, adds Kagan. Another is to maximize similarity to an adult role model. A third is anxiety. A fourth relates to expectancy of success or failure. He continues:

Children quickly develop different expectations of success or failure in intellectual tasks. Unfortunately, the most frequent and prepotent reaction to an expectancy of failure is decreased involvement in the task and subsequent withdrawal. Educators have been guilty of minimizing the critical role which a child's expectancy of failure plays in shaping his behavior in a school situation. The child's motives are contingent on expectation of success or failure, and motives are sloughed or adopted with zeal depending on the degree to which the child believes he can attain the goals that gratify the motive. Growth of specific motives and persistence at task mastery hang delicately on the balance between hope and fear.

During infancy, Kagan continues, the child acquires schemata and learning to orient to the external world. Variables controlling attention include movement and contrast characteristics of the stimuli, the acquired reward value of the stimuli, the degree to which the stimuli violate earlier learned schemata, and the degree to which the stimuli are conditioned to fear.

We shall argue that the most important determinant of attention in the human infant is based on prior learning and varies with the degree to which external stimuli match or mismatch the familiarity of the schema that the infant has developed. [We view a schema as] a cognitive representation of an external stimulus. This representation contains an arrangement of elements. Both the arrangement and the elements are critical. . . .

[During infancy] the most important determinant of attention is the age of the schema in the child's mind. With age a child comes to know a stimulus more completely, which is another way of saying that a schema for a stimulus pattern becomes firmer. If we were able to slice into the child's mind at any time and study the collection of schemata and the rate of development of each, we would see some very old schemata, some moderately old schemata, and some emergent schemata. An emergent schema today (one that has just been freshly formed) may be an old one next week or next month. As schemata mature, the child becomes capable of assimilating new related stimulus patterns and the process proceeds. A basic principle of attentional involvement states that well-established schemata [and] extreme violations of schemata will elicit minimal attention because they have too much or too little uncertainty in them.

When recognition is immediate there is minimal uncertainty, for the stimulus matches the schema perfectly and attention is not necessary. *Attention will be maximal to moderately uncertain stimuli that match emergent schemata or stimuli that elicit moderate uncertainty.* When the stimulus does not match the schema at all, attention wanes. . . . Material that has already been learned is regarded as boring to the child; material that is too difficult is also avoided because the child has no cognitive structures to assimilate the information. It is of importance to note this ... relation between age of schema—or age of conceptual structure—and attention holds as well at 16 weeks of age as it does at 16 years. [Experienced schoolteachers recognize this.] After a principle has been presented to a fifth grader there is often drill on different arrangements of that principle before new components are added. The infant data validate the implicit wisdom of this approach.... An infant's attention is attracted to those stimuli that have been associated with primary gratifications.

On the one hand, Kagan contends that the child may learn things even though he makes no outward behavioral response. He notes that "one can tell a child to watch the action of a teacher but not make any overt rehearsal himself and then the next day ask the child to act out a response he learned through attention but never issued during the attentional phase." On the other hand, he asserts that "it is more delicate and difficult to study the dynamics of the perceptual system; but individual differences in these variables, in the rate of habituation and differentiation and information processing, may be more prognostic of future levels of cognitive development than motor coordinations that are so public during the first year and a half."

Between the ages of eighteen months and entrance to school, Kagan adds, "the child acquires a set of symbols that allows him to categorize and conceptualize aspects of his environment." There is growth of a labeling vocabulary, and there are three fundamental ways of organizing stimuli. First, "objects are regarded as similar because they are functionally related to each other in terms of their action upon one another or their geographical or temporal contiguity"; for example, "a hole is to dig." A second is analytic: "an orange is an object with a skin." A third is categorical: "an orange is a fruit."

During the early school years, before age ten, growth occurs in the formulation of rules and in the habit of evaluation. Kagan cites how children at this stage solve problems, and relates this stage to reading:

In the first phase the child labels or comprehends the initial information. At this point the adequacy and richness of his labeling vocabulary is most critical. Notice, however, that there is a phase of evaluation in which the child should pause to consider the validity of his initial coding. When most adults are reading a newspaper or a book, they seldom make mistakes, and we minimize the role of evaluation in initial coding. For a child learning how to read or mastering basic vocabulary forms, however, the role of evaluation is critical. If the child reads *nickel* for *pickle, 10 cents* for *5 cents, cat* for *bat,* he is not likely to arrive at the correct solution of the problem. The initial decoding or comprehension phase is followed by a proliferation of hypotheses. Now the role of evaluation is most important, for in many problem situations two or three hypotheses may occur in close succession and each one may appear appropriate. Now the child must evaluate the differential validity of each of these hypotheses. The next stage involves the implementation of the chosen hypothesis, and now the possession of rules is important, whether the rules be formal algorithms, as in the case of arithmetic, or informal mediational nests, as in the case of questions such as, "How many ways can you use a newspaper?" Evaluation of the validity of the final response is important, for it appears that the children called "high-creative" often do not evaluate the accuracy of their responses and emerge with more "creative" answers. In the final phase an answer is reported to an examiner or written on a piece of paper, and once again evaluation of the validity of the response is an important process. In sum, evaluation of the validity of a cognitive act touches the problem-solving process at three places—in the initial coding and comprehension phase, in the selection of a correct hypothesis to implement, and, in the end, in the evaluation of the accuracy of the transformation solution performed.

Kagan concludes:

A child's intellectual performance in or out of school [may be viewed] as the result of the interaction of five factors—elemental skills, strategies of processing information, motives, standards, and sources of anxiety. The elemental skills involve a primary set of labeling symbols and rules. The child must have a minimal vocabulary level in order to understand speech, comprehend the written word, and report orally the product of his thinking. He must also have learned certain rules that represent combinations of symbols. . . . Rules and vocabulary are the basic equipment for the production of thought.

VYGOTSKY'S VIEW OF CONCEPTUAL DEVELOPMENT

A second view of the developmental nature of the conceptual process is provided by Vygotsky.[21] At first the young child views words as properties of objects. However, Vygotsky contends that as the child develops inner speech (which stems from differentiation of social and egocentric functions), the speech structures become the basic structures of the child's thinking.

Before puberty, the child does not possess concepts as such, but complexes, and words really denote a vague syncretic conglomeration of objects: in fact, the word is part of such a conglomeration.

Vygotsky designates stages of conceptual development. In the first stage, the child categorizes by trial and error, or he organizes things because of their spatial relationships in his visual field, or he takes elements from different heaps and lumps them together.

In the second stage, he thinks in complexes. Says Vygotsky:[22]

Individual objects are united in the child's mind not only by his subjective impressions but also by *bonds actually existing between these objects*. [The child] has partly outgrown his egocentrism. . . . Remains of complex thinking persist in the language of adults. Family names are perhaps the best example of this. Any family name, "Petrov," let us say, subsumes individuals in a manner closely resembling that of the child's complexes. The child at that stage of development thinks in family names, as it were; the universe of individual objects becomes organized for him by being grouped into separate, mutually related "families."

The child discovers the bonds underlying complexes by direct experience, and "any factually present connection may lead to the inclusion of a given element into the complex." Thus a child develops "associative complexes." Vygotsky defines them this way: "To the child at that stage the word ceases to be the 'proper name' of an individual object; it becomes the family name of a group of objects related to one another in many kinds of ways, just as the relationships in human families are many and different."[23]

The child sometimes groups objects by the one trait in which they differ. He will also form groups on the basis of "participation in the same practical operation": knives, forks, and spoons, for instance. Then there is the chain complex, in which each link is as important as the next. The child does not accord any significance to a single trait as he would in forming a concept. "Often a remote similarity is enough to create a bond." Next there is the diffuse complex. There is a kind of fluidity of attributes; in fact, this amounts to the child's version of a generalization. This leads to the pseudo-concept, which is functionally equivalent to a concept. This is "predetermined by the meaning a given word already has in the language of adults. . . . The pseudo-concept serves as the connecting link between thinking in complexes and thinking in concepts. . . . Verbal intercourse with adults thus becomes a powerful factor in the development of the child's concepts."[24]

The child, now approaching adolescence, is about to develop the ability to perform conceptual thinking. The difference between thinking in complexes and advanced thinking is this:[25]

The principal function of complexes is to establish bonds and relationships. Complex thinking begins the unification of scattered impressions; by organizing discrete elements of experience into groups, it creates a basis for later generalizations.

But the advanced concept presupposes more than unification. To form such a concept it is also necessary *to abstract, to single out* elements, and to view the abstracted elements apart from the totality of the concrete experience in which they are embedded. In genuine concept formation, it is equally important to unite and to separate. Synthesis must be combined with analysis.

So during the third stage in the child's development, the child will group on the basis of maximum similarity but will shift to grouping on the basis of a single attribute. He is forming potential concepts. Vygotsky concludes:[26]

Our investigation has shown that a concept is formed, not through the interplay of associations, but through an intellectual operation in which all the elementary mental functions participate in a specific combination. This operation is guided by the use of words as the means of actively centering attention, of abstracting certain traits, synthesizing them, and symbolizing them by a sign.

The processes leading to concept formation develop along two main lines. The first is complex formation: The child unites diverse objects in groups under a common "family name"; this process passes through various stages. The second line of development is the formation of "potential concepts," based on singling out certain common attributes. In both, the use of the word is an integral part of the developing processes, and the word maintains its guiding function in the formation of genuine concepts, to which these processes lead.

There is empirical evidence to support these developmental views. Gleason reports:[27]

We asked some questions about a number of compound nouns we had noticed in the children's vocabulary list, words like *birthday* and *blackboard* and *football* and *Thanksgiving* that are clearly made up of two separate words put together. They all seemed to be fairly obvious. At least we thought that all adults would be able to tell us that a handkerchief is called a handkerchief because it is a kerchief that you hold in your hand. We wanted to know if the children had noticed the separate parts of the word. The general form of the question was "Why do you think a birthday is called a birthday?" Unless the name happened to coincide with some very important feature, to the child, of the thing referred to, the children ignored the parts of the word and mentioned what to them was most important. A fireplace is called a fireplace because you make a fire in it, but there is not really much else to say about fireplaces. On the other hand, to children a birthday is called a birthday not because you are celebrating the day of your birth but because you eat cake or get presents, and that is how they responded. And six out of ten first graders think that Thanksgiving is called Thanksgiving because you eat lots of turkey. While there was less agreement about these words than there was in the production of plurals and past tenses, there was still a great deal of agreement in the *types* of response we got.

Some of the subjects seemed to have completely private meanings for some of these words. They knew what the words referred to and how to use them, but their ideas about the words were rather amusing. One little boy said that an airplane is called an airplane because it is a plain thing that goes in the air. Another child said that breakfast is called breakfast because you have to eat it fast to get to school on time. Several subjects thought that Friday is called Friday because it is the day you eat fried fish. And two of our subjects thought that a handkerchief is called a handkerchief because you hold it in your hand and go "kerchoo." One of them was six years old and the other was a college graduate. Of course all of our subjects used these words perfectly correctly in their speech, and this part of the experiment was quite separate from asking them to demonstrate their control of the use of the plural, the past tense, or other English inflexions. Here we were asking them what they thought about words that we knew were already in their vocabularies. In a sense it would appear that to speak English it does not matter what you think a word means as long as you use it correctly.

By and large, the type of response we got depended very much on the age or stage of development of the subjects. Four-year-olds saw no sense to the questions. For them the name of a thing is a part of it. A birthday is called a birthday because it *is* a birthday. Five-year-olds said a birthday was called a birthday because you got presents. Some six-year-olds had begun to notice at least the *day* part, and adults mentioned both parts of the word.

CAN CONCEPT DEVELOPMENT BE FOSTERED?

We have seen the developmental nature of the child's conceptual processes and that, as far as Vygotsky is concerned, the child does not develop genuine concepts until he is eleven or twelve. This idea is similar to the one expressed by Piaget: the child does not develop formal thought, or logical thinking, until he is eleven or twelve. What, then, is the role of the school in terms of teaching concepts?

"Practical experience ... shows that direct teaching of concepts is impossible and fruitless," Vygotsky asserts. "A teacher who tries to do this usually accomplishes nothing but empty verbalism, a parrotlike repetition of words by the child, simulating a knowledge of the corresponding concepts but actually covering up a vacuum."[28]

However, Vygotsky believes something can be done. He agrees with Piaget on the importance of social interaction for the development of thought, but he points out that Piaget was studying the development of spontaneous concepts. What about nonspontaneous concepts? For example, what about scientific concepts? Vygotsky says:[29]

The development of nonspontaneous concepts must possess all the traits peculiar to child thought at each developmental level because these concepts are not simply acquired by rote but evolve with the aid of strenuous mental activity on the part of the child himself. We believe that the two processes—the development of spontaneous and of nonspontaneous concepts—are related and constantly influence each other. They are parts of a single process: the development of concept formation, which is affected by varying external and internal conditions but is essentially a unitary process, not a conflict of antagonistic, mutually exclusive forms of mentation. Instruction is one of the principal sources of the schoolchild's concepts and is also a powerful force in directing their evolution; it determines the fate of his total mental development.

Vygotsky cites Piaget's reasoning as to how the child becomes aware —and master of his own thoughts: We become aware of what "we are doing in proportion to the difficulty we experience in adapting to a situation." And "to become conscious of a mental operation means to transfer it from the plane of action to that of language, i.e., to re-create it in the imagination so that it can be expressed in words."[30]

But he counters that children become aware of differences earlier than they become aware of similarities "because awareness of similarity requires a more advanced structure of generalization and conceptualization than awareness of dissimilarity."[31]

Vygotsky agrees with Piaget that the schoolchild is not aware of his conceptual operations, but he cites what he terms "laws governing psychological development. One of them is that consciousness and control appear only at a late stage in the development of a function, after it has been used and practiced unconsciously and spontaneously. In order to subject a function to intellectual and volitional control, we must first possess it." And by "consciousness" he means "awareness of the activity of the mind ... self-reflective awareness."[32]

Therefore, school instruction does have a function in terms of developing the child's conceptual processes. Says Vygotsky:[33]

[It] induces the generalizing kind of perception and thus plays a decisive role in making the child conscious of his own mental processes. Scientific concepts, with their hierarchical system of interrelationships, seem to be the medium within which awareness and mastery first develop, to be transferred later to other concepts and other areas of thought. Reflective consciousness comes to the child through the portals of scientific concepts.... To us it seems obvious that a concept can become subject to consciousness and deliberate control only when it is part of a system.

Vygotsky concludes that what distinguishes spontaneous concepts from scientific concepts is "absence of a system"; the child lacks a system for his spontaneous concepts. He asserts that "all the peculiarities of child thought described by Piaget ... stem from the absence of a system in the child's spontaneous concepts—a consequence of undeveloped relations of generality."[34]

Piaget certainly agrees. He notes "absence of a system and coherence" in the language and thinking of children younger than seven or eight and he asserts that "its disappearance coincides with the advent of genuine argument," for argument causes the need for inner unity of thought and the systematization of opinions.[35]

Manifestations of this "absence of a system" would indicate the need for systematic instruction. For example, Cynthia P. Deutsch reports:[36]

The deficiencies which seem to exist in the slum child have to do in part with cognitive and concept-formation behavior, and these are skills which underlie many problem-solving abilities, even in nonverbal areas. If, as is hypothesized, it is impoverishment of experience which negatively affects the development of these skills, then that impoverishment is associated with a debilitation at the center of the growth of basic learning skills, and not with more superficial, and presumably more easily compensated, skills.

She warns that in the areas of training and curriculum,

it is highly likely that experience alone is not enough to enable the disadvantaged child to overcome the poverty of his background. That is, what is probably necessary is experience that is engineered, labeled, verbalized, and repeated in such a way that it is made relevant both to the child's previous experience and to his later activities. In other words, simply a trip to the zoo will not make up for the child's lack of previous trips, acquaintance with animals, with the use of transportation to get there, and the like.

In support of her contention that structured and systematized instruction is necessary, she notes that migrant children who travel great distances have as little concept of distance, geography, and mileage as slum children who have never been more than ten blocks from home. Both groups of youngsters are termed "disadvantaged," and the unorganized experience of the migrant children apparently had no impact on developing their concepts of distance, geography, and mileage.

To be most effective, it would seem, in systematizing the presentation of concepts (that is, developing categorizing behavior leading to the growth of logical thinking), these questions must still be answered: how to optimize a presentation, and what to present?

SUMMARY

Concept learning is a mental process that arises through discrimination of stimuli and their placement in classes. To form discrimination there must be a series of pertinent events permitting the individual to note critical at- tributes that indicate the ways in which various stimuli are similar and the ways in which they are different. Stimuli with like attributes are grouped into the same category. Thus, contrary to an often-held belief, a concept is not a convention socially agreed upon, but an abstraction formed by the mind. Language, although not required in concept formation, permits the labeling and sharing of concepts.

Concepts vary with development. Children pass through different stages in deriving them. Categories of concepts may be functional, analytical, or categorical. At first children categorize concrete experiences through their subjective impressions. Later they think according to families of experiences in which individual elements are grouped. Approaching adolescence, they are capable of abstraction, which synthesizes attributes of concepts apart from concrete experiences. Thus children do not process true concepts until they are eleven or twelve.

Examples of concepts are evident in vocabulary development, since words are often used as labels for concepts. For example, when someone says, "Pull up a chair," it is possible that what will be pulled up will have four legs, one leg, or no legs, something with or without a back, something made out of a variety of materials. So we have a generalized concept of "chair." If need be, our concept of chair could be further differentiated into categories and labeled "stool," "bench," "wheelchair," "desk chair," and the like.

Categories, and therefore concepts, are also formed in other areas related to reading; phonemes, grammatical structures, and letters are all examples of categories. They are all learned essentially in the same way. From various kinds of experience the human mind identifies critical common attributes that permit a categorization. The job of the teacher is to provide the pertinent experiences necessary, order them, draw children's attention to the critical attributes, and, if necessary, help label the concept. Note that the teacher need not teach generalizations; if the range of instances of the concept is sufficient and suitably redundant, then generalizing comes naturally to the child. What must be highlighted by careful planning are critical differences to support discrimination.

SUMMARY OF CHAPTERS 8 THROUGH 12

Let us review what we have said about mental development.

Using the point of view of Piaget we have learned that the individual acts on incoming data so as to keep his inner organization in line with the state of organization he is able to perceive in the outside world. Thus he works to maintain a state of mental equilibrium. Being a seeker of stimuli, he gathers in (assimilates) through the senses perceptible data from the environment. These new learnings do not fit neatly into the existing mental structure, so the mental structure must be rearranged through the process of accommodation. Physically manipulating objects is necessary for the young child in forming his mental structures. Later the child can perform verbally what he has learned to do in actions. Requiring children to verbalize before they are ready will lead to frustration or to verbalization without real understanding.

Before reaching the age of eleven or twelve the child cannot justify things logically; he sees them only from his own viewpoint. While between six and twelve he may perform problem-solving actions (experiments) accurately, he cannot explain them logically, nor perform them in his mind when concrete referents are not available. Formal reasoning comes about when the individual is able to detach himself from his own viewpoint and the reality of the moment. Reasoning from the viewpoint of another and from mere assumption gradually becomes possible. Direct manipulation of events, discussion, and argument are essential for this development and should play a central part in all curriculum between the ages of six and twelve.

Basic to both language and thought are actions. Language cannot be considered as the source of all thought, but it does structure thought. It serves as a system of notation for thought. Language constructs thought because it is a socially imposed convention. However, language detaches thought from action. Thus language is both a facilitator and a constructive force in thought.

Piaget agrees with the Gestaltic view that there is an innate internal regulatory mechanism structuring and organizing thought, but he believes that this is developed through the activity of the individual in exploring and manipulating the environment. Mental organization comes about not merely by an automatic and fully developed inherited mechanism for equilibrating internal states in response to incoming perceptual data, but also by the activity of the developing child. Both Piaget's view and the Gestaltic view are in agreement that thought comes about through an interaction of the individual with the environment.

Whereas the behaviorist sees behavior as being modified through extrinsic rewards, Piaget believes that the individual actively seeks stimuli and that rewards result internally when equilibrium is reestablished. In addition to sensory stimuli, Piaget believes that motor activities are important in learning.

Concept learning results from the natural propensity to organize the data of perception by grouping. It involves discriminating stimuli, placing them in classes, and at times labeling them. The nature of concepts varies with the child's development. At first categorization is based on subjective, concrete experiences and leads to biased complexes rather than concepts; abstraction becomes possible when the child reaches the age of eleven or twelve.

We are now ready for our discussion of instruction.

NOTES FOR CHAPTER 12

1. Robert M. Gagné, "The Learning of Principles," in *Analyses of Concept Learning*, edited by Herbert J. Klausmeier and Chester W. Harris (New York: Academic Press, 1966), pp. 81–83.
2. F. C. Bartlett, *Thinking: An Experimental and Social Study* (London: Allen & Unwin, 1958).
3. D. E. Berlyne, *Structure and Direction in Thinking* (New York: Wiley, 1965), p. 45.
4. H. H. Kendler, "The Concept of the Concept," in *Categories of Human Learning*, edited by A. W. Melton (New York: Academic Press, 1964), pp. 211–36.
5. Charles E. Osgood, *Method and Theory in Experimental Psychology* (London and New York: Oxford Univ. Press, 1953).
6. John B. Carroll, "Words, Meanings and Concepts," *Harvard Educational Review* 34, 2 (1964), 178–202.
7. James J. Jenkins, "Meaningfulness and Concepts; Concepts and Meaningfulness," in *Analyses of Concept Learning,* p. 68.
8. E. James Archer, "The Psychological Nature of Concepts," in *Analyses of Concept Learning,* p. 37.
9. John B. Carroll, "Words, Meanings and Concepts," 180–90.
10. Earl B. Hunt, *Concept Learning: An Information Processing Problem* (New York: Wiley, 1962).
11. Roger W. Brown and Eric H. Lenneberg, "A Study in Language and Cognition," *J. Abnorm. Soc. Psychol.* 49 (1954), 454–62.
12. John H. Flavell, *The Developmental Psychology of Jean Piaget* (New York: Van Nostrand, 1963).
13. Charles E. Osgood, George J. Suci, and Percy H. Tannebaum, *The Measurement of Meaning* (Urbana: Univ. of Illinois Press, 1957).
14. B. F. Skinner, *Verbal Behavior* (New York: Appleton-Century-Crofts, 1957).
15. C. L. Hull, "Quantitative Aspects of the Evolution of Concepts," *Psychol. Monogr.,* no. 123 (1920).
16. L. Bouthilet, "The Measurement of Intuitive Thinking," unpublished Ph.D. thesis, Univ. of Chicago, 1948.
17. J. L. Freedman and S. A. Mednick, "Ease of Attainment of Concepts as a Function of Response Dominance Variance," *J. Exp. Psychol.* 55 (1958), 463–66.
18. Eric H. Lenneberg, *Biological Foundations of Language* (New York: Wiley, 1967), pp. 331–37.
19. B. L. Whorf, *Language, Thought and Reality,* edited by John B. Carroll (Cambridge: MIT Press, 1956).
20. Jerome Kagan, "A Developmental Approach to Conceptual Growth," in *Analyses of Concept Learning,* pp. 97–112.
21. Lev S. Vygotsky, *Thought and Language* (Cambridge: MIT Press, 1962).
22. Ibid., p. 61.
23. Ibid., p. 62.
24. Ibid., pp. 63–69.
25. Ibid., p. 76.
26. Ibid., p. 81.
27. Jean Berko Gleason, "Language Development in Early Childhood," in *Oral Language and Reading,* edited by James Walden (Champaign, Ill.: National Council of Teachers of English, 1969), pp. 25–26.
28. *Thought and Language,* p. 83.
29. Ibid., p. 85.
30. Ibid., p. 88.
31. Ibid.
32. Ibid., pp. 90–91.
33. Ibid., p. 92.
34. Ibid., p. 116.
35. Jean Piaget, *The Language and Thought of the Child* (Cleveland: World Publishing, Meridian, 1955), p. 91.
36. Cynthia P. Deutsch, "Learning in the Disadvantaged," in *Analyses of Concept Learning,* pp. 201–2.

the child begins to read

Thus far we have studied two perspectives for an understanding of the nature of competence in reading. First, we have offered information on the nature of language. Second, we have discussed the nature of the learner and how concepts and meaning become a part of the learner. Let us now consider in what ways these two fields might guide us in developing methods of instruction. We must remind ourselves that a critical issue in reading instruction is to help children reach a stage where they can read words, phrases, sentences, and paragraphs that they have never seen before.

That the child knows most, if not all, of the sounds of language when he comes to school has been well established through research by Gleason, Miller, and others. The child uses these sounds in speaking and understanding spoken language. Although he knows the sounds in the language context, recognizing them in isolation is another learning task. Vygotsky gives an example of a child who is unable to articulate *sk* by itself, although he is quite capable of pronouncing the sound in actual words. A beginning task for the child in learning to read is to develop the concept that there are units of sound in spoken language and that these units have a written representation—the letters of the alphabet. He must then perceive that these sounds and letters are arranged as words and thus provide spoken and, indirectly, written cues for meaning.

The above process is accomplished through groupings (the *groupements* discussed by Piaget), or mental abilities developed in and making possible the stage of concrete operations. The groupings provide a means of discovering invariant properties of the data of perception regardless of order, context, size, form, and the like. For instance, in the word *baby*, the first *b* is an initial form and an initial sound. Does it seem the same when it occurs in writing in the second position? Does it sound the same? In the transfer from written to spoken form, can the child hold the concept of invariance of letters and sounds in the necessary orderings? Will the *b* in the context of *table* still look and sound like the same *b*? The existence of these mental abilities or groupings distinctive of concrete operations seems necessary for actual decoding in beginning reading.

Building a sight-word vocabulary depends on having the child associate the spoken word with its total written form. The written word is a complex configuration. The child may learn it on the basis of some preferred aspect of the total configuration reflecting what he notices about the written form of the word; such an individually derived perception is commonly referred to as a stimulus bias. This procedure in learning to read does not help the child to discover sounds of language and their written representations. He may eventually discover them for himself. He will certainly need to in order to read words and sentences he has never seen before.

What then is the nature of the concepts necessary for achieving the ability to transfer from the written to the spoken sounds of a word? What helps and what hinders the formation of these concepts? Various research studies will be reviewed at this point to help us discover how the child learns to select and group sounds and relate this knowledge to reading.

We turn first to Underwood's work on concept formation. He describes conjunctive concepts as those relating to maximum similarity of two or more stimuli (or minimal contrast). In learning, the presentation of maximally similar stimuli "will produce positive transfer, and the amount of positive transfer is directly related to stimulus similarity (Hamilton, 1943)."[1] On the other hand, disjunctive stimuli in learning produce negative transfer. Says Underwood:[2]

It probably is no coincidence that subjects find conjunctive ... concepts easier to learn than disjunctive concepts (Hunt and Hovland, 1960).[3] When viewed from the transfer studies in verbal learning, ... conjunctive concepts have the necessary similarity among the positive instances of the concepts to produce positive transfer, whereas the disjunctive concept does not.

Consider, now, problems of learning to read words. Suppose a child is presented with four new words that he is to learn to read: *Saturday, happy, dime,* and *near.* These words are disjunctive: they have minimal similarity when analyzed in terms of sound pattern to spelling pattern. It could be speculated that learning to read these words would be more difficult and have less transfer value than learning to read a list such as *puppy, happy, snappy.* As to transfer, we might speculate that a child studying the families would be more likely to be able to read *Pappy* and *snippy* than would a child presented with words having minimal similarity.

Underwood also notes:[4]

In order for a relationship among stimuli to be perceived (e.g., for a concept to be formed), responses to the stimuli representing different instances of the concept must be contiguous. . . . Inserting other irrelevant concepts between two instances of the same concept makes it more difficult for the subject to bring the responses to the instances of the same concept into a contiguous relationship. . . . The principle is that the more contiguous the responses to instances of the same concept the more likely it [is] that the subject would detect similarities among the stimuli, hence learn to recognize the concept involved. It is clear, however, that contiguity of responses is of no consequence unless the stimuli associated with the responses can be remembered.

Thus, the learner apparently is unable to assimilate too many differences that occur simultaneously.

An examination of the sequencing of words in some common basal readers, however, indicates that this is just what happens. The child may be introduced to *came* in a primer, then not be introduced to *game* until the 2-1 reader. The lapse in time may be six months. Hence there is the need for initial consonant substitution (changing the initial consonants for *-ame*). But a focus on initial consonant substitution as the learning task—that is, on the conjunctive concept rather than the disjunctive concept—assumes that the child is at the concrete operational stage and possesses certain logical and infralogical groupings. At this stage the child probably will not have those mental abilities at his disposal.

Introducing words with similar spelling patterns would seem to provide greater response contiguity—for example, *came, game, same,* where the repeated *-ame* is to be learned.

Underwood also discusses backward associations: following learning, can a subject produce the stimulus pattern? Says Underwood:[5]

As is known, backward associations do, indeed, exist following the acquisition of forward associations; . . . backward associations are operationally real; the subject can recapture the stimulus term in greater or lesser detail following the learning of the forward association. . . .

During this stage the achievement of reversibility would allow the child to learn that the stimulus configuration *-at* stands for sound occurrences in various words in his speaking vocabulary such as *bat, cat, fat, hat, mat,* and *pat;* it can be expected that he could also learn that various words in his speaking vocabulary are spelled *-at.*

Underwood turns his attention to stimulus selection and stimulus bias. He asserts:[6]

If the stimuli of a paired-associate list consist of two or more discrete elements (e.g., two letters, two words), the association may be formed between only one of the elements of the stimulus and the response term. Such stimulus selection may be demonstrated by transfer tests in which the second-list stimuli consist of only one of the stimulus elements. In extreme cases the selection may be complete and nearly universal across subjects.

Underwood continues describing stimulus biases:[7]

Certain stimulus biases or preferences must to a certain extent determine stimulus selection. . . . Different attributes or characteristics of stimuli have different degrees of dominance for the subject, and concept learning is difficult when the dominant attributes are incorrect.

There are unfortunate consequences of stimulus bias in beginning reading instruction. A teacher may, for example, tell a child that *astronaut* is a long word. The child selects "long word" as the bias and reads every long word as *astronaut.*

Venezky describes what may happen when a child is learning to read:[8]

A very typical thing that happens in a child who is learning to read is that he is doing very well through word recognition. He crams 30, 40, 50 words into memory. At a certain point there is almost complete breakdown. He has overloaded memory. He has not learned to generalize, and he can't go much further. So an additional strategy is that which leads to generalization. . . .

We have asked a tremendous number of teachers and remedial reading people and educators about this particular problem. First, where does the poor reader go wrong, at what stage? Are there really children who truly learn grapheme-phoneme correspondences, segment sounds, who get up to third or fourth grade level, as a group—that is, not just one or two kids, but a large number of poor readers—who break down at that point? Everything we can find so far says that the main point where children go wrong is very early, at the beginning of the reading process. They break down almost immediately when they are told to work with sounds in words. That is, they generally don't understand the task. There is something that stops them at this very early phase.

The child with reading problems probably has not yet developed the groupings and is unable to differentiate the global concept of word-sound relationship. As a result, he may very well resort to some other strategy in attempting to learn to read words. The resort to an alternative strategy—and one that is erroneous and will break down—is fostered by the classroom teacher who reminds the child of the long word. But there are also other reading methods that foster development of erroneous strategies. Suppose a child is asked to read "Tom climbed to the top of the tree" and he can't decode *tree*. If the teacher says "Look at the picture. Where is Tom?" or if she resorts to context and asks "Now where do you think Tom is?" she is directing the child's attention away from the word she wants him to read.

Underwood also observes:[9]

We noted at the outset that verbal learning could be seriously retarded if words obviously belonging to the same class were stimuli for different responses. The moment the same response is used for all instances of the class, however, learning will occur in one trial.

Again considering concepts and their relevance as a link between a theory of learning and a theory of instruction, Archer, too, has some important comments. He believes that concepts differ from simple to complex.[10]

On the one hand, the simple concept has but one bit of relevant information and no irrelevant information, whereas, on the other hand, the complex concept involves a set of many relevant attributes and is embedded in many irrelevant attributes.

Archer notes a number of research studies that "make it abundantly clear that increasing the amount of irrelevant information degrades the speed with which a concept can be identified."[11] It should be obvious that in traditional approaches, when a teacher introduces a new word as part of a story, talks about it, and accompanies it with a picture, there is a surfeit of irrelevant attributes.

Archer also notes that "increasing the amount of relevant information required also degrades the speed with which a concept might be identified."[12] For example, it can be argued that instead of presenting lists of words with minimal contrasts such as *bat, cat, fat, hat, mat, pat, rat,* and *sat*, children should be presented with lists such as *fat-fate, hat-hate, mat-mate,* and *rat-rate*. But we could predict that it would take children longer to learn the latter lists.

Archer also reports that "the identifiability of a concept will be facilitated if the relevant information is obvious and the concept will become more difficult to disentangle from its context if the irrelevant is obvious."[13] Consider the use of service words such as *of, is,* and *come*. The child is swamped with irrelevant information; and the relevant information may not be apparent, leading to the selection of the wrong stimulus.

Thus we would expect high transfer of *-at* in a list such as *bat, cat, fat, hat, mat,* and *pat,* but low transfer of *b, c, f, h, m,* and *p*. To obtain high transfer (again assuming the groupings), we would have to have lists such as *bad, bed, bud; can, cat, cap; fan, fat, fit*. We would expect high transfer of *f* in *fair, farm, fat,* and *father,* though, again, the remainder of the spelling-sound relationships seem to lie between conjunctive and disjunctive concepts. We would expect minimal transfer for a word list that included *please, thank you,* and *mother*.

Considering transferability, Archer notes that "the acquisition of one concept can have a positive or negative effect upon the acquisition of a second concept."[14] We would expect that once the child develops a strategy for attacking words, he would apply this strategy to attacking words he has never seen before. Archer notes[15] that

subjects apparently learn not only the specific concept at hand but they also learn something about *how* to form concepts. If the concepts are of the same general type, there will be a considerable improvement in performance over successive concepts apparently because of transfer of certain nonspecific skills from one problem to another.

This statement exemplifies Piaget's concept of "horizontal shift."

Archer's phrase "the same general type" has special import in beginning reading. Again it points to the efficacy of word families over service words and phonic lists where only one spelling-sound relationship is controlled.

Next, Archer turns to forgetting. Nonuse of a concept leads to forgetting. Hence repetition is important. This points especially to the importance of sequence in arranging lists of words regardless of the system. Also, it can be seen that repetition is greater in a list controlling *-et-*/et/ than in a list with only one word: *sled*.

The role of feedback also is important, Archer states. The longer the interval between response and feedback, the more difficult—and slower —the acquisition of the concept. Learning may be slow when a teacher collects children's worksheets and workbooks and fails to give the youngsters prompt feedback. The function of feedback can be viewed theoretically as an indication to a child that he has successfully assimilated the stimulus and accommodated to it.

Against the backdrop of the studies of language acquisition, developmental psychology, and concept-formation research, it is interesting to speculate about the difficulties that might arise in learning to read with the traditional system of instruction often used in schools today. Let us explore these difficulties.

Around 1920, having children learn to read silently became an important goal in beginning reading instruction. It was, and often still is, assumed that because the skilled reader reads silently, that is what beginning readers should do. This line of reasoning obscures the fact that children who use and understand spoken language seem to need to read aloud in the beginning stages. Venezky proposes[16] that the reason for this lies in the nature of the beginning-to-read process, which he sees as a process of "translating from written symbols to a form of language to which the person already can attach meaning." He points out that "somehow, in teaching reading, the child must first learn to read aloud." He cites research indicating that even very good adult readers subvocalize when they encounter difficult passages; "it seems they utilize this speech representation in a subvocal form."

The literature suggests several reasons why oral reading is important to the young child. First, we have seen from Piaget that when a person encounters an event for the first time, he attends to it by assimilating it into an existing schema; he does, in fact, fall back on a schema that already works. This seems to explain why adults on encountering difficult reading matter resort to an earlier schema—subvocalizing, moving their lips, or writing the material down. Second, we have seen in Vygotsky that the function of egocentric speech—talking to oneself—is to organize action. The child learning to read is apparently at the stage of speech moving inward and requires oral reading to organize his discovery of spelling-sound relationships.

Another common aspect of current methods of reading instruction is that of preparing the children with interpretation and meaning for a new word before it is introduced in its written form. There are variations, of course, but in general, teachers commonly use the following technique.

The teacher gathers a small group of children about her. With an oversize picture next to her in full view of the children, she tells a story about what's happening in the picture. Let's say the picture shows a boy running down the street to a store. In telling the story, the teacher says, "You can see Jimmy run down the street to the store." As she says "run," she may display a word card with *run* on it, or print *run* slowly and in large letters on the chalkboard, or place a card with *run* on it in a pocket chart or on the ledge of the chalkboard. She may ask a child to come up and frame the word with his hands. Then she goes on with the story and repeats the procedure when she comes to the next word. After all the words have been introduced—three or four or five—she gives the children their readers and asks them to turn to the page containing a "story" of three or four lines that include perhaps one of the new words and some of the words previously introduced. The picture on the page may be the same as or similar to the oversize picture next to her. Both pictures show Jimmy running to the store, and the child is supposed to associate the story he heard with the picture he sees, and the word *run* with the picture and the story.

Next, the teacher may ask the children to read the story to themselves to find out why Jimmy is going to the store. This gives them a purpose for reading. She may tell the children to raise their eyes when they finish the page. In a few minutes, she says, "Now let's find out why Jimmy was going to the store. Beth, will you read for us." Thus interaction and status often become a part of the situation for the children.

Now suppose Tommy is reading and he comes to the sentence, "Jimmy, run to the store." He reads: "Jimmy, run to the—" and he stops. What the teacher does now is crucial. Tommy does not yet have a method of word attack, at least one taught by the teacher. Suppose you're the teacher. Consider the alternatives.

1. You say, "Now you sit there and think about that, and we'll come back to you." This is known as the take-a-good-hard-look technique, as though somehow, Tommy will get it if he thinks about it. Imagine yourself sitting in an audience at a symphony concert. You start to cough; suddenly the conductor raps his baton and the orchestra stops. The conductor turns to the audience and announces that the concert will continue when you stop coughing. How would you feel? Well, that's how Tommy feels. Usually, out of kindness, one of his classmates places a book in front of her face—it's usually a her—and whispers the word to him while you're not looking.

2. You say, "Now who will help Tommy?" A girl's hand goes up, you call on her, and she says, "Store." You say, "Very good, Gwendolyn." You have just used your first teacher aide, Gwendolyn. She told Tommy the word; you didn't. In Tommy's eyes, you are now someone who points out to his friends that he is stupid, rather than someone to help him over the rough spots.

3. You say, "Look at the picture. Where is Jimmy running?" Tommy replies, "Down the street." You say, "Yes, but where to?" Whether or not Tommy answers "store," you have just taught him that reading is a guessing game. In the weeks and months ahead, Tommy will show you that he has learned this lesson well and will apply it often.

4. You decide to use the context clue and say, "Now remember our story? Where was Jimmy running?" The results will be the same as for number three.

5. You say, "Now what was the short word we had today?" or "What was the word with the snake on the front of it?" This and various similar techniques direct Tommy's attention to the wrong attributes of the written word (which is stimulus bias): he may just as likely try *sore, shore,* or *snore* as *store.*

6. You simply say, "Store. Go on, please." Not likely to have much effect.

7. You say, "Tommy, look at the word. It's 'store.' Now read it and say it. No, don't look at me and read it; look at the word. Store. Good. Now read the sentence over, please, and go on from there." You note that Tommy needs more work with *store.*

From the above discussion we can see that the use of pictures as a major tool for cuing meaning for the written word may introduce complications that will slow down and even confound the discovery of the relationships of the written to the spoken word.

There is another possibly deleterious effect of programs that use a high ratio of pictures to words. This concerns the nonlinguistic aspects of the child's cognitive behavior. Moshe Anisfeld has hypothesized that "the child's behavior is governed more intensely by the effects of immediate stimuli than by ideational processes such as sets, rules, and plans."[17]

He continues:[18]

The child's cognitive behavior can thus be characterized as submissive to sensory stimulation and disrespectful of the authority of plans, guiding principles, and rules.... In learning to read, the child has to form a relation between orthography and speech. One would suspect the establishment of a relation between these two systems to be affected by the nature of the relation for the child between speech and reference.

The manner in which writing represents speech is based almost exclusively on the properties of speech, and the association between speech and reference has little relevance to the way in which speech is coded in writing. The fact that the word 'chair' refers to a sit-on-able rather than an eat-off-able object has no bearing on the spelling of this word. In reading, 'chair' falls into one category with 'child' on the basis of its initial sound, and another category with 'fair' on the basis of the middle and final sounds. Obviously, the referents of these words do not fall into common categories. Thus, when a child learns the code for a phonetic orthography he has to maintain a set of responding to the auditory properties of words. Of course, when the constellation of stimuli arouses him the child does spontaneously respond in this manner, as evidenced by his rhyming activities. But the present question is whether the auditory set can gain control over the child's responses so that he is consistently guided by it even when the immediate stimuli are not favorable. *It seems that such an unfavorable situation may arise when pictures are present in the reading text, thus emphasizing the referential aspect of the words. Additional complications in the reading task may be due to the fact that in order to understand what he is reading the child has to attend simultaneously to two competing sets, the auditory and the semantic set.* [Emphasis ours]

On the basis of Anisfeld's hypothesis and its implications, by reducing the ratio of words to pictures, textbooks may well be adding a further obstacle to the development of the child's ability to become an independent reader, since the child must attend to two competing sets of stimuli, one auditory and the other semantic, thus delaying his learning to relate written symbols to spoken sounds.

Most methods of reading instruction do include some phonic instruction. They do, however, show much variation in the nature of, and the emphasis placed on, the phonic instruction. Studies by linguists, reported earlier, have shown us that there are many regular patterns of word forms in the English language, certainly enough to design early learning materials that will provide sufficient samples on which the child can build letter-sound concepts and develop strategies for reading new words. The writings by learning theorists reinforce the view that mastering the written code is facilitated when redundancy and minor variation, as found in word families, occur in the learning task.

When reading instructors emphasize meaning and context as necessary conditions for word recognition, they tend to select the reading content which is thought to be most familiar and most interesting to children. In such programs the manuals for teachers suggest flash-card drills, chalkboard games, pocket-chart drills, and so forth for follow-up activities after the group reading session. The words selected for such repetitious presentation, and shortly after for the beginning steps of the program of phonic instruction, are those expressive of interesting stories and events and not samples of the recurring word forms of the language.

When phonic instruction is included in the traditional program of reading instruction, the program often proceeds according to the following steps. First grade contains sight words and the repetition-for-recognition games described above. (Teachers often supplement this instruction with a phonics program even in this grade.) In second grade, what teachers term "blends," "short and long vowels," and "digraphs" are introduced in the teachers' handbooks and in workbooks. Grade three sees dipthongs and prefixes and suffixes. A major emphasis within the traditional programs remains on the meaning and interpretation of high-interest words and stories. Recently published reading programs have compressed this sequence and have moved it downward in grade level.

It can be argued that one reason children who are learning to read in such programs may have trouble even with a complementary phonic program is that a great deal of time is spent talking about stories: "Now whom did we read about, boys and girls? What was the name of the boy? What did he do? Where did he run?" Or "We read about whom? The boy's name was what? Jimmy did what? Jimmy ran where?" Also, a great deal of time may be spent playing word games, with little time spent learning how to read words or actually reading words. The argument can be countered, however, by contending that the discussions and games develop thinking and language skills, and that as these become sharper and more mature, the child is better equipped developmentally to get more out of the reading program.

But what about the words themselves? Examine words customarily selected and the learning problem becomes apparent. One might find:

home	done	here	bear	do	five
come	gone	there	hear	go	give
		were			

have	rough	should	lemon	tar
save	though	shoulder	demon	war
	through			

The words look alike but they do not sound alike. They are introduced at such intervals that the beginning student may have great difficulty developing rules about spelling-sound relationships. One word in a pattern, such as *game,* might come in one reader, whereas the next pattern word, such as *came,* would be introduced many months later in another reader. Such a system makes it difficult for the child to do any kind of categorization of spelling-sound relationships. The common, or similar, conceptual attributes are few and far between.

There are a number of kinds of phonic programs ranging from those which, particularly in the beginning phase, are paced and developed from the meaning-interest priority of the reading instruction, to materials developed to take advantage primarily of the findings of linguistics concerning the patterns and regularities of spoken language as it appears in written form. Some further examples of approaches to phonic instruction follow.

Another kind of phonic program is one in which the child may first learn only vowel spelling-sound relationships as single sounds and then apply these to patterns of words. Stories may be built on these patterns alone. These programs tend to be complicated by the fact that there are more vowel sounds than there are vowel names and because five vowel spelling-sound relationships may be introduced at one time.

In still another form of phonic instruction the child, after some experience with reading, is given lists of families of words. He is asked to detect and verbalize a rule, generalization, or exception to a common spelling-sound relationship. For example, consider these words: *treat, sneeze, throat, green, dried, daisy, snow.* What do they have in common? In each word, the first vowel says its name and the second is silent. Discovering this generalization, the child is expected to apply it when he reads. In some other programs the process is reversed; children must memorize rules, generalizations, and exceptions, and then examine lists of words illustrating what they have memorized. In the complementary reading material, however, the presentation of spelling-sound patterns is not controlled. Therefore, the child is likely to encounter many words in which the generalizations won't work—for instance, "great bread for breakfast." The result may well be interference in the development of a decoding strategy.

Clymer studied forty-five phonic generalizations as they occurred in four basal readers—generalizations that had long been considered applicable to the English language. Only eighteen of the forty-five met his criteria of usefulness as defined in his study. His criteria were, first, that there must occur within the basal readers at least twenty words to which the generalizations might apply and, second, that the generalizations must display a percentage of utility for the sample of at least seventy-five.

Emans replicated the Clymer study, reasoning that "although some phonic generalizations may not be useful with words in the primary grades, these same generalizations might have utility for the words the child is required to recognize later."[19]

However, although a number of generalizations do apply, the question must be asked whether or not it is helpful to have the child verbalize them. For example, Reed asserts that "most linguists who have looked into the matter are in agreement ... that the memorization of rules of phoneme-grapheme correspondence is not helpful and takes time away from more important activities."[20]

It seems important to recall at this time Anisfeld's comment that children are probably guided more by immediate stimuli than by rules or principles. It is likely that the lists of words children encounter as illustrations of rules, generalizations, and exceptions are more effective in teaching the children how to decode than the rules, generalizations, and exceptions per se.

For instructional purposes, the issue about planning for the learning of phonic rules or generalizations must take into account the development of the child. Piaget contends that during the stage of concrete operations and just preceding it the child may have difficulty performing an action in words that he can already perform nonverbally. However, Vygotsky contends that once the action can be performed, being able to describe it in words may give the child conscious awareness—hence control—over the action. One may hypothesize, therefore, that the child may be able to decode words well before he can ever describe the action—deductively or inductively—in terms of the applications of rules, generalizations, exceptions, and so on. However, it is possible that in the later grades materials planned for good sampling opportunities may allow for verbalized rules and possibly increased ability to use orthographic cues accurately.

A special case in the study of rules, generalizations, and exceptions is the study of syllabication. Since good readers are able to recognize the syllables of words and poor readers cannot, it is sometimes contended that to help poor readers read multisyllabic words, we must teach them how to syllabicate. Wardhaugh cautions us that "the precise point at which one syllable may be said to end and another begin is often impossible to determine." For, "when English words are divided in writing according to their syllables, the division points have little or no relevance to the phonological facts." The conventional division points have been arbitrarily determined for purposes of proofreading and appearance in printed matter. Wardhaugh takes exception to the fact that such divisions "are constantly referred to in spelling manuals, reading texts and pronunciation guides as though they had much wider application."[21]

Wardhaugh concludes that "exercises which require students to say how many syllables a word has have some value; exercises which insist that students decide where syllables really begin and end cannot be justified on linguistic grounds."[22] He suggests that if hyphenation is to be taught, a good dictionary should be used.

Another level of difficulty would be phonic programs in which the child is required to learn to identify letters as consonants or vowels. Then come phonic programs in which children mark vowels and consonants with symbols to stand for short, long, stressed and unstressed, hard, soft, and so forth. In all of these the child encounters many words—far more than in any reading without a supplementary phonic program—and his attention is drawn to spelling-sound relationships and patterns, especially in the skill development exercises.

In some phonic programs the child is expected to learn individual spelling-sound relationships and to be able to use them to sound out words. In fact, what the child must learn is a "word" for each letter, but these "words" vary according to the "word" or letter on either side. Consider the *g* in *sign-signify-significant.* Consider the *s* in *reserve-conserve,* or the *a* in *fat, father, fate,* and *fall.* The child also must be able to equate the syntax of these "words" with a specific phonological representation. He must recognize the /bæ/-/æ/-/tæ/ equals /bæt/. If he can detect the one-to-one correspondence, he can read the word. If he can't, he may develop what is known as phonic disability. That is, he will be able to sound out words but he will not be able to read them. To avoid this complication, there is frequent practice in reading words without sounding them out (or naming the letters) and frequent reading of stories to develop rapid word recognition. Blending, sounding, and naming are used only when necessary.

In still another kind of phonic program, lists of words are used with only one spelling-sound relationship in common. Consider this list: *face, fair, farm, fat, father.* Or this one: *ball, bat, baby, brother.* Both lists deal with what may be called "the beginning sound."

The words may have been selected on the assumption that the child already knows how to read *ace, air, arm, at, all,* and *other.* Chances are that if he does, he may very well not be having any trouble with *f*-/f/ or *b*-/b/. If he does not, then he is likely to discover that, in the first list, *a* represents five different sounds and *t* is involved with two, and in the second list, *a* represents three sounds. We have already seen that disjunctive lists such as these are more difficult to learn than conjunctive lists such as those in minimal-contrast phonic families.

Frequently the reading material used for learning-to-read instruction juxtaposes words that have no similarity in spelling-sound relationships and patterns and gives little evidence of planning for the occurrence of conjunctive patterns such as *came, game,* and *name* in its reader levels. As a result, the cognitive demand on the child to decode pairs such as *home* and *come, rough* and *though,* is extensive.

The efficiency of programs will vary to the extent that they cope with this problem, for they must deal with words that look alike but do not sound alike. The problem is partially solved by sequencing. On the one hand, each new pattern is an extension of the previous pattern. And on the other hand—and more important—a conflicting pattern is not introduced until the child has mastered the pattern with which it would conflict. *Home* belongs to the CVCe pattern; *come* does not. The child should develop rapid recognition of one before he tackles the other. There are a number of words such as *done, won, son, Monday, monkey, month, color, cover, company,* and *nothing* in which *o* stands for the short *u* sound in *up.* But there are many more words in which *o* stands for the sound in *not, hot,* and *pot.* Sequencing the introduction of these relationships is important, apparently because of the danger of interference at the beginning stage of reading instruction and because at that stage the child may be unable to use the syntactic and semantic information in the message to help him choose the correct sounds that the letters stand for. Later, when he is more skilled at decoding, the greater the likelihood of his being able to use context of meaning to help him decode various spelling patterns.

A second variable is related, and this deals with the amount of information the child can assimilate at a time. Both the chapters on Piaget and those on concept formation regarding discrimination indicated that the more attributes to be accounted for, the more difficult the concept-attainment task. Thus one would expect that in beginning reading, learning patterns of words containing five different vowel spelling-sound relationships would be more difficult than learning the same patterns taught sequentially.

To summarize: in developing word-attack skills, the teacher should be concerned with the sequencing of information, contradictory information, and the amount of information.

But why do so many children learn to read with all these programs? Probably because, as the child is in the concrete operational stage, the teacher's chalkboard games and activities help him develop his cognitive skills, lead him to have encounters with many words, and lead him to go from the global nature of written words to their differentiated, alphabetic elements. Piaget hypothesizes the child's ability to *organize* assimilated elements. It would be expected that reading programs that facilitate this organization would be more effective with more children than those that don't.

At least at the beginning stage of reading, this would explain why children are able to learn to read thousands of words in code-emphasis programs where one printed word seems similar to the next, when they are only able to learn a few hundred words in programs where the words are dissimilar. Some children can probably organize spelling-sound relationships pretty much on their own. The child who lags in maturational development probably needs a more organized approach in terms of sequence, consistency, and quantity of information.

In addition children see—and learn—many words other than those in the reading program: on signs, packages, billboards, bulletin boards, in other textbooks, and from TV. For example, eight kindergartners in a study conducted by George E. Mason[23] learned 122 words watching TV, and 33 first-graders learned 107 words. Actually, one authority estimates that children may learn to read as many words outside school that are not in the reading program as they would in conventional programs. Another source of words is library books. The more trade books a child receives in and outside school, the greater the likelihood he will be exposed to words not in the look-say program. For this reason, he is especially fortunate if his parents read to him.

The child still has one other chance, however, and that occurs if the teacher uses co-basals. Arthur V. Olson compared the vocabularies of seven commonly used basal reader series at the pre-primer, primer, and first-reader level. The basal readers introduced different words at different rates (new words per 100 words of text). The cumulative totals differ. The percentage increase of words from book to book differs. Only 12.06 percent (92 words) of the total vocabulary appeared in five or more of the series. At the first-reader level, only 8.65 percent of the total vocabulary appeared in five or more series. Olson reports:[24]

A study of the vocabulary showed that there were a total of 763 different words introduced. One hundred sixty different words were introduced at the pre-primer level, 256 at the primer level, and 347 at the first reader level.

A core vocabulary of 92 words common to five or more of the series was found. Thirty-two words were common at the pre-primer level, 31 at the primer, and 30 at the first reader.

In comparing this list to the *Dolch Basic Sight Vocabulary of 220 Service Words,* it was found that 79 words, or 35.91 percent of the words, appeared in five or more of the series and also appear on the Dolch list.

Because the basals have such a small core of words in common, Olson reasoned that the use of co-basals to reexpose students to words they were having trouble with might actually harm poor or below-average readers. Actually, by increasing the number of words—increasing the data—it might help the poor reader discover spelling-sound relationships. This may be one reason why, in teacher terms, co-basals "work."

But what if the child doesn't get to see other words in books because his school doesn't have a library? Or what if the first-grade curriculum uses mostly pictures and spoken language and nonwritten materials. Suppose his parents can't read or if they can, suppose they don't have books or don't have time to read to the child? In that event, the child is not likely to encounter enough words to develop an unconscious system of rules dealing with spelling-sound relationships.

SUMMARY

In this chapter we have noted that knowledge regarding the nature of the learner and the nature of language can serve as a guide for instruction in beginning reading. We have suggested that the primary task for the young child is to recognize that spoken language is comprised of units of sounds of a limited number and to relate them to their written form. This chapter has been concerned with drawing attention to instructional programs that can best aid the child to learn to associate speech sounds with their written form and to have the written form serve as a cue for the necessary sounds.

The role of instruction is to construct the environment to foster the child's active discovery of regularities and differences in the learning task. A number of principles involving concept learning are useful in this regard.

Since the child does not know which events are important, the content of instruction must be ordered. There is need for appropriate repetition and feedback to help the child check what he has learned. Simple concepts, those containing fewer bits of information, need to be introduced before more complex concepts. The number of different concepts introduced at any one time needs to be reduced. Irrelevant information must be avoided. The concepts to be learned should be sequenced so that they are repeated without extraneous concepts being interspersed. Similar concepts need to be taught in sequence.

We have shown that many modern reading programs fail to construct adequately an environment that facilitates learning. They present too many different concepts and do not sequence them properly; for example, service words representing many different groups of sounds are often introduced at one time. In beginning reading, irrelevant concepts are presented when too much reliance is placed on pictures or when discussion is centered on matters other than learning the relations between sounds and symbols.

This chapter has dealt with beginning reading. The next, and last chapter, will deal with reading beyond the beginning stages.

NOTES FOR CHAPTER 13

1. Benton J. Underwood, "Some Relationships between Concept Learning and Verbal Learning," in *Analyses of Concept Learning,* edited by Herbert J. Klausmeier and Chester W. Harris (New York: Academic Press, 1966), p. 53. The reference is to R. Jane Hamilton, "Retroactive Facilitation as a Function of Degree of Generalization between Tasks," *J. Exp. Psychol.* 32 (1943), 363–76.
2. Underwood, p. 53.
3. E. B. Hunt and C. I. Hovland, "Order of Consideration of Different Types of Concepts," *J. Exp. Psychol.* 59 (1960), 220–25.
4. Underwood, pp. 54–55.
5. Ibid., p. 56.
6. Ibid., pp. 56–57.
7. Ibid., pp. 57–58.
8. Richard L. Venezky, "Communicating by Language: The Reading Process," *Proceedings of the Conference on Communicating by Language,* February 11–13, 1968, New Orleans (Department of Health, Education, and Welfare: Public Health Service—National Institute of Child Health and Human Development, Bethesda, Md.), pp. 166, 210–11.
9. Underwood, pp. 60–61.
10. E. James Archer, "The Psychological Nature of Concepts," in *Analyses of Concept Learning,* p. 38.
11. Ibid., p. 40.
12. Ibid.
13. Ibid.
14. Ibid., p. 44.
15. Ibid., p. 42.
16. Venezky, pp. 16–18.
17. Moshe Anisfeld, "Language Skills in the Context of the Child's Cognitive Development," *Project Literacy Reports* 2 (September 1964), p. 37. (Cornell University).
18. Ibid., pp. 40–42.
19. Robert Emans, "When Two Vowels Go Walking and Other Such Things," *Reading Teacher* 21, 3 (December 1967), 262.
20. David W. Reed, "Linguistics and Reading, Once More," in *Oral Language and Reading,* edited by James Walden (Champaign, Ill.: National Council of Teachers of English, 1969), p. 80.
21. Ronald Wardhaugh, "Syl-lab-i-ca-tion," *Elementary English* 43, 7 (November 1966), 786.
22. Ibid., p. 788.
23. George E. Mason, "Children Learn Words from Commercial TV," in *Elementary School Journal* 65, 6 (March 1965), 318–20.
24. Arthur V. Olson, "An Analysis of the Vocabulary of Seven Primary Reading Series," *Elementary English* 42, 3 (March 1965), 263–64.

14

competence in thought, language, and reading

In chapter 8 we noted that reading skills are acquired in stages. At the initial stage the child needs to recognize the shapes of the code symbols—the letters—and then he needs to discover the alphabetic nature of written English. He needs to establish a relationship between each word that he sees and its underlying phonological representation.[1]

Goodman notes:[2]

One may think of a hypothetical stage in reading in which the fledgling reader recodes graphic input as speech which he then treats as aural input and decodes for meaning as he does in listening. Research has indicated that this view is not appropriate for proficient readers (Goodman and Burke, 1968)[3] and may not fully apply even to beginners (Y. Goodman, 1967).[4]

However, Goodman suggests the existence of three levels of proficiency. The first is the "recoding" stage, in which written words are translated into word names. In the second stage, the reader comes to be able to decode and comprehend the entire meaning of large language units. In the third stage, the process is further telescoped so that recoding and decoding are simultaneous.[5]

Hence reading "is not a process of sequential word recognition. A proficient reader is one so efficient in sampling and predicting that he uses the least (not the most) available information necessary."[6] Goodman continues:[7]

All the information must be available for the process to operate in the reader and for the sampling strategies it requires to develop in the beginner.

Three basic kinds of information are used. They are:

1. *Grapho-phonic*. This is the information from the graphic system, and the phonological system of oral language. Additional information comes to the reader from the interrelationships between the systems. Phonics is the name for those relationships.
2. *Syntactic information*. This is the information implicit in the grammatical structures of the language. The language user knows these and, therefore, is able to use this information before he learns to read his native language. Reading, like all language processes, involves a syntactic context.
3. *Semantic information*. As he strives to re-create the message, the reader utilizes his experiential conceptual background to create a meaning context. If the

reader lacks relevant knowledge, he cannot supply this semantic component and he cannot read. In this sense, all readers regardless of their general reading proficiency are incapable of reading some material in their native language.

Since the value of any bit of the three types of information must be related to the other available information, the choice of which bit to select can only be made in full context and the strategies for making those selections can only be learned in response to real language materials (not flash cards or spelling matrices or phonics charts).

It appears that as the child develops proficiency in decoding, he also develops his ability to use the syntactic and semantic information in the printed message. This ability, in turn, exerts a cognitive influence on his perceptual strategies. The child develops the unconscious ability to perform sampling with his eyes. It is a mistake, therefore, to assume that just because a child can decode fluently, he is ready to plunge into all types of reading. He still has more reading skills to develop. Let us consider an excerpt from an article by Anne D. Pick:[8]

The last stage of learning to read ... continues over a period of several years during which the child learns to process larger and more complex units of writing. These units are based on the grammatical surface structure of the written language.

Several investigations of the function of grammatical structure in reading have been carried out by Harry Levin and his colleagues. Levin and Mearini (1964) asked whether a reader's attention is focused on the more important or informative parts of a word. If so, they suggested, readers of a language like Italian should attend more to the ends of words than readers of English because there are many more inflectional suffixes in Italian than in English. They compared the performance of Italian and American school children on a word sorting task designed to show where the children directed their attention. The task required sorting groups of nonsense words on the basis of characteristics whose location in the words varied. When the criterial attribute was located at the beginning of the word, the two groups of children performed equally well in the sorting task. When the criterial attribute was located at the end of a word, however, the Italian readers performed the task better than the American children did. These results demonstrate that the morphological structure of a language directs a reader's attention to the informative or critical parts of written words.

It is obvious to any observer that a reasonably skilled reader processes written text in larger units than parts of words. His eyes do not fixate even on every word, and it is reasonable to suppose that the pattern of his eye fixations in relation to the structure of the material being read may reflect the units in which he is processing the material.

Levin used the "eye-voice span" to investigate the function of another aspect of grammatical structure in the perceptual processing of material being read (Levin & Kaplan, 1967; Levin & Turner, 1966). The eye-voice span is the distance, in words, that the eye is ahead of the voice when one is reading aloud. This distance can be determined simply by removing the text from the reader's sight while he is reading aloud and counting the number of additional words of the text he is able to say correctly.

These investigators have measured the eye-voice span both for children and for adult readers. As might be expected, fast readers show a greater span than slow readers do and older readers show a greater span than younger, less skilled readers do. Other, more interesting results show the effect of syntactical structure on the eye-voice span. When the material being read consists of unstructured strings or lists of words, the number of words in the span remains quite stable for each particular reader. However, when paragraphs composed of sentences are read aloud, the number of words in the span varies, and its size depends on the syntactical structure of the part of the sentence where it is measured. For example, the eye-voice span tends not to stop before phrase boundaries but rather it increases to reach the ends of phrases. Also, the span is smaller for the active forms of sentences than for the corresponding passive forms which are more constrained or predictable.

One other study by Weber (1967) demonstrates that even young, beginning readers are sensitive to grammatical structure. First grade children were given a simple text to read aloud and the investigator simply observed the children's errors and corrections of errors. She found that when an error occurred which was incompatible grammatically with the sentence being read, the error usually was corrected. Errors which were not corrected were usually compatible grammatically with the sentence. These effects were even more striking for the children who were judged to be the better readers of the group than for the poorer readers. Such a difference would be expected if, as the evidence suggests, one acquires increased skill in reading by utilizing grammatical structure.

In summary, the units of perceptual processing in reading beyond a beginning level are not single letters. Spelling structure and various aspects of grammatical structure all function to form perceptual units in reading. The young reader becomes increasingly skilled by utilizing progressively more of these structural regularities in the written language. No doubt other structural characteristics, as yet unidentified, are used in perceptual processing and also serve to increase efficiency, and hence skill, in reading.[9]

According to Sumner Ives, "no one can read an English sentence by recognizing words alone, only by recognizing them in a syntactic frame." He notes that "it is immediately obvious that the pattern, or arrangement of parts, in an English sentence is one factor contributing to its meaning as a whole and, in some instances, the meanings of individual parts." He concludes that much of the core of the grammatical structure of English "can be taught very early in the school program, and the teaching of syntax and the teaching of reading can be mutually supporting activities."[10]

Reed also recognizes the importance of syntax to comprehension. He asserts[11] that

this problem is often not recognized for what it is. If a child reads every word in a sentence as if it were an item in a list, a linguist would say that he has not identified such grammatical structures as noun phrases, verb phrases, and sentence adverbials. Reading teachers seem to make one of two assumptions—either that the problem is one of elocution, in which case the child will be exhorted to "read more naturally" or to "read the words as if talking to a friend," or else that the problem is one of understanding, in which case the advice will be to "think what the words mean as you read." Both of these assumptions are correct as far as they go. The child's oral reading *is* faulty as regards intonation, and he probably *has* failed to understand any sentence that he reads as if it were a list of syntactically unrelated items. But both of these facts are merely superficial symptoms of an underlying failure to identify grammatical structures.

In Carroll's analogy of a computer cited earlier, if a sentence is a program for the brain of relationships between concepts, the child's failure to identify grammatical structures may mean that he is not yet programmed. There is some evidence that the child's syntactical patterns become increasingly complex as he matures.

Hunt studied the grammatical structures written by fourth-, eighth-, and twelfth-graders, using the T-unit as an item of analysis. A T-unit is "one main clause expanded at any of many different points by structures that are modifiers or complements or substitutes for words in the main clause."[12]

His study of subordinate clauses[13]

showed that adjective clauses, rather than noun clauses or movable adverb clauses, are the ones used more often by older students. In equal numbers of words, eighth graders used one and a half times as many adjective clauses as fourth graders, and twelfth graders used more than twice as many as fourth graders. Per T-unit, eighth graders used twice as many as fourth graders, and twelfth graders used more than three and a half times as many as fourth graders. But superior adults used virtually the same number of subordinate clauses per T-unit as twelfth graders (though the proportion of adjective clauses was still larger). So the amount of T-unit expansion that can occur through the addition of subordinate clauses seems to have fairly definite practical limits, and those limits seem to be reached already by the average twelfth grader. If further expansion of the T-unit is to occur—and already we have seen that it does occur—that expansion must be achieved in the other way: by increasing the number of nonclause e optional elements that are added to the minimal essentials of the clause such as subject and finite verb, etc.

The remaining chapters were addressed to nonclauses. Though the clauses of the twelfth graders average only half a word longer than those of the eighth graders, the fact that the clauses of superior adults average about three and a half words longer suggests that clause length is especially worth studying as a place where substantial growth can occur. First, nominal structures were examined, then verb structures (the auxiliary and then main verb), then nonclause adverbial structures not modifying nouns, and, last, predicate adjectives. From that study three facts stand out.

1. At several places there are increases which, though significant, are insufficient to affect clause length appreciably, as, for instance, with predicate adjectives.

2. The total number of nonclause adverbials related to verbs as complements or modifiers decreases overall from grades four to twelve. But there is an increase of about one tenth of an adverbial per clause from grades four to eight and then a decrease of nearly two tenths per clause from grades eight to twelve. About half these adverbials were prepositional phrases several words long. The effect of this decrease in words per clause from grades eight to twelve was more than offset by gains in length elsewhere.

3. The major lengthening of the clause occurs as an expansion of the nominals used as subjects, objects of verbs, objects of prepositions, etc. For instance, eighth graders, as compared with fourth graders, use about a third more modifiers of nouns per clause, and twelfth graders, as compared with fourth graders, use more than twice as many per clause.

The same adjectives, prepositional phrases and verbal forms that appear as modifiers of a noun can also appear as predicate elements, usually after a form of *be,* with the same noun as subject. (The man is tall, the tall man; the book is on the table, the book on the table; the car is painted red, the car painted red; the tide is rising, the rising tide.) One gets the impression from studying these materials that the younger students tend to use short clauses to express these meanings, whereas older students tend to reduce such clauses to mere modifiers which are consolidated with the same noun in another clause, thus achieving greater length.

Many of the genitive modifiers result from the nominalizing of clauses. (Someone nominalizes clauses; some*one's* nominalizing *of* clauses. Two genitives.) To convert a clause to a nonclause nominal is a characteristic of older writers, as the increase of infinitival nominals and gerunds testifies. Eighth graders write twice as many of these per clause as fourth graders, and twelfth graders write two and a half times as many per clause as fourth graders do.

So the chief factor which lengthens clauses appears to be the increasing of nonclause modifiers of nouns and the nominalization of clauses. This factor and the increase in adjective clauses account in the main for the increased length of T-units.

According to this sample, the student of average IQ, when he gets his high school diploma, writes T-units about 160 percent as long as those he wrote eight years earlier. If ever he learns to write like a "superior adult" his T-units will be some 230 percent of what they were in fourth grade.

The older student can incorporate and consolidate more grammatical structures into a single grammatically interrelated unit. The younger student produces short separate units. His span of grammatical concern or attention is narrow. As he matures that span broadens, so he casts the net of consolidation over larger and larger bodies of material. As he consolidates, he also discards needless words. His redundancy lessens and his succinctness gains. Unless we suppose that there is less thought per word in the writing of older students, then we must suppose that as students mature they learn to incorporate a larger and larger body of thought into a single intricately related organization. . . .

It might be useful to look at three different versions of the same passage, each version more mature in the terms of this study.

Suppose that a student wants to say these several things.

> The sailor finally came on deck. He was tall. He was rather ugly.
> He had a limp. He had offered them the prize.

Written thus we have five T-units, with an average length of 5.4 words, shorter than the fourth grade average of 6.6 words.

These five T-units might all have been strung together with too many *and*'s, but none of the fourth graders in this study produced anything quite that anomalous. But a fourth grader might have reduced two of them to nonclausal structures coordinated with *and.*

> The sailor finally came on deck. He was tall *and rather ugly and had a limp*. He had offered them the prize.

As a result, the average clause length has been increased from 5.4 words to 7.3 words, something between the fourth and eighth grade averages. One clause is now 12 [*sic*] words long, longer than the average clause of superior adults. The average T-unit length has been increased too. It is 7.3 words, still below the fourth grade average; but now one of the three T-units is "middle-length," whereas originally all five would have been counted with the "shorts."

Of course any one of the original five T-units could have become an adjectival clause, but four can hardly be attached to a single noun. The limit on nonclausal modifiers, if there is one, is much higher.

Actually these five T-units can be all consolidated into a single T-unit. Three units will be reduced to nonclausal structures: one to an adjective, one to an adjective with an adverbial modifier, one to a prepositional phrase. A fourth is here reduced to a subordinate clause, an adjectival.

> The *tall, rather ugly sailor with a limp, who had offered them the prize,* finally came on deck.

This T-unit is now 18 words long, longer than the 14.4 word average for twelfth graders. The number of clauses is 2, whereas the average for twelfth grade T-units is only 1.67. The two clauses average 9 words in length, whereas the twelfth grade average is 8.6. Five "short" T-units have been consolidated into a "middle-length" one. The nominal has been "complicated" four times, and fourth graders in this study produced only 9 like that in 18,000 words. Eighth graders produced 31 of them and twelfth graders 36. All in all, then, this is a moderately mature sentence, clearly more mature than the average sentence produced by the average twelfth grader; but by no means impossible for him, nor impossible for the average eighth grader either.

It seems natural enough to suppose that the fourth graders and the twelfth graders all get their ideas expressed, but apparently the younger writers spread their ideas out more thinly over more clauses and more T-units.

The three alternate versions show one thing more: the increased succinctness and economy which comes with the reducing of clauses (or sentences or T-units) to nonclausal structures. The first version, even without *and*'s to join the five sentences together, took 23 words. The second version, though it adds two *and*'s, took only 22 words. The third version took only 18 words. The length is thus reduced by one fourth. The consolidation of T-units saves words. Older students say more in a thousand words.

O'Donnell, Griffin, and Norris also studied the syntax of children at different grade levels. In a preface to their report, Richard Braddock noted:[14]

In their study, O'Donnell, Griffin, and Norris analyzed the language of 180 boys and girls from white middle class families in Murfreesboro, Tennessee—30 children each in kindergarten and in grades 1, 2, 3, 5, and 7. The language samples were collected during March, 1965, by having three children at a time view a motion picture (with the sound track turned off), then privately tell the story of the film to an interviewer and answer certain questions related to the narrative, these oral responses being recorded on tape. The children in grades 3, 5, and 7 were also asked to write the story of the film and answers to the same questions.

This procedure was followed with each of two animated cartoons of Aesop's fables. Typescripts of the oral and written responses (the oral responses typed without punctuation) were then divided into T-units, each of which was analyzed for the type of sequential pattern of the main clause and for the number, kinds, and functions of sentence-combining transformations the T-unit contained. The mean number of words per T-unit and the mean number of sentence-combining transformations per 100 T-units were also calculated.

Here are their conclusions:[15]

GENERAL CONCLUSIONS AND IMPLICATIONS

Several considerations ought to be kept in mind when findings of this investigation are applied to the questions that motivated it, or when further implications are drawn from those findings.

The language samples analyzed may be supposed comparable, for they were produced under similar conditions as responses to moving-picture cartoon versions of Aesop's fables simple enough and lively enough to be followed with interest by even the youngest children. It is not, however, certain that the 180 white, middle class children in six grade groups in Murfreesboro, Tennessee, spoke and wrote about those films in March, 1965, in language just like what would be used in such discussion by other children at other times and places.

In the second place, this study did not by any means deal with all aspects of language that might be of interest, or with the full range of grammatical structures and functions. Except for main-clause patterns, the structures and functions selected for attention were only those taken to be dependent on sentence-combining transformations.

It should be remembered, too, that though the children in Murfreesboro were encouraged to interpret and support their interpretations of two stories seen silently enacted, by far the largest part of all responses simply recounted the stories as they had been understood. Language used by children for different purposes would very likely display somewhat different patterns. General representativeness of the behavior of subjects of this study is at various points suggested by remarkable parallels with that reported by other investigators of the language of other children under other circumstances. Nevertheless, it is with due tentativeness that, on the basis of observations made in the course of this research, answers to some broad questions are offered.

Are Measurable Differences to Be Found in Grammatical Structures Used by Children at Various Age-Grade Levels?

Taken in its simplest possible sense, the first question motivating this study is gratuitous. Numerous researchers have given quantitative accounts of syntactic differences in language used by children at varying chronological and educational stages. The problem was whether or not the particular series of analyses contemplated would reveal significant differences among the particular groups of children to be studied. So understood, the question was a real one, and it has been affirmatively answered.

Implied in the question was concern not only with the nature of any differences that could be identified, but also with common features of children's syntax that might be disclosed where variance was not found. Special importance, indeed, may be attached to the fact that little diversity was observed in relative frequencies of grammatically complete basic structure patterns of main clauses. The eleven patterns identified in the language samples ... were all used in the speech of kindergarten children, although six of them occurred very infrequently. Two of the rarer ones (that involving an object complement and that in which an initial adverb is followed by the inverted order of verb and subject) were sometimes missing in oral responses in later grades, but all the patterns were used by seventh graders at about the same rate as they had been used in kindergarten—with one exception. The one significant difference was a 60 percent reduction in use of nominal complements following linking verbs. This pattern, incidently, was used still less frequently in Grades 2, 3, and 5 than in Grade 7. In writing, all eleven patterns were used, at least occasionally, in each of the three grades studied. The only three significant variations in frequencies all related to the commonest clause structures. It is probably more revealing to note that there was a steady and significant reduction in incidence of grammatically incomplete patterns in speech from kindergarten through Grade 7, and a significant reduction in their use in writing in Grade 5.

The suggested generalization that relative uses of basic structures in main clauses do not vary much through the elementary school years is not necessarily invalidated by reports of differential employment of "sentence patterns" that have been made by certain other investigators. Strickland (1962), Hocker (1963), and Riling (1965) distinguished such patterns not only by reference to basic structure but also to various types and positions of adverbial modifiers and to connections between clauses. Sam and Stine (1965) tabulated total occurrences of six structure patterns such as are dealt with in this study, and they reported large increases in the use of four of them in fifth and sixth grade writing; but they did not take account of the fact that children in successive grades wrote longer compositions. Loban, who identified "patterns of communication units" roughly comparable to main clause structures discussed here, computed their use in percentages of total amounts of oral language produced, but his reports (1961, 1963, 1964) are almost wholly confined to comparisons of behavior of the most and least linguistically proficient children in the various grades. Nevertheless, it is pertinent to cite his conclusion (1963, p. 84) that, except in uses of linking verbs and in general decreases of incomplete structures, "differences in structural patterns are not notable." He remarked, *"Not pattern but what is done to achieve flexibility within the pattern proves to be a measure of effectiveness and control of language. . . ."*

Numerous notable grade level differences *were* found in the course of the present study in proportional uses of syntactic structures describable as formed from sentence-combining transformations. To speak first of one of the less impressive, after a constant rise in the rate of main-clause coordination in speech through Grade 5, the trend was significantly reversed by the seventh graders. Seventh graders also employed such coordination in writing less frequently than did either fifth or third graders. What is probably more important, in both speech and writing there were significant overall increases across the grade spans in the use of the whole classes of transformation-produced nominals and adverbials. The overall increase in use of the whole class of coordinations within T-units was also significant in speech, though not in writing.

The statements just made do not imply that notable increases were found in the use of all construction types distinguished within the three general classes. Nor do they mean that the classes as wholes were more frequently represented in each successive grade, though that was true in all but four instances. Increments were not equal in all grades where they appeared, either. Statistically significant increases in use of the nominals and adverbials (as whole classes) occurred in speech only in Grades 1 and 7; such increases were found in writing in both fifth and seventh grades. Coordinations within T-units increased significantly in seventh grade speech; in writing, their increase in Grade 5 was significant, but the rate of their use was reduced by seventh graders.

Among eighteen specific kinds of structures comprised in the three general categories, some were used little more in one grade than another, and some were used less frequently in more advanced grades. Three (the gerund phrase and nouns modified by adverbs and by infinitive phrases) were used infrequently and with little variation over the grade spans represented by speech and writing samples. Noun clauses were a little less often employed in the writing of fifth and seventh graders than in that of third graders. Relative clauses were used in speech at a higher rate by kindergarten children than by any other grade group. There were wide fluctuations in the incidence of infinitives with subjects in speech, but fifth and seventh graders used them a little less frequently than kindergarten children did.

With these exceptions, however, the specific constructions identified showed marked overall increases in use in speech and writing across the grade ranges. The greatest and most frequently significant increases in speech occurred in Grades 1 and 7; in writing, increases were common in both the later grades but were most impressive in Grade 5.

Greatest overall increases and most frequently significant increments from grade level to adjacent grade level were found in the use of adverbial infinitives, sentence adverbials, coordinations within T-units, and modifications of nouns by adjectives, participles, and prepositional phrases. In the theory of transformational grammar, all these constructions are explained as being produced by application of deletion rules. They may be contrasted with constructions that require transformational substitutions or additions. Relative clauses, as we have already noted, were used in speech most frequently by kindergarten children, though in writing they occurred least often in the papers of third graders. Noun clauses were increased modestly in speech from kindergarten through the seventh grade, but they were used in writing most frequently by third graders. Though adverbial clauses were used twice as frequently in seventh grade speech as in kindergarten and almost twice as often in seventh grade writing as in third grade writing, at no point was there a significant increase from one grade to another just above it. To the group of transformations requiring addition and possibly substitution, but not deletion, must be added the coordination of main clauses. It has been shown that the rate of use of such coordination was increasingly high through the fifth grade, but that it was significantly reduced in Grade 7.

IS IT POSSIBLE TO DEFINE A SEQUENCE IN CHILDREN'S ACQUISITION
OF A PRODUCTIVE REPERTORY OF SYNTACTIC STRUCTURES?

To speak of children's acquiring a syntactic repertory does not here imply any notion that they mechanically accumulate a structure-hoard. Without concern, at the moment, about how children come by their competence to use syntactic resources in speech and writing, the question asked is simply whether we may discover a characteristic order in the development of actual uses of those resources. Do some types and functions of structures typically appear earlier and others later?

A general kind of sequential development in productive command of syntax has been indicated by studies of very young children. Individual rates of advancement vary, but the order appears remarkably constant. Brown and Fraser (1964), for example, found that among thirteen two-year-olds they studied, use of *be* in progressive verb phrases was delayed; it never appeared in speech of children whose utterances had a mean length of less than 3.2 morphemes, but was used by all the others. Use of *can ... will* as modal auxiliaries developed still later, and only when utterances had reached a mean length of at least 3.5 morphemes. Lenneberg (1964) has also shown that among single-base transformations, the passive presents particular difficulty to immature minds; it is always late in appearing in children's speech. Menyuk (1961, 1963a, 1964b) has identified some sequential trends in syntax of children from nursery school age to first grade. Can further evidence be found relating to order in the development of older children?

This investigation offers no simple, direct answer to that question. If some item of syntax had been found absent in the speech of younger children but present in increasingly frequent use in more advanced grades, it would have seemed evident that it was a characteristically later acquisition. No such instance was observed. Among the thirty-nine specific structures and functions identified for attention, the three completely missing in kindergarten speech were not much used by older children, either. We could argue that these items (noun modification by an adverb and transformation-produced constructions used as indirect objects and object complements) had not yet been firmly incorporated into repertories of even the seventh graders. It seems more probable that the situation the children responded to furnished little opportunity for their use—or, indeed, that expression generally makes little use of them.

An inference, however, may possibly be drawn from the fact that some items were used much more frequently in kindergarten than in the later grades. It can be reasoned that these features were early incorporated into the children's expression patterns and were partially displaced by others later added. Items in question were the relative clause, noun modification by an infinitive phrase, the main clause in which an adverb is followed by inverted order of verb and subject, the main clause in which a linking verb is followed by a nominal complement, and the transformation-produced nominal functioning as subject complement. To this list, as an obviously early acquisition, we may add main-clause coordination, which was reduced in frequency only in the seventh grade.

On the other hand, there was a group of items that appeared more than sporadically in kindergarten speech but were used from about three to ten times oftener by seventh graders. At various levels, there were significant increments in their use. These would appear good candidates for identification as generally later acquisitions. They were noun modification by a participle or participial phrase, the gerund phrase, the adverbial infinitive, the sentence adverbial, the coordinated predicate, and the transformation-produced nominal functioning as object of a preposition.

Theoretically, it seems reasonable to suppose that these constructions (unless acquired as formulas) would be mastered relatively late. Transformational grammar derives them all by application of deletion rules, and some of them indirectly from their sources by way of strings that could more directly yield subordinate clauses. Thus, *The man wearing a coat ...* may be more difficult than *The man who was wearing a coat* .... and *A bird in the tree* ... more difficult than *A bird that was in the tree.*... Noting that noun clauses did not vary much in frequency after the first grade, while participial modifiers of nouns were used by seventh graders three times as often in speech and nearly eight times as often in writing as they were used by kindergarten children, we may contend that such clauses (The dove saw *that the ant was drowning*) are easier to manage and earlier added to the child's repertory than is the reduction of them to a single participial modifier (The dove saw the ant *drowning*). And common observation supports the supposition that conjunction of two independent clauses as wholes is easier for children than deletion of the subject of one and coordination of the predicates. All such argument, however, goes beyond the data collected in this study.

Inconclusiveness of the findings bearing on sequential enlargement of syntactic repertoires may indicate that study of individual language production would be more fruitful than a cross-sectional investigation.

DO CHILDREN DEVELOP PRODUCTIVE CONTROL OF SYNTAX GRADUALLY, OR DO THEY
GO THROUGH STAGES OF RELATIVELY RAPID DEVELOPMENT?

The data collected and analyzed in this study indicate that there may, indeed, be particular periods when children's expansion of their use of syntactic resources proceeds at a relatively rapid pace. Among the children observed, such periods in oral expression were located at the extremes of the grade range—the time spans between kindergarten and the end of the first grade, and between the end of the fifth grade and the end of the seventh. Progress, of course, was made between Grade 1 and the end of Grade 5, but it appears to have been slower and fluctuating in rate. In writing, development was impressive in both of the higher grades, but the overall expansion was more striking in Grade 5.

In first grade speech there were numerous increments in structures and functions dependent on sentence-combining transformations that may reasonably be supposed to reflect syntactic control. Increases large enough to be statistically significant were observed in first graders' use of two of the general classes of constructions studied: nominals and adverbials. Significant increments were found also in the use of adverbial clauses, infinitives with subjects, and nominals functioning as direct objects.

Increments of such magnitude were not again so frequently discovered in the speech of any grade group before the seventh. Seventh graders showed very large gains over fifth graders in the use of all three of the general classes of constructions, and also in the use of noun clauses, noun modification by means of adjectives and prepositional phrases, adverbial clauses, sentence adverbials, coordinate nominals, and coordinate predicates. Further, they notably exceeded fifth graders in the use of transformation-produced nominals functioning as subjects, direct objects, and objects of prepositions.

It is certainly not assumed here that multiplication of uses of any particular syntactic structures or functions is always a mark of language control. Naturally, effective language varies with circumstances; appropriateness depends on such factors as subject, context, purpose, and anticipated listeners or readers. In this report, it has only been supposed that when large groups of children respond under similar circumstances arranged to give them considerable scope for expression, if older groups more frequently employ features of syntax such as have been mentioned in the last two paragraphs, they demonstrate (as groups) their firmer command of resources of the language. Admittedly, the supposition is related to some subjective notions about adult skill in handling language. Those notions also suggest that restraint in the use of some syntactic possibilities is a demonstration of control.

In the first grade, development of control may be seen in reduced frequency of grammatically incomplete clause patterns, though similar decreases were somewhat greater in Grades 2 and 3. First graders also reduced by about 40 percent the use of main-clause patterns in which predicate nominals follow linking verbs. It is argued here that this fact reflects growth toward maturity, for the simple pattern in question serves the very elementary purposes of indicating identification or equation. (Examples: *It was an ant. He was a hunter. It was a rainy day.*) This pattern was used still less frequently in later grades than in Grade 1. Another, though indirect, evidence of first graders' marked growth in manipulating syntax is their more than 10 percent reduction of the proportion of clauses containing less than nine words. No other equally great reduction was found in speech until the seventh grade.

Besides the decrease in the proportion of short T-units that has just been mentioned, the speech of seventh graders was distinguished by an equally great reduction in the incidence of main-clause coordination; it was the only such reduction observed.

In writing, the syntax of third graders could be judged inferior to that of the older children at almost every point at which analysis was applied. It seems possible to conclude, also, that the advancement gap was greater between Grade 5 and Grade 3 than between Grade 7 and Grade 5. That judgment is based in part on the more impressive fifth grade decrements in incomplete clauses and short T-units. It is also supported by the facts that, though significant increments in the whole classes of transformation-produced nominals and adverbials occurred in both grades, there were much greater fifth than seventh grade increases in the use of genitive forms, relative clauses, adverbial clauses, and complex structures functioning as direct objects.

In fifth grade writing, there were also significant increments in the use of all types of coordinations within T-units, by contrast with a small general reduction in their use by seventh graders. The handling of such coordinations, however, is not here interpreted as showing differential development of writing skill in the two grades. It seems more likely, as earlier discussion suggested, that by about the fifth or sixth grade, children exploit such coordinations in writing at a rate they will not exceed in later years.

ARE THERE SIGNIFICANT DIFFERENCES IN CHILDREN'S HANDLING OF SYNTAX IN SPEECH AND WRITING?

Distinct and dramatic differences were found in the syntax of speech and writing in all three grades from which writing samples were collected. On almost all counts, it was clear that where notable differences appeared in Grade 3 (and there were many), they indicated weaker control in writing. The one important exception was in coordinations of main clauses, which occurred more than three times as often in speech as in writing.

Unexpectedly uniform evidence, however, showed that advances in the control of syntax in Grades 5 and 7 were accelerated in writing far beyond those reflected in speech. The crossover in the relative degrees of skill in the two modes of expression was marked in the later grades by a lower proportion of short T-units (those less than nine words in length); by significantly greater use of the whole classes of transformation-produced nominals, adverbials, and coordinations within T-units; by notably more frequent use of seven of the twelve specific types of nominal structures identified; by greater use of adverbial clauses and adverbial infinitives; and by much greater use of coordinate predicates, particularly in Grade 5. It may also be reflected in the lower incidence in writing of clause patterns in which linking verbs are followed by nominal complements.

It seems quite possible that general trends described here may be characteristic among school children. Lull (1929), on the basis of quite different, essentially subjective observations, reported that children in Kansas began at the 5B grade level to write better than they spoke. Harrell (1957, p. 70) concluded that Minnesota children aged 9 through 15 demonstrated greater control of syntax in writing than in speech on almost all the measures he applied.

DO BOYS AND GIRLS DIFFER SIGNIFICANTLY IN THE USE OF SYNTACTIC STRUCTURES
AT VARIOUS GRADE LEVELS?

Numerous differences were observed in syntactic structures and functions in the language of boys and girls at the six grade levels studied, and a good many of them were large enough to be statistically significant. In speech, however, the differences so fluctuated that no distinct, consistent pattern was indicated. About the only generalization warranted is that when the honors were not even, they more often favored the boys. Taken as a whole, the findings of this investigation do not support the widely held notion, formulated by McCarthy (1954, p. 577), that among American white children the development of girls characteristically outruns that of boys "in nearly all aspects of language." Absence of clear, consistent sex distinctions can also be noted in recent reports by Templin (1957), Harrell (1957), Strickland (1962), Loban (1963), Menyuk (1961, 1963b), and Riling (1965).

In writing, however, girls in Grades 3 and 5 appeared to be clearly superior to the boys. Their greater writing skill would seem to be reflected in their less frequent coordination of main clauses, the smaller proportion of their T-units containing fewer than nine words, and their greater use of transformation-produced nominals and adverbials (considered as whole classes). Among specific structures, noun clauses were used with significantly greater frequency by girls in both Grade 3 and Grade 5; adverbial clauses were used oftener by girls in both grades, and significantly so in Grade 5; and coordinate predicates had notably greater use by girls in Grade 3. All these facts suggest that girls more readily adapt themselves to the practice of writing than boys do. The suggestion is reinforced by various data offered in the study by Hunt (1965) of compositions written in Grades 4, 8, and 12.

In the seventh grade writing reported on here, however, the relative positions of the sexes were clearly reversed on the scales taken to indicate syntactic skill. Differences almost uniformly favored the boys; some of the most impressive are seen in the much greater use of transformation-produced nominals and in the considerably less frequent use of short T-units and main-clause coordination. The comparison of the sexes in Grade 7, of course, should take into account the fact that the mean age of the boys was seven months greater than that of the girls.

IS THERE A SIMPLE OBJECTIVE MEASURE THAT HAS SPECIAL CLAIM TO VALIDITY AS
AN INDICATOR OF CHILDREN'S DEVELOPMENT OF SYNTACTIC CONTROL?

Both casual observation and careful studies, many of them reviewed by McCarthy (1954), indicate that mere volubility is a fair measure of preschool children's development of a productive mastery of their native language. Observation and common sense, on the other hand, prevent us from supposing that it is a very meaningful gauge of control of syntax by adult speakers and writers. The present study confirms earlier comparable reports in showing that up through the elementary grades there is a general, positive correlation between age-grade advancement and increasing word-length of total responses to a particular stimulus situation. Does this mean that for such children volubility is still a useful index to the degree of linguistic maturity attained?

This study, in fact, appears to justify an intuitive reluctance to regard a gross word-count very seriously as a measure of language mastery in school age children. Quite apart from such matters as appropriateness of word choice, pertinency of remarks, and general organization, it shows that development of power to manipulate syntactic structures is very imperfectly reflected in comparisons of mean length of total responses at various grade levels. Evidently, development of syntactic control may be most clearly marked at stages where increases in total wordage are least notable, and *vice versa*. If this is true of groups of children, it is no doubt more conspicuously true of individuals. The length of total response is probably a function of complex interaction of many factors, among which control of syntax may be one, but one of quite limited explanatory significance.

The claims of clause length as an easily observed, objective indicator of development in syntactic control have not been explored in this investigation. Objections to the validity of length of "sentences" or "phonological units" as measures of such development, however, were inferentially supported by observation of very high rates of main-clause coordination in both speech and writing. Those rates increased regularly up to the seventh grade, and even there they were (by any conceivable standards of educated adult usage) excessive. Whatever ordinary practice of identifying "sentences" might be adopted, it can surely be presumed that such coordination as has been described here would adversely affect sentence length as an index of syntactic skills.

Various calculations based on relative frequencies of subordinate clauses in children's language have long been favored devices for gauging development toward maturity in use of syntactic resources. That they have some discriminative power has been repeatedly demonstrated. Findings of this study, however, raise a question about their sensitiveness as measures of growth. Nominal, adjectival, and adverbial clauses were all used quite often by kindergarten children, and none of the types was employed in speech in any grade at a rate significantly higher than in the grade below. Relative clauses, in fact, were used most frequently in kindergarten. In writing, there were no significant increases in the use of noun clauses; significant increments in adverbial and relative clauses occurred only in Grade 5. If the older children had improved their command of syntax, they did not show it very clearly in expanded use of subordinate clauses.

It has been pointed out that with advances in grade, the children often increased significantly their use of certain types of structures that can be identified as transformations involving deletion rules. It might reasonably be proposed that growing power to manipulate syntax is better measured by relative uses of such structures than by subordination indexes. Better still, we may argue, is a computation of the relative frequency of all sentence-combining transformations, including subordinate clauses—but excluding main-clause coordination. Such a measure is objective, and there appear to be good grounds for believing it to have a high degree of validity. It is, however, far from being simple and easily applied.

The readily performed calculation of mean lengths of T-units, however, appears to give a close approximation to results of the more complicated accounting of sentence-combining transformations. Differential lengthening of T-units in successive grades studied in this research reflected varying degrees of expansions in the exploitation of syntactic resources. Comparisons of subgroup means of T-unit length also indexed just such distinctions between the speech and the writing of boys and of girls as were observed in the more detailed analyses.

This investigation supports the finding by Hunt (1964, 1965) that when fairly extensive samples of children's language are obtained, the mean length of T-units has special claim to consideration as a simple, objective, valid indicator of development in syntactic control. Confidence in its usefulness when applied to the language of children is enhanced by evidence that even high school students typically write in T-units shorter than those produced by skilled adults. Hunt (1965, p. 57) has reported a sampling of articles in *Harper's* and *The Atlantic* in which T-units were 40 percent longer than those in the twelfth grade writing he studied.

SOME IMPLICATIONS FOR TEACHING AND FOR FURTHER RESEARCH

Unlike earlier reports on children's language, but confirming more recent accounts, this study found in speech no evidence of linguistic superiority of girls over boys at comparable ages. It seems possible that changes in social, cultural, and educational environments have reduced differential behavior of the sexes. If there are English teachers who assume that they must naturally expect less language maturity in boys than in girls in the same grade, they may need to reexamine their assumption.

Judging both by syntactic features and volubility, however, girls in Grades 3 and 5 appeared to be a good deal more adept in writing than the boys were. If the findings of this study are generalizable, they raise the question of why girls acquire writing skill more rapidly. Is their earlier adaptation to writing related to finer motor adjustment, or do the school's methods better fit them? Could, or should, special planning be given to the initiation of boys into the practice of writing? These questions probably deserve attention.

As Loban (1963, p. 87) has pointed out, earlier research (including his own) has not resulted in identification of clearly defined stages of development in language proficiency in the elementary school years. Techniques of analysis employed in this study have led to the observation that in the population sampled, the first grade year was one of rapid and extensive development in exploiting language structures. Then, from the end of Grade 1 to the end of Grade 5, growth in control of syntax in speech proceeded at a much slower pace, though advances in writing were very considerable by the end of the fifth grade. Approaching adolescence, the children apparently made most important advances in the handling of oral expression; their growth toward physical maturity was accompanied by a corresponding development in language structure.

If the periods of striking development identified here are indeed stages of natural growth, it would seem appropriate to take advantage of them. Teaching materials and techniques designed to heighten awareness of the structural resources of the language might be particularly effective at those stages.

On the other hand, it is not impossible that the generally unimpressive progress in syntactic control in the middle grades may be in part a function of the educational program during those years. Would more carefully planned and efficiently managed programs in the school accelerate development of syntactic mastery in those grades? This is a question that calls for experimental investigation. Some other questions demanding research are these: Does deliberate instruction at any level contribute a great deal to mastery of syntax, or does the child just absorb a functioning knowledge of language practices from his general environment? If deliberate instruction does result in increased facility with language, what materials and methods are most efficient and effective? Is the gap between development of syntactic control in speech and writing in the upper grades desirable? If not, is it possible to close it by accelerating growth toward mastery in speech?

The present study provides valuable information about types of grammatical patterns and constructions that are used often and with increasing frequency by children as they advance in school, but perhaps equally valuable is its evidence of infrequent uses. Relative to the amount of speech and writing analyzed, the variety of sentence patterns and the variety of constructions filling the pattern slots were fairly restricted at all grade levels. The fact that at each level, however, most of the possible patterns and constructions did occur in the language of some of the children suggests that it is reasonable to suppose they would have been useful to others and that their use is within the potential capacity of elementary school children.

We need, of course, to know a great deal more than we do about the hierarchy of difficulty involved in both the production and interpretation of various grammatical structures. Results of penetrating research on this subject could surely improve the designing of instructional materials to develop systematically the child's ability to manipulate structures and thus to increase flexibility and power in expression. Naturally, the development of judgment about what is appropriate ought to accompany growth in ability to manipulate syntax. It is also obvious that concern with structure must not be separated from the concern with other aspects of language growth, but improvement in control of syntax is certainly a crucial interest of English teachers.

Fuller understanding of the nature and implications of transformational grammar will probably be a valuable aid to the perception of problems and possibilities of English teaching. That grammar generates insights into language structure not easily accessible by other means; it also suggests techniques of language analysis that seem efficient and productive.

Such techniques have been applied within a limited scope in this investigation. Their application has led to at least tentative answers to a number of questions, but it has left many others untouched. It has not, for example, explored stylistic differences between oral and written uses of language. Very probably, methods used in this study could be further refined and applied to many other aspects of language behavior. Similar research conducted at the high school and college levels might also have an important bearing on language instruction.[16]

Another longitudinal study was performed by Walter D. Loban.[17] He analyzed the language of the same children from kindergarten through sixth grade, and then compared the language of the low-ability group with that of the high-ability group. He found[18] that during the first four years of schooling, the subjects as a whole decrease the number of mazes [utterances of egocentric speech] and words in mazes, but the average number of words in mazes increases for the low subgroup. Subjects rated as skillful in language are reducing both their incidence of mazes and the number of words per maze. In other words, the lower group says less than the high group and some of them have more difficulty in saying it.

An implication of the maze is that the child is in the process of what Vygotsky called speech moving inward: the child is developing inner speech—the ability to think in words. But apparently this process is slower in low-language-ability children than it is in high-language-ability children. One would anticipate, therefore, that the low group would have greater difficulty applying, analyzing, and evaluating written language than the high group.

Loban also found[19] that

although differences in structural patterns are not notable—with the exception of partials and linking verbs—very important differences do show up in the dexterity with which subjects use elements *within these structures*. The nominals, whether in subject or object position, and the movable elements show marked differences when low and high groups are compared. This holds true consistently for any syntactical nominal structure. It is assumed, from this, that predication, when it is studied, will also show similar marked differences. This finding on the elements of structural patterns is considered to be one of the important findings of this study and should be considered in relation to the findings (above) on the similarity of structural patterns. *Not pattern but what is done to achieve flexibility within the pattern* proves to be a measure of effectiveness and control of language at this level of language development.

Apparently, the child who is more mature in the development of inner speech is also more mature in the development of certain transformational rules; that is, he has a greater number of ways to relate deep structures to surface structures.

Loban also concluded that "in the movable elements of the patterns, the high group consistently shows a greater repertoire of clauses and multiples (movables within movables)."[20]

He explains[21] that

essential sentence elements, those determining the structural patterns in the First Level Analysis, occupy fixed positions. In English, word order determines meaning. English speakers can say *Mary ate the rhubarb* ... but they cannot say *The rhubarb ate Mary* and make sense. Even in poetic inversion they risk misunderstanding. ... The essential sentence elements, then, have a fixed order in our language.

There are, however, some less essential elements which are relatively unfixed, adverbial modifiers like *usually, in the meantime,* and *if you don't really like it*. In this study these have been classified as words, phrases, clauses, and multiple movable constructions (movables within movables such as *holding the clowns in his hands* or *whoever in the excitement manages to keep from laughing*). The high and low groups show little difference in the use of words and phrases as movables, but ... the high group consistently shows a greater repertoire of *clauses and multiples* used as movable elements in the sentence....

The high group exceeds the low group in the number of more complicated constructions used as subjects. . . .

In the low group, during the years from kindergarten through grade six, there occur only eight instances of subject nominals more complicated than a noun, pronoun, or noun-headed nominal phrase. Of these eight, half are prepositional phrases and none are clauses. The boys in the low group contributed only two of the eight instances (two infinitives).

For nominals used as complements the same situation develops. Both groups . . . use nouns, noun-headed nominal phrases, and pronouns as complements with about the same frequency. The difference lies in the use of infinitives and clauses where the high group invariably exceeds the low group.

The study indicates that the high-language-ability boys used almost three times as many verbals and prepositional phrases as complements as did the low-language-ability boys. And though the high-language-ability girls used more verbals as complements than did the low-language-ability girls, the latter used more prepositional phrases as complements. Said Loban:

The boys in the low group are the ones who have the smallest repertoire, the least dexterity. Also, in the high group there is the interesting phenomenon of boys exceeding the girls. . . .

As in the previous analyses, the high group exceeds the low group in using any form of nominal except single noun or pronoun. Nouns amplified by modifiers, compound nouns, clauses, infinitives—all these characterize the high group rather than the low group. Once again the high boys manifest slightly greater flexibility than the high girls, and the low boys are even more restricted in their repertoires than are the low girls.

Loban next points out that "effectiveness with language often requires an ability to use those conventions characterizing standard English," that is, the language used by persons in the mainstream of playing various roles in the major institutions within a social system. Loban stresses that school texts often describe as errors language habits that superior writers and speakers, even those of prestige, employ. He continues:

The analysis of usage and grammar in this research [indicates] that the use of verbs—and in particular, agreement of verbs with subjects—was the major category of deviation from convention.

For Negro subjects whose parents have migrated from the rural South, using the verb *to be* as it is employed in standard English proved to be twelve times as troublesome as for the Caucasian or Negro subjects whose parents were from the urban California background. Use of present for past tense impresses one as another difficulty to be attacked in the middle grades as well as earlier by those subjects with a rural background. By noting the incidence of southern Negroes' nonstandard usage in relation to those of the northern subjects, one can locate those deviations that will require the greatest help in schools with a number of children similar to this special group. . . .

That sensitivity to the conventions of standard English is related to skill in language shows up in the significant differences on conventional usage in the analysis of spoken style. Statistically the high group is significantly superior to the random group. . . .

Ineptness with language is far less serious than malicious perjury or slander, no matter how skillfully or beautifully phrased. The purposes for which human beings use language deserve study. For children's language, as for all language, function is still relatively uncharted. Piaget's disputed analysis of function finds children's language to be primarily egocentric before age seven or eight and more social and analytical in nature after age eleven or twelve.... Other experimenters have noted requests, threats, criticism, commands, and questions. In the present study expression of tentativeness proved to be a function of language which distinguished effective and ineffective users of language. Apparently the functions of language are varied and numerous, even in childhood.

Results of all research into function of language depend upon the situation from which language samples are derived. Only when two language investigations sample similar situations will their classification of function be comparable. This points up a limitation of all research into language, including the present study. [He notes that he used an interview situation that limited opportunities for threats, commands, or deception.]

Despite the limitations expressed above, the analysis of linguistic function in this research does reveal one fact of considerable import. Those subjects who proved to have the greatest power over language—by every measure that could be applied ... were *the subjects who most frequently used language to express tentativeness.* Supposition, hypotheses, and conditional statements occur much less frequently in the language of subjects lacking skill in language.

The low subgroup furnishes only a few examples of this use of language whereas the high subgroup uses language in this way from the kindergarten year through the sixth grade, employing such words as *perhaps* and *maybe* more often than do the subjects who have difficulty in expressing themselves. These most capable speakers often use such expressions as the following:

> It might be a gopher, but I'm not sure.
> That, I *think*, is in Africa.
> But maybe they don't have any dogs in Alaska.
> I'm not exactly sure where that is. It looks like it might be at school.
> That's white grass—unless there's snow or the sun is reflecting.

The child with less power over language appears to be less flexible in his thinking, is not often capable of seeing more than one alternative, and apparently summons up all his linguistic resources merely to make a flat dogmatic statement.

Loban's description is reminiscent of Piaget's description of the egocentric children asserting the meanings of proverbs: what Piaget called "justification at any price."[22] This, he observes, is similar to autistic thought described by psychoanalysts. Autistic thought is undirected; intelligent thought is logical, directed. Says Piaget:[23]

Directed thought, as it develops, is controlled more and more by the laws of experience and of logic in the stricter sense. Autistic thought, on the other hand, obeys a whole system of special laws (laws of symbolism and of immediate satisfaction) which we need not elaborate here. Let us consider, for instance, the completely different lines of thought pursued from the point of view of intelligence and from that of autism when we think of such an object as, say, water.

To intelligence, water is a natural substance whose origin we know, or whose formation we can at least empirically observe; its behavior and motions are subject to certain laws which can be studied, and it has from the dawn of history been the object of technical experiment (for purposes of irrigation, etc.). To the autistic attitude, on the other hand, water is interesting only in connection with the satisfaction of organic wants. It can be drunk. But as such, as well as simply in virtue of its external appearance, it has come to represent in folk and child fantasies, and in those of adult subconsciousness, themes of a purely organic character. It has in fact been identified with the liquid substances which issue from the human body, and has come, in this way, to symbolize birth itself, as is proved by so many myths ..., rites ..., dreams and stories told by children. Thus in the one case thought adapts itself to water as part of the external world; in the other, thought uses the idea of water not in order to adapt itself to it, but in order to assimilate it to those more or less conscious images connected with fecundation and the idea of birth.

Now these two forms of thought, whose characteristics diverge so profoundly, differ chiefly as to their origin, the one being socialized and guided by the increasing adaptation of individuals one to another, whereas the other remains individual and uncommunicated. Furthermore—and this is of the very first importance for the understanding of child thought—this divergence is due in large part to the following fact. Intelligence, just because it undergoes a gradual process of socialization, is enabled through the bond established by language between thoughts and words to make an increasing use of concepts; whereas autism, just because it remains individual, is still tied to imagery, to organic activity, and even to organic movements. The mere fact, then, of telling one's thought, of telling it to others, or of keeping silence and telling it only to oneself must be of enormous importance to the fundamental structure and functioning of thought in general, and of child logic in particular. Now between autism and intelligence there are many degrees, varying with their capacity for being communicated. These intermediate varieties must therefore be subject to a special logic, intermediate too between the logic of autism and that of intelligence. The chief of those intermediate forms, i.e., the type of thought which like that exhibited by our children seeks to adapt itself to reality, but does not communicate itself as such, we propose to call *egocentric thought.*

We begin to form a picture that a lagging ability to think in words and a lack of the ability to manipulate movables within movables is reflected in a lack of tentativeness in thought of children in the low language group. This, in turn, is similar to the egocentric, unsocialized thought described by Piaget.

Loban also noted[24] that

those who are high in general language ability (the high group in this study) are also high in reading ability. Those who are low in general language ability (the low group in this study) are also low in reading ability. In addition, the gap between the high and the low groups is apparently widening from year to year.

Loban also made a transformational analysis of the grammatical complexity of a sample of language from a low language ability youngster and one from a high youngster. He found[25] that

the girl from the low group was shown to be at least two years behind the boy from the high group in development of grammatical complexity.

Both the index of subordination and the transformational analysis show complexity of grammatical structure to be associated not only with chronological age but also with proficiency in language and with socioeconomic status.

Recently sociolinguists have suggested that the language of lower socioeconomic class black Americans is as systematic and rich as that of middle-class white Americans, but that in an encounter between members of the two groups, especially black child with white middle-class teacher, sociocultural differences lead the black child to keep language interaction to a minimum. This theory, subscribed to by many sociolinguists, including William Labov, is in some ways consistent with the language-deprivation theory espoused by Basil Bernstein.[26]

Let us now examine the implications of these studies for the teaching of the language arts, including reading, beyond the beginning stage of reading instruction. For example, Loban concludes:[27]

Not basic sentence pattern but what is done to achieve flexibility within pattern proves to be a measure of proficiency with language at this level. Since formal instruction in grammar—whether linguistic or traditional— seems to be an ineffective method of improving expression at this level of development, one can conclude that elementary pupils need many opportunities to grapple with their own thought in situations where they have someone to whom they wish to communicate successfully. Instruction can best aid the pupils' expression when individuals or small groups with similar problems are helped to see how *their own* expression can be improved. This instruction would take the form of identifying elements which strengthen or weaken communication, increase or lower precision of thought, clarify or blur meanings. For the pupils, the approach would usually be through models, meaning, and reasoning rather than through the application of rules. On the other hand, the teacher would need to be aware of the structural problems behind the semantic difficulties and would be guided by research in determining what to emphasize or to ignore. Inductive reasoning toward generalizations would be more frequently encouraged than deductive applications to sentences not of the pupils' own creating. Occasionally the effectiveness or ineffectiveness of important ideas read or heard (e.g., recorded on tape) would be examined as a profitable reversal of self-expression through speaking and writing. Attention to structure at the expense of emphasizing successful communication could be a dangerous contribution of research not carefully interpreted.

In this study the superiority of the high group in handling oral signals effectively—their skill at using pitch, stress, and pause—combined with their relative freedom from using partial structural patterns is impressive. It would be difficult not to conclude that instruction can yet do more than it has *with oral language*. Many pupils who lack skill in using speech will have difficulty in mastering written tradition. Competence in the spoken language appears to be a necessary base for competence in writing and reading. Modern equipment for recording and studying the spoken word makes possible marked advances in such instruction.

And Hunt adds:[28]

This study provides no evidence at all on the question of whether the abstract description of sentence structures should have any part in the English curriculum. That question must be debated on grounds quite apart from the findings of this study. During the past two decades "schoolroom grammar" has been vigorously assailed by language specialists as being vague, confusing, and self-contradictory. Yet school texts have stood ironclad and unregenerate against such Lilliputian barbs. Whether the grammar now being taught is both clear and true is not the concern of this study, though that question is of vital importance.

In the schools where the description of grammatical structures is to be taught, this study has one very strong implication as to how it should not be taught. At present the study of grammatical structures is cut up into little gobbets and scattered widely over several years of the English curriculum. One consequence of this scattering is that "grammar is always reviewed but never taught." No English teacher knows which fragments previous teachers have undertaken. Every teacher discovers that in a given class of children some know considerable grammar and others just as able know virtually none. Perhaps by always passing the buck to some other teacher we escape seeing how unsuccessful we are collectively.

This scattering appears to be motivated at least in part by the notion that some structures are used only by older children and so should be taught only to them. Against such motivation this study provides strong evidence. The structures studied here are at least as complex as those studied in most school grammar courses. Indeed they are probably more complex than those taught in most college courses called "Advanced Grammar." Yet they are virtually all used by fourth graders and are used often enough and successfully enough to indicate that fourth graders command them. This study provides no justification for teaching some structures early and others late. Indeed it provides no justification for not going straight through a description of grammatical structures once such a course is begun. The student's practice is years ahead of the course anyway. The course need not pretend to be waiting for his practice to catch up.

Although the average child in the fourth grade produces virtually all the grammatical structures ever described in a course in school grammar, he does not produce as many at the same time—as many inside each other, or on top of each other—as older students do. He does subordinate some clauses to others, but not as many. He does reduce some coordinated clauses to coordinations inside a single clause, but not enough. He does put several clauses into a T-unit, but not as many as older students do. He does write some complicated nominals, but his are never most highly complicated. It is what the older student does *in extremis* that especially distinguishes him.

Take an oversimplified analogy: suppose you taught a youngster first to juggle two tennis balls. Suppose then you taught him to juggle two baseballs. In a sense, he could now be said to be able to juggle two tennis balls and two baseballs, four balls in all. But if you suddenly told him to juggle all four at the same time you can be sure he would drop them all. Only years later will he be able to handle all four at once successfully.

The following passage is perfectly grammatical. Furthermore it is clear, and, in a way, effective. But no reader of this study can fail to see that it is not written the way an older student would write it or would want to write it. What would the English curriculum do if it chose, as one of its primary tasks for eight years, the job of converting to normal mature writing this piece of perfectly normal fourth grade writing?

> We rode some more and finally we got there.
> Right away we started to fish.
> We couldn't fish where we were because some other people came
>   and they had two babies with them.

You know how babies are.
We moved over onto another point.
I could see little minnows in the water.
I got my pole and got a worm.
I put my pole in the water and waited.
Finally I got a bite.
I pulled on the pole.
My brother was excited.
I caught a little fish.
He was about four inches long.
Right after I caught a fish my brother caught a fish.
His was about five inches long.
Then I caught another fish.
He wasn't big at all.
He was about two inches long.
After we fished awhile we went to the car to eat.

This study suggests a kind of sentence-building program that probably has never been produced, or at least not systematically and fully. The aim would be to widen the student's span of grammatical attention and concern. The method would be for him to reduce independent clauses to subordinate clauses and nonclauses, consolidating them with adjoining clauses and T-units. He could work up to structures of considerable depth and complexity comparable to those exhibited by twelfth graders and superior adults.

He might or might not also break down complicated structures into simple clauses, though the whole process has both deductive and inductive aspects. To a certain extent writing teachers have always used this method. It would be possible of course to do a great deal more of it, using the student's own writing, other writers' sentences, and of course specially prepared exercises.

Persons familiar with transformational grammar will see immediately that the process here suggested is analogous to the process first described by Zellig Harris and then more precisely by Chomsky: "In addition to the transformations ... which convert sentences into sentences ... we must construct others which convert pairs of sentences into single sentences." (*Proceedings of the Third Texas Conference,* p. 142)[29] The longer and more complicated T-units written by older students require more and more of these recursive "sentence-combining transformations" which used to be described as operating on the strings underlying "kernel sentences."

Obviously the kind of program envisioned here could be incorporated into a course in transformational generative grammar. But surely it need not be. Surely any reader of this report has been able to see the possibility for consolidating certain clauses and T-units as they were presented. If those examples have been clear, then the whole matter could be approached in somewhat that fashion. In teaching English to foreigners it is now customary to provide a great deal of drill in producing the language, but a minimum of abstract analytical description. Production is the sole aim. Perhaps a comparable program is feasible for native speakers and writers.

If proficiency in this process is the most significant factor of growth in sentence maturity, then a teacher is certainly tempted to try to hasten that growth. Perhaps the student with a broad repertoire of equivalent structures has the same advantage as a student with a high vocabulary.

Of course, forced growth is not always firm growth. Perhaps the older students' proficiency comes only as a result of years of psychological and experiential maturing. It may come only with the development of all thought processes. In that event, attempts to force the growth will be futile. It is even possible that injudicious forcing is worse than futile. The centipede who ceased to crawl because he never knew which leg it was best to move first is no fiction. More than one child has been debilitated by excessive self-consciousness. Nonetheless, some extensive experiments need to be made.

O'Donnell, Griffin, and Norris also suggest that "teaching materials and techniques designed to heighten awareness of the structural resources of the language might be particularly effective" at grade one and again at grade five, during stages of natural growth in language development.

Also, a study by John C. Mellon indicates that transformational sentence-combining practice could enhance the syntactic fluency of junior high school students. However, Mellon suggests that the greatest dividends from such practice might be obtained through a program of sentence-combining transformations in the elementary grades rather than in junior high school. He points out that no grammar, in the traditional sense, is required, but he leaves open the questions of whether "enhanced syntactic fluency would begin to be reflected in judgmental responses of the general reader, and whether the motivational attraction of the sentence-combining problems can be maintained over several years of use."[30]

All these studies would indicate, then, that beyond the beginning stage of reading instruction, reading programs ought to contain, as one component, systematic opportunity for the development of syntactic fluency. According to Bever and Bower:[31]

An implication of these suggestions would appear to be this: by developing the child's syntactic structures and transformational rules, a reading program ought to enable children to interpret written messages that they have never seen before—it ought to develop sentence attack, just as earlier it developed word attack; and it ought to develop grammatical, structural recognition, just as earlier it developed word recognition. If this were done, children might be able to read faster with better comprehension.

THE READING CURRICULUM

It should be apparent that a major focus of the reading curriculum beyond the beginning stage is on the uses of reading: reading literature, reading in the content areas and, in general, reading to obtain, record, and organize information.

In general, here is how American reading programs have been handling this issue, as described by James Moffett:[32]

The traditional practice is to pose questions to the pupil about what he read, comprehension questions designed to find out how well he understood (test) and to make him think more about it (teach). The latter is what is important, of course —to invite him to relate facts and draw inferences he may not have while reading silently, and therefore to help him do so the next time he reads a new text alone.

But it would be hard to find a child who does not resent the inevitable quizzing, by the teacher or the printed questionnaire, on what he has just read. He has enjoyed the story and now he must face the music, endure the commercial, pay the piper. Has anyone attempted to estimate the damaging effect of this on children's will to read? In rat-and-pigeon psychology, this administering of a pain after a certain act would be called "negative reinforcement," when it is intended to discourage the act. Indeed, how many *adults* would read if they had to face a battery of questions afterwards?

Earlier we saw the importance of social interaction to the development of the process of thinking. This importance was especially underscored by Piaget, who noted that child interacting with child is more important than teacher-pupil interaction. Moffett also recognizes this point:[33]

In order to dramatize or discuss a text, pupils have to think about the meaning of it and follow out implications. Enacting a story or poem is translating a text into voice, movement, and space. Characterization, sequence of actions, mood, setting, build-up, and climax have to be grasped in order to be rendered by the children. Disagreements in interpretation have to be discussed. Inventing details of action and dialogue and extending stories are based on implications and potentialities of the text. They help pupils render future texts in their own minds.

Small-group discussion of texts should take off from children's own questions and spontaneous comments, as allowed for in the reading groups, or take off, in the trained, topic-centered groups, from subjects the pupils have drawn from common reading. Asking the group for help in understanding some point in the text should become a natural habit. There are some things a pupil *knows* he did not grasp; he should have plenty of opportunity to find out what he missed, and perhaps even why he missed it. Comparing reactions and interpretations is also of vast importance, for it allows the reader to discover other things he has misunderstood *without* knowing it. It also shows that his reaction or interpretation may not be the only one justified by the text. Comparison itself often starts good discussion, because each child can refer to the text to support his reading of it. It is in this way that textual examination should occur. The teacher may suggest sometimes that members of the reading group take turns reading aloud a single poem or story and talk about the varying renditions. This discussion, too, may cause them to look back closely at the text.

A possible procedure for the small groups trained especially for topical discussion is to bring to the meeting their copies of something read in common, agree on one or two things in the selection they want to talk about, and then start discussion. Or, during the conclusion of one session, when the group is settling on a topic for next time, they may propose something in their current reading.

In this way, reading is no longer a passive act. In this way, language becomes, as Jerome Bruner[34] has pointed out, "a major instrument of thought.... It can equally be said that the combinatorial or productive property of language is an invitation to take experience apart and put it together again in new ways." As a result, teaching language

may well be teaching the calculus of thought.... Indeed, I should like to urge that the closest kin to the teacher of English composition is the teacher of mathematics. The latter is teaching a somewhat artificialized calculus of thought that applies principally to what are called well-formed problems. The ill-formed problems for which the calculus of grammar is most useful are incalculably more interesting and strenuous.

"Language," he contends, "provides an internal technique for programming our discriminations, our behavior, our forms of awareness."[35] Language can be used in compelling stories that demand the attention of children, and language can be an active expression of their natural curiosity. Too often, however, the first lesson that the child learns "is that learning has to do with remembering things when asked, with maintaining a certain undefined tidiness in what one does. . . ."[36]

To counter this negative attitude,[37]

the teacher must be . . . a day-to-day working model with whom to interact. It is not so much that the teacher provides a model to *imitate*. Rather, it is that the teacher can become a part of the student's internal dialogue—somebody whose respect he wants, someone whose standards he wishes to make his own. It is like becoming a speaker of a language one shares with somebody. The language of that interaction becomes a part of oneself, and the standards of style and clarity that one adopts for that interaction become a part of one's own standards.

The will to learn can be nurtured by the need to respond to others to work toward a common objective. This, Bruner insists, is reciprocity.[38]

What can most certainly be encouraged—and what is now being developed in the better high schools—is something approximating the give and take of a seminar in which discussion is the vehicle of instruction. This is reciprocity. But it requires recognition of one critically important matter: you cannot have both reciprocity and the demand that everybody learn the same thing or be "completely" well rounded in the same way all the time.

As children think, and talk, and argue, their interaction leads them to organize their thoughts. And this, according to both Piaget and Vygotsky, leads to the development of logical thinking.

To foster this kind of interchange, the teacher must restructure her role as a classroom leader. She becomes a discussion leader, asking provocative questions, probing, calling on youngsters to support assertions by citing evidence. She seldom asks a question that can be answered with a straight yes or no. Sometimes several answers are correct, and sometimes there is no one correct answer. Because discussion is so important to the child's cognitive growth, the teacher who likes to do all or most of the talking may well need to reevaluate her role.

This new role as discussion leader finds support in the views of the late Hilda Taba.[39] On the one hand, she noted, many educators believe that a child cannot do reflective thinking until he has enough factual information. On the other hand, other educators believe that thinking is a by-product of the study of certain subjects such as mathematics. Memorize, and you learn how to think.

She believed, however—as do Piaget and Vygotsky—that thought *does* consist of describable processes and that it *can* be developed. Believing that "cognitive operations are an active transaction between the individual and his environment or the material," she conceived of thought as "an active organization of mental processes." Citing Piaget, she decided that first students would be given a sufficient amount of information—they would be able to assimilate "the 'stuff' to think with." Then teachers questions would evoke discussions, and the demands of the questions would lead the students to higher and higher thought processes.[40]

She foresaw, too, the existence of individual differences, but in a light different from that held by many educators who believe that differences are reflected by the speed at which children demonstrate mastery of certain rote-learning tasks. She asserted[41] that

it is not beyond possibility that by far the most important individual differences may be found in the amount of concrete thinking an individual needs before formal thought can emerge. This difference may distinguish the slow but capable learner from one who is incapable of abstract thought. It is not beyond possibility, therefore, that many slow learners can achieve a high level of abstract thought, provided that they have the opportunity to examine a greater number of concrete instances than the teaching process typically allows. The employment of teaching strategies which are scientifically designed for the development of cognitive skills may make it possible to develop cognitive processes at a much higher level and in a greater number of students.

Finally, she realized that this kind of discussion strategy could be evaluated by interaction analysis, a system of coding teacher-pupil interaction developed by Ned A. Flanders of the University of Michigan.[42] Thus the classroom teacher could obtain a measure, from time to time, of the level of cognitive functioning for each student.

It should be obvious that if action and concrete operations lead to the attainment of concepts and words for specific conceptual processes, and that if denotative or societal meanings are to develop, then discussion has another role to play. For interaction leads to the conventionalization of language, as Werner and Kaplan have pointed out:[43]

Gross deviations from conventional meanings become lessened and corrected in young children mainly by the reactions of elders to singular usages of words. In the growing child conventionalization occurs to an increasing extent also through the child's observance of a discrepancy between his own and other people's word usage. Our results bear witness to the considerable influence of private experience coloring the content of words of children of elementary school ages. . . . many childish words are subjected to the developmental process of conventionalization till their meanings are fairly congruent with the word content of adults.

Concept formation, vocabulary development, and conventionalization of word meanings seem to require a classroom procedure quite different from that now being pursued by teachers in intermediate grade reading programs.

Many teachers appear to be unduly committed to a belief that there is something normative about vocabulary—that is, that you can give a child a vocabulary test and if he doesn't know the meaning the testmaker had in mind for a specific word, the child should somehow be taught that word. Some teachers also seem to believe that a child develops his vocabulary by consulting a dictionary or glossary every time he comes across a word he doesn't know the meaning of.

These are questionable assumptions. For one thing, there are no valid studies dealing with the size of a child's vocabulary at any grade level or with identifying words that he absolutely must know or with the number of meanings that he must know for any given word.

Studies *do* indicate that before children come to school, they acquire a vocabulary of 2000 to 25,000 words. Estimates indicate that before the child enters school he uses in speech and understands, on the average, about 8000 different words out of the 600,000 words in the English language, not counting proper nouns.[44] One might ask, "How did he learn them?"

Despite encouragement to use glossary or dictionary, teachers report that children seldom do. This is probably just as well, for the use of a glossary interrupts the child's reading of a selection and presents him with a synonym for a word (and he may not know the meaning of the synonym either) or with a simple definition. The latter case may reinforce the child's view that meaning is static, that there is only one meaning for a word, rather than promote a realization that the acquisition of meaning is a dynamic process.

In the intermediate grades, reading material can present positive and negative instances to help the child attain concepts and words for those concepts. Materials can present definitions in context such as parenthetical definitions, and can use redundancy, synonymy, and antonymy in context to help develop the child's concept and word-acquisition processes. In using redundancy, for example, a selection might describe an explorer who gets lost after wandering this way and that. Then the author explains that the explorer retraced his "devious" path in his mind. Discussion can provide the children with opportunities to express newly acquired concepts and to use their newly acquired words. The teacher, in turn, can lead them to become consciously aware of the ways in which writers communicate the properties of concepts and explain words, including their parts, so that the reader will be able to interpret the message.

What is important, therefore, is not that the child can pass his weekly vocabulary test, but that he becomes increasingly aware of the nature of semantics and syntax. As his thinking becomes more and more social—less and less egocentric—the child should become aware that language is addressed to an audience, that audiences differ, and that the words and sentence structures a writer uses may vary with the audience, the situation, the message, and the reaction the writer desires to obtain. This awareness can be developed by leading the child to read material of various types: advertising, radio and TV scripts, essays, humor, law briefs and court opinions, and so on. These should not be introduced as unique experiences, however. Rather, there should be a sufficient quantity in any one area to allow the child to perceive the similarities within the domain and the differences between domains.

In such a curriculum for reading, study skills would no longer be an end in themselves but a means to an end: a means of helping the child acquire the information he wants in order to satisfy his own needs, whether individual or social. Each skill should be developed as the child—or preferably a group of children—manifests a need for it. Organization is a key.

If the child knows the alphabet in order, the teacher can lead him to discover that words can be arranged in alphabetical order. This process is the key to using the dictionary, encyclopedia, atlas, almanac, telephone book, and library cards. The child should encounter enough different reference books so that he can become aware both of the function of alphabetizing and of the vast numbers of interesting and useful reference books.

Notetaking becomes a condensation—a sampling of information in which the child examines a selection and perceives it as a concept because of the conjunctive or disjunctive information it contains.

He then labels the concept—whether obtained in a paragraph or selection—with a word. Principles are handled the same way. Outlining becomes a means of organizing notes, and the child is led to perceive outlining in terms of its function: what it does for him in his attempts to systematize his acquired information, his discovery of information, and his development of the insights and hypotheses he obtains from the information.

SUMMARY

In this chapter we have noted what a reader must do in addition to reading words, for reading is more than word identification. He must process complex morphological and syntactical structures. We have seen that as the child matures and becomes more skilled with language he uses more complex grammatical patterns. The growth for the school-age child is not in the use of a greater variety of sentence patterns but in the use of greater flexibility within the various patterns. For example, he uses an increasing number of modifiers and complements and an increased clause length. He consolidates grammatical structures. In all this, the child shows a developing language competence.

Since general language ability is related to reading, findings in this area carry some important implications for reading instruction. It would seem that the child should have many opportunities to express himself and to explore his own language both in oral expression and in writing. To increase his syntactic fluency, he needs to participate in an environment planned to encourage his use of more complex structures such as subordinate clauses, unit consolidation, and sentence combination. He needs to discover in his reading a variety of grammatical structures. Reading materials should be carefully selected to provide learning opportunities that support and encourage his competence, thinking, and language. Yet, if the complexity of the reading materials is beyond his level of competence, he will not have developed the principles or rules or learning skills needed to make use of them to further his development. Since language and thought display a common course in development, the concepts and meaning of reading materials must be those which support and encourage thought. In this way the child will be motivated to learn, and his efforts to master the materials will meet with success. Reading materials that validate and expand the child's hypotheses and efforts to understand concepts and meaning lead him into higher and higher levels of competence. Most importantly, both language and reading development need to be supported by social interaction. Children need to be actively involved in discussion, talking, and arguing to improve their thought processes. The teacher thus takes the role of discussion leader: discovering and supporting contrasting viewpoints, clarifying areas of bias and overgeneralization, and guiding experimentation and other sources for verification. Study skills become an aid for discussion rather than merely an aid for remembering.

SUMMARY OF BOOK

In summary, it will be well to call to mind two very important and fundamental facts of learning to read: (1) many different approaches and methods have been and are now being used for reading instruction and many children in all the approaches are learning to read; and (2) all the children who learn to read are able to read matter they have never seen before. Some authors refer to the reading of new material as a "creative" activity. Regardless of the term we use to describe this phenomenon, we must nevertheless account for it in an explanation of the learning-to-read process.

Because different approaches to reading instruction work, and because individuals become capable of reading new material, we must look for an explanation in terms of the "nature" of the learner. We have tried to depict a learner who receives all the data that is fed in through the senses and organizes it. The child actually sorts out the data to which he has access to discover regularities and acquire a system of principles that can be generally applied. As the child, by nature, discovers rules or principles, he also learns how to go about and become more efficient at detecting the rules or principles: he learns how to learn!

His progress in understanding the regularities of the environment is developed through application and successive refinement of the rules and principles. By his own activity he learns. The errors he makes are indicative of the rules or generalizations he is exploring at any particular time.

Language learning gives clues as to how a child learns to read. The child discovers the rules of language by sampling language from his environment. How he discovers these rules is determined by the nature of the child as well as the nature of the language. It is the nature of the child to systematize the data received by the senses and to generalize from his own system to new data. Both the information and the qualities of the relatedness of successive information become a part of his mental equipment and build his internal competence. He has by nature the mental ability to increasingly elaborate and differentiate his internal information and his system. Thus the child views and acts upon his environment—of which language and reading are a part—in accordance with his competence. This competence in the child is different from the competence of the adult.

The child's learning must wait for and is dependent on his development. He must proceed through global and inappropriate rules and make apparent errors of performance, though not errors of competence, to become increasingly competent. That is his nature as a learner. He alone can gauge when he has grasped an approximate rule sufficiently well to revise it. As the child develops, there is a sequence in how he learns: learning at the age of two is different from learning at six; learning at six is different from learning at twelve. Although there are individual differences between children, the similarities are greater than the differences. For example, the early perceptions of children are based on their subjective view of the environment as they know it. This view changes and becomes less subjective as the children develop and learn. Their earliest thoughts are restricted to their immediate environment as it is experienced directly through the five senses, and new information gathered through their own motor activities. Gradually, children separate thought from its tie to the physical world of the here and now and engage in abstract thought.

Returning specifically to language, most efficient language learning seems to occur in a situation of one child in intimate relationship with one adult, the mother. This seems to afford optimal redundancy and variation. In learning language, the young child emits innate sounds. He explores these sounds, producing all the sounds of all the languages in the world. This exploration of the child proceeds in a specific way. He emits contrasting sounds, making first one sound and then another, refines each, and focuses on the differences. As he becomes aware of his linguistic environment, he matches (does not copy) the sounds he produces with the sounds he hears. Eventually, he drops those sounds he does not hear. He learns the grammar of his particular language in much the same way. At birth he has the potential to grasp the grammars of all languages. He explores his own language environment and matches what he is capable of doing with what he hears. However, this takes time. He is limited by his developing capacity—by what he is capable of doing at any given time. He is also limited, and advantaged, by the principle, which is innate, that he can learn general rules or patterns, not specifics. The general nature of these rules is what permits him to be creative in his language, allowing him to produce and understand what he has never previously heard or seen. However, it also means that he must apply these rules generally. Since the rules, at first, are only approximations, he appears to make errors in applying them. But these errors actually indicate that he is learning the general rules, and he continues to interact with the environment to refine the rules further. The desire to refine the rules comes about when he is confronted with the realization that his broad generalizations do not work.

In reading instruction, the school helps the child by selecting and preparing the environment so there are not too many exceptions to the early, broad generalizations. As in all learning, the child needs redundancy, or repetition, to facilitate his formulation of the generalizations, and to give him familiar samples on which to test his own generalizations. This provides feedback and the intrinsic reward of successful reading based not on wild guessing but on strategic approaches. On the one hand, if there is too much redundancy the child may readily achieve generalization but will become bored. On the other hand, if there is not enough redundancy he will be inefficient in discovering the rules or patterns, and learning will be reduced; in the extreme, he will become frustrated. Or he will try to imitate like a parrot, without relating the new data to his internal system of generalization. Both frustration and imitation may lead to failure. Thus the child seems to have an optimal rate of learning and an optimal environment.

NOTES FOR CHAPTER 14

1. Richard L. Venezky, "Communicating by Language: The Reading Process," *Proceedings of the Conference on Communicating by Language,* February 11–13, 1968, New Orleans (Department of Health, Education, and Welfare: Pubilc Health Service—National Institute of Child Health and Human Development, Bethesda, Md.), p. 208.
2. Kenneth S. Goodman, "Analysis of Oral Reading Miscues: Applied Psycholinguistics," *Reading Research Quarterly* 5, 1 (Fall 1969), 16.
3. Kenneth S. Goodman and Carolyn Burke, *Study of Children's Behavior while Reading Orally,* report of project no. 5425, U. S. Department of Health, Education, and Welfare, 1968.
4. Yetta M. Goodman, "A Psycholinguistic Description of Observed Oral Reading Phenomena in Selected Beginning Readers," unpublished doctoral dissertation, Wayne State University, 1967.
5. Kenneth S. Goodman, "The Psycholinguistic Nature of the Reading Process," in *The Psycholinguistic Nature of the Reading Process,* edited by Kenneth S. Goodman (Detroit: Wayne State Univ. Press, 1968), pp. 15–26.
6. Kenneth S. Goodman, "Analysis of Oral Reading Miscues: Applied Psycholinguistics," 17.
7. Ibid., pp. 17–18.
8. Anne D. Pick, "Some Basic Perceptual Processes in Reading," *Young Children* 25, 3 (January 1970), 176–78.
9. References for the Pick article:
   • Levin, H., and Kaplan, E., "Studies of oral reading: X. The eye-voice span for active and passive sentences," unpublished manuscript, Cornell Univ., 1967.
   • Levin, H., and Mearini, M., "The incidence of inflectional suffixes and the classification of word forms," *Journal of Verbal Learning and Verbal Behavior* 3 (1964), 176–81.
   • Levin, H., and Turner, E., "Sentence structure and the eye-voice span," *Project Literacy Reports* (Cornell Univ.) 7 (1966), 79–87.
   • Weber, R., "Grammaticality and the self-correction of reading errors," *Project Literacy Reports* (Cornell Univ.) 8 (1967), 53–59.

10. Sumner Ives, "Syntax and Meaning," in *Recent Developments in Reading,* Proceedings of the Annual Conference on Reading, Univ. of Chicago, 1965, edited by H. Alan Robinson *(Supplementary Educational Monographs* 95, December 1965, Univ. of Chicago Press), pp. 129–33.
11. David W. Reed, "Linguistics and Reading, Once More," in *Oral Language and Reading,* edited by James Walden (Champaign, Ill.: National Council of Teachers of English, 1969), pp. 81–82.
12. Kellogg W. Hunt, *Grammatical Structures Written at Three Grade Levels,* Research Report 3 (Champaign, Ill.: National Council of Teachers of English, 1965), p. 141.
13. Ibid., pp. 141–45.
14. Roy C. O'Donnell, William J. Griffin, and Raymond C. Norris, *Syntax of Kindergarten and Elementary School Children: A Transformational Analysis,* Research Report 8 (Champaign, Ill.: National Council of Teachers of English, 1967), p. v.
15. Ibid., pp. 87–99.
16. References for the O'Donnell, Griffin, and Norris article:
   • Anastasi, Anne, and D'Angelo, Rita, "A Comparison of Negro and White Preschool Children in Language Development and Goodenough Draw-a-Man IQ," *Pedagogical Seminary and Journal of Genetic Psychology* 81 (December 1952), 147–65.
   • Anderson, John E., "An Evaluation of Various Indices of Linguistic Development," *Child Development* 8, 1 (March 1937), 62–68.
   • Bear, Mata V., "Children's Growth in the Use of Written Language," *Elementary English Review* 16, 7 (December 1939), 312–19.
   • Brown, Roger, and Fraser, Colin, "The Acquisition of Syntax," *Monographs of the Society for Research in Child Development* 29, 1 (1964), 43–79.
   • Bushnell, Paul P., *An Analytical Contrast of Oral with Written English,* Teachers College Contributions to Education, no. 451 (New York: Teachers College, Columbia Univ., 1930).
   • Carroll, John B., "Language Development in Children," in *Encyclopedia of Educational Research,* edited by Chester W. Harris (New York: Macmillan, 1960), pp. 744–52.
   • Chomsky, Noam, *Syntactic Structures* (The Hague: Mouton, 1957).
   • Chomsky, Noam, "A Transformational Approach to Syntax," in *Third Texas Conference on Problems of Linguistic Analysis of English,* edited by Archibald A. Hill (Austin: Univ. of Texas Press, 1962), p. 124–58.
   • Chomsky, Noam, *Aspects of the Theory of Syntax* (Cambridge: MIT Press, 1965).
   • Davis, Edith A., *The Development of Linguistic Skill in Twins, Singletons with Siblings, and Only Children from Age Five to Ten Years,* Institute of Child Welfare Monograph Series, no. 14 (Minneapolis: Univ. of Minnesota Press, 1937).
   • Davis, Edith A., "The Location of the Subordinate Clause in Oral and Written Language," *Child Development* 12, 4 (December 1941), 333–38.
   • Day, Ella J., "The Development of Language in Twins: I. A Comparison of Twins and Single Children," *Child Development* 3, 3 (September 1932), 179–99.
   • Ervin, Susan M., and Miller, W. R., "Language Development," in *Child Psychology,* Sixty-second Yearbook, part I, National Society for the Study of Education, edited by Harold W. Stevenson et al. (Chicago: Univ. of Chicago Press, 1963), pp. 108–43.
   • Hahn, Elise, "An Analysis of the Content and Form of the Speech of First Grade Children," *Quarterly Journal of Speech* 34 (October 1948), 361–66.
   • Harrell, Lester E., Jr., "A Comparison of Oral and Written Language in School-Age Children," *Monographs of the Society for Research in Child Development* 22, 3 (1957).
   • Heider, F. K., and Heider, G. M., "A Comparison of Sentence Structure of Deaf and Hearing Children," *Psychological Monographs* 52, 1 (1940), 42–103.
   • Hocker, Mary Elsa, "Reading Materials for Children Based on Their Language Patterns of Syntax, Vocabulary, and Interests," unpublished master's thesis, Univ. of Arizona, 1963.
   • Hoppes, William C., "Considerations in the Development of Children's Language," *Elementary English Review* 11, 3 (March 1934), 66–70.
   • Hunt, Kellogg W., *Differences in Grammatical Structures Written at Three Grade Levels, the Structures to Be Analyzed by Transformational Methods,* report to the U.S. Office of Education, Cooperative Research Project no. 1998, Tallahassee, Fla., 1964.
   • Hunt, Kellogg W., *Grammatical Structures Written at Three Grade Levels,* Research Report 3 (Champaign, Ill.: National Council of Teachers of English, 1965).

- LaBrant, Lou, "A Study of Certain Language Developments of Children in Grades 4–12 Inclusive," *Genetic Psychology Monographs* 14, 4 (November 1933), 387–491.
- Lees, Robert B., "The Grammar of English Nominalizations," *International Journal of American Linguistics* 26, 3, part 2 (1960).
- Lees, Robert B., "Grammatical Analysis of the English Comparative Construction," *Word* 17, 2 (August 1961), 171–85.
- Lenneberg, Eric, "Speech as a Motor Skill with Special Reference to Nonaphasic Disorders," *Monographs of the Society for Research in Child Development* 29, 1 (1964), 115–27.
- Lindquist, E. F., *Design and Analysis of Experiments in Psychology and Education* (Boston: Houghton Mifflin, 1953).
- Loban, Walter D., *Language Ability in the Middle Grades of the Elementary School,* report to the U.S. Office of Education, contract no. SAE 7287, Berkeley, Calif., 1961.
- Loban, Walter D., *The Language of Elementary School Children,* Research Report 1 (Champaign, Ill.: National Council of Teachers of English, 1963).
- Loban, Walter D., *Language Ability: Grades Seven, Eight, and Nine,* report to the U.S. Office of Education, Cooperative Research Project no. 1131, Berkeley, Calif., 1964.
- Lull, H. C., "The Speaking and Writing Abilities of Intermediate Grade Pupils," *Journal of Educational Research* 20, 1 (June 1929), 73–77.
- McCarthy, Dorothea A., *Language Development of the Preschool Child,* Institute of Child Welfare Monograph Series, no. 4 (Minneapolis: Univ. of Minnesota Press, 1930).
- McCarthy, Dorothea A., "Language Development in Children," in *Manual of Child Psychology,* 2d ed., edited by Leonard Carmichael (New York: Wiley, 1954), pp. 492–630.
- Menyuk, Paula, "Syntactic Structures in the Language of Children," unpublished doctoral dissertation, Boston Univ., 1961.
- Menyuk, Paula, "A Preliminary Evaluation of Grammatical Capacity in Children," *Journal of Verbal Learning and Verbal Behavior* 2, 5–6 (December 1963a), 429–39.
- Menyuk, Paula, "Syntactic Structures in the Language of Children," *Child Development* 34, 2 (June 1963b), 407–22.
- Menyuk, Paula, "Alternation of Rules in Children's Grammar," *Journal of Verbal Learning and Verbal Behavior* 3, 6 (December 1964a), 480–88.
- Menyuk, Paula, "Syntactic Rules Used by Children from Preschool through First Grade," *Child Development* 35, 2 (June 1964b), 533–46.
- Riling, Mildred E., *Oral and Written Language of Children in Grades 4 and 6 Compared with the Language of Their Textbooks,* report to the U.S. Office of Education, Cooperative Research Project no. 2410, Durant, Okla., 1965.
- Roberts, Paul, *English Syntax* (New York: Harcourt, Brace & World, 1964).
- Sam, N. H., and Stine, E. S., *Structural Analysis of the Written Composition of Intermediate Grade Children,* report to the U.S. Office of Education, Cooperative Research Project no. S-057, Bethlehem, Pa., 1965.
- Shire, Sister Mary Louise, "The Relation of Certain Linguistic Factors to Reading Achievement in First-Grade Children," unpublished doctoral dissertation, Fordham Univ., 1945.
- Slobin, Dan I., "Grammatical Transformations and Sentence Comprehension in Childhood and Adulthood," unpublished doctoral dissertation, Harvard Univ., 1963.
- Smith, Madorah E., "An Investigation of the Development of the Sentence and the Extent of Vocabulary in Young Children," *Child Welfare* 3, 5 (1926), University of Iowa.
- Stormzand, Michael, and O'Shea, M. V., *How Much English Grammar?* (Baltimore: Warwick and York, 1924).
- Strang, Ruth, and Hocker, Mary Elsa, "First Grade Children's Language Patterns," *Elementary English* 42, 1 (January 1965), 38–41.
- Strickland, Ruth G., *The Language of Elementary School Children: Its Relationship to the Language of Reading Textbooks and the Quality of Reading of Selected Children,* Bulletin of the School of Education, Indiana University 38, 4 (July 1962).
- Templin, Mildred, *Certain Language Skills in Children: Their Development and Interrelationships,* Institute of Child Welfare Monograph Series, no. 26 (Minneapolis: Univ. of Minnesota Press, 1957).
- Watts, A. F., *The Language and Mental Development of Children* (Boston: Heath, 1948).

17. Walter D. Loban, *The Language of Elementary School Children*, Research Report 1 (Champaign, Ill.: National Council of Teachers of English, 1963).
18. Ibid., p. 82.
19. Ibid., p. 84.
20. Ibid.
21. Ibid., pp. 46–54.
22. Jean Piaget, *The Language and Thought of the Child* (Cleveland: World Publishing, Meridian, 1955), p. 156.
23. Ibid., pp. 63–64.
24. Walter D. Loban, *The Language of Elementary School Children*, p. 85.
25. Ibid., p. 86.
26. Basil Bernstein, "Social Class and Linguistic Development: A Theory of Social Learning," in *Education, Economy and Society: A Reader in the Sociology of Education*, edited by A. H. Halsey, Jean Floud, and C. Arnold Anderson (New York: Macmillan [Free Press of Glencoe], 1961), pp. 288–314.
27. *The Language of Elementary School Children*, p. 88.
28. Kellogg W. Hunt, *Grammatical Structures Written at Three Grade Levels*, pp. 155–58.
29. Chomsky, Noam, "A Transformational Approach to Syntax," in *Third Texas Conference on Problems of Linguistic Analysis of English*, edited by Archibald A. Hill (Austin: Univ. of Texas Press, 1962).
30. John C. Mellon, *Transformational Sentence-Combining: A Method for Enhancing the Development of Syntactic Fluency in English Composition*, report no. 1, Office of English Education and Laboratory for Research in Instruction, Graduate School of Education, Harvard University, Cooperative Research Project 5-8418, 1967, p. 112.
31. Thomas G. Bever and T. G. Bower, "How to Read without Listening," *Project Literacy Reports* (Cornell Univ.) 6 (1966), 13–25.
32. James Moffett, *A Student-Centered Language Arts Curriculum, Grades K–6: A Handbook for Teachers* (Boston: Houghton Mifflin, 1968), p. 103.
33. Ibid., pp. 103–4.
34. Jerome S. Bruner, *Toward a Theory of Instruction* (Cambridge: Harvard Univ. Press, Belknap Press, 1966), pp. 104–5.
35. Ibid., pp. 108–9.
36. Ibid., p. 123.
37. Ibid., p. 124.
38. Ibid., p. 126.
39. Hilda Taba and Freeman F. Elzey, "Teaching Strategies and Thought Processes," *Teachers College Record* (Columbia Univ.) 65 (March 1964), 525–34.
40. Ibid., p. 527.
41. Ibid., p. 528.
42. Ned A. Flanders, *Analyzing Teacher Behavior* (Reading, Mass: Addison-Wesley, 1970).
43. Heinz Werner and Edith Kaplan, "The Acquisition of Word Meanings: A Developmental Study," *Monographs of the Society for Research in Child Development* 15, serial no. 51, no. 1 (1952), 102–3.
44. Irving Lorge and Jeanne Chall, "Estimating the Size of Vocabularies of Children and Adults: An Analysis of Methodological Issues," *Journal of Experimental Education* 32 (1963), 147–57.

index

about the authors

Justin Fishbein is director of basal language arts for Science Research Associates and has been primarily responsible for editing and managing many of the publisher's reading and language arts programs since 1963. He is a graduate of Harvard University and before joining SRA was for ten years a reporter for the *Chicago Sun-Times,* where his coverage of state and local government was cited by the American Political Science Association. Mr. Fishbein was named Outstanding Young Man by the Highland Park (Illinois) Junior Chamber of Commerce for his work with various civic groups, and cited by the American Association of Colleges for Teacher Education for his contributions to the organization's Media Project. His articles on reading have appeared in the *Instructor,* the *Grade Teacher, Texas School of Business,* and the *Quill.* He is a member of the International Reading Association, the National Council of Teachers of English, the National Reading Conference, the United Kingdom Reading Association, Sigma Delta Chi, the National Association of Science Writers, and the Chicago Newspaper Reporters Association.

Robert Emans is chairman of the Ohio State University Department of Early and Middle Childhood Education. He received his doctor's and master's degrees in education from the University of Chicago and his bachelor of arts degree, with honors, from the University of Wisconsin, where he was the first undergraduate ever elected to Phi Delta Kappa. Before coming to Ohio State, he was associate professor of education at Temple University, associate professor at Chicago Teachers College, and assistant professor at the University of Wisconsin, Milwaukee. He has served as a visiting professor at the University of Hawaii and the University of Chicago. His articles on reading and education have appeared in *Elementary English,* the *Elementary School Journal,* the *Reading Teacher,* the *Journal of Teacher Education,* the *Reading Research Quarterly,* the *Journal of Reading Specialists,* and the *Journal of Educational Research.* He writes a column for the *Ohio Reading Teacher* and has contributed reviews to *Adult Leadership* and written chapters in the Conference Proceedings of the IRA and the University of Chicago *Monograph.* Dr. Emans is a member of the International Reading Association and serves as chairman of its subcommittee on research awards. He is also a member of the National Council of Teachers of English, the American Educational Research Association, the American Association of Colleges for Teacher Education, and the National Society for the Study of Education.

This book was designed by Naomi Takigawa
set in Century Schoolbook with Helvetica Bold display
by Holmes Composition of San Jose
printed and bound by Kingsport Press of Kingsport Tennessee
edited by George Oudyn
sponsoring editor Karl Schmidt
cover by Takigawa

2345/987654321